MW01538253

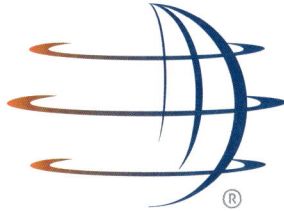

SHIPLEY CAPTURE

GUIDE™

Fifth Edition

LARRY NEWMAN, CPP APMP FELLOW

Shipley Associates
532 North 900 West
Kaysville, UT 84037
888.772.WINS (9467)

www.shipleywins.com

No part of this publication may be reproduced, stored in a retrieval system, or transmitted, in any form or by any means (electronic, mechanical, photocopy, recording, or otherwise) without prior written permission from Shipley Associates.

Trademarked names may appear in this book. Rather than use a trademark symbol with every occurrence of a trademarked name, we use the names only in an editorial fashion and to the benefit of the trademark owner with no intention of infringement of the trademark.

©2022 Shipley Associates

Fifth Edition

ISBN: 978-0-9990168-7-9

THIS CAPTURE GUIDE HAS THREE OBJECTIVES:

1 Help individuals and organizations capture competitive business opportunities more effectively, economically, and consistently.

2 Guide individuals in capture planning and sales roles to understand and adapt best practices for opportunities in any market.

3 Document best-practice capture management and planning guidelines.

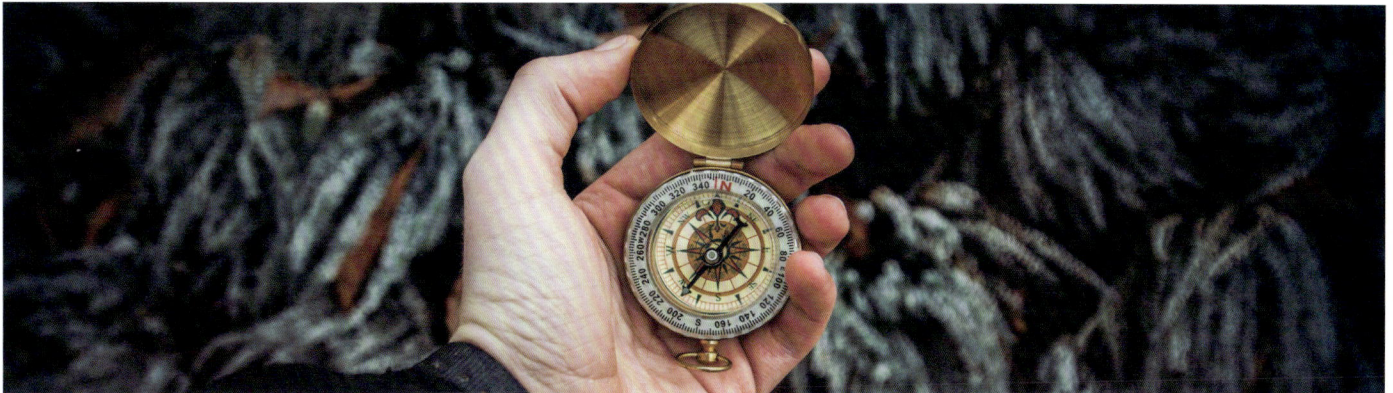

The most effective organizations are 10 times more effective in winning competitive new business than industry averages, based on several industry benchmarking studies dating back to the late 1980s. Researchers have concluded that the most effective organizations follow defined framework processes based upon fundamental principles. Less-effective organizations follow defined processes but lose sight of principles that help them adapt to individual opportunities.

Help individuals and organizations capture competitive business opportunities

Guidelines are based on fundamental principles revealed by business development research:

- Align capture activities with the customer's needs and selection process.
- Influence the customer to prefer your organization and solution early, and maintain that preference through selection, award, and delivery.
- Base your strategy on the customer's perspective of reality.

- Align your actions and messages throughout the business development cycle.
- Use decision gate reviews of potential business opportunities for determining the best manner in which to proceed.

Follow these principles to win more business more effectively, economically, and consistently.

Guide individuals in capture planning and sales roles to understand and adapt best practices.

This *Capture Guide* is designed to be a quick reference for individuals assigned as capture managers or assigned to contribute to capture teams. Individuals can learn of their roles during key capture activities and develop best-practice skill sets more quickly.

Document best-practice capture management and planning guidelines

At Shipley Associates, we have observed and recommended industry best practices in business development consulting, training, and process reengineering for more than 50 years. We endeavor to follow these guidelines in our consulting practice, teach them in our professional development practice, and share them in our series of *Guides*.

This *Capture Guide*, like the companion *Proposal Guide* and *Business Development Lifecycle Guide*, offers guidelines, not rules. Reality encompasses more variations than can be covered in a guide intended to be concise. When in doubt, consider the underlying principles.

What's New in the Fifth Edition

This *Capture Guide 5th Edition* includes updated graphics and design elements as well as updates to the Color Team Reviews section.

We hope individuals newly assigned to capture roles, their managers, and experienced practitioners will find this 5th Edition to be a valuable tool.

ACKNOWLEDGEMENTS:

Many thanks go to industry practitioners, experts, and Shipley global colleagues who collaboratively developed the *Shipley Capture Guide*.

Feedback from our global clients and consultants through our consulting practice, business process reengineering practice, and training participants has prompted numerous, ongoing improvements.

This *Guide* is regularly revised to incorporate additional content and cross-referenced to the *Shipley Business Development Lifecycle Guide* and *Shipley Proposal Guide*.

ABOUT THE AUTHOR:

Larry Newman is a founding partner of Shipley Associates. He joined Shipley Associates in 1986 as a consultant and training facilitator, helping clients win competitive business in over 30 countries and varied selling environments.

Mr. Newman authored all three Shipley *Guides: Proposal Guide, Capture Guide,* and *Business Development Lifecycle Guide*.

Mr. Newman is an APMP Fellow, is APMP accredited at the Professional level, and has presented at more than 20 professional association conferences.

USING THE *SHIPLEY CAPTURE GUIDE*

Capture planning guidelines are designed to help business development and sales professionals answer common questions about how to position their solutions and organizations to win competitive business more effectively, efficiently, and consistently.

Like the companion *Proposal Guide* and *Business Development Lifecycle Guide*, this *Capture Guide* is designed to be an easy-to-use reference. In the midst of repeated competitive pursuits, most business development professionals lack the time to read entire books that discuss capture planning from beginning to end. If you need immediate help winning important business opportunities, read on.

While capture planning originated within and is practiced predominantly by large organizations pursuing strategic, competitive, complex government programs, the fundamental principles are adaptable to most market sectors and selling environments.

For new users of the *Capture Guide,* consider the following time-saving suggestions:

Read An Introduction to Capture Planning if you are unfamiliar with the concept or term. If you are looking for specific guidance, go directly to the topic sections:

- Use the alphabetical topic arrangement to find a specific topic. You might have to try several titles before you find the information you need. If you cannot find a topic, refer to the Index.

- After finding the relevant topic, review the short summary and the numbered guidelines in the shaded box at the beginning of the entry. Then turn to the guideline or guidelines that appear to learn best practices.

- Read the guidelines and text. Review the examples, where available. Because capture planning is more conceptual than preparing a proposal, the examples are predominantly tools rather than excerpts from capture documents. Many specific examples would only apply to one market or selling environment and, therefore, would be less useful to readers with diverse perspectives.

Review the notes and cross-referenced entries in the page margins. Topics are cross-referenced within the *Capture Guide*, *Proposal Guide*, and *Business Development Lifecycle Guide*.

If you are developing or adapting a capture plan template to be used in your organization, turn to Sample Templates and Checklists Capture Plan Templates. The first template explains the presentation template, accompanied by adaptation suggestions by market and selling environment.

Different individuals, organizations, market sectors, and countries use similar and potentially confusing terms to mean different things. The following terms are used in this *Guide:*

- Bid request vs. Request for Proposal (RFP), Request for Tender (RFT), Request for Quote (RFQ), Invitation to Tender (ITT), or solicitation

- Customer vs. prospective customer, prospect, prospective buyer, buyer, or client

©*Shipley Associates*

ALPHABETICAL LISTING

CONTENTS

SAMPLE TEMPLATES

©Shipley Associates

AN INTRODUCTION TO CAPTURE PLANNING

Capture planning can progress an organization from an "unknown" to a "favored" position with a customer. This positioning is achieved by influencing the customer throughout the sales cycle to prefer your company and your solution. The most successful capture planning includes using an adaptable, repeatable process.

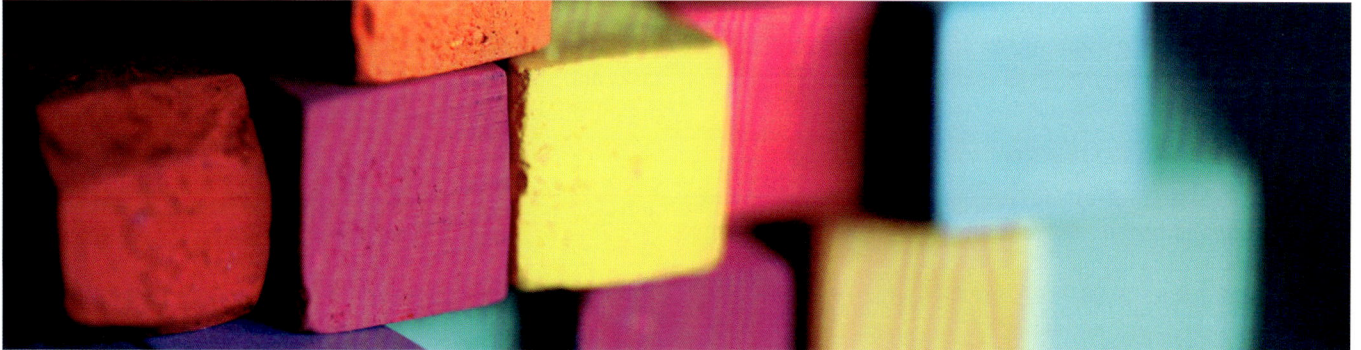

Capture planning originated in the 1980s as a phrase describing a recognized discipline. Capture planning became more recognized in the 1990s inside organizations primarily focused on large U.S. Department of Defense opportunities. However, the concept of influencing a customer prior to a procurement is as old as selling.

As the terminology of capture planning spread to organizations of various sizes serving a variety of markets in multiple countries, business development professionals noted that it was synonymous with complex sales cycles. Concurrently, commercial organizations pursuing large, complex opportunities were developing and practicing similar disciplines they called account or sales planning. Both are different ways of referring to the practice of engaging with a customer early in the business development process to improve win probability.

What Is Capture Planning?

To understand capture planning, consider the aim, potential outcomes, origin, context, and relationship with established selling methodologies.

The aim of capture planning is to progress from an initial unknown position to a favored position as viewed by the customer. Initially, the customer is unknown by the seller and the seller is unknown by the customer. Your initial unknown seller's position is ignorance about customer needs, the customer's view of your organization, and your relative competitive position.

Because the customer's view is the only relevant view, the aim of the seller is to progress from unknown, to known, to an improved position, and eventually to a favored position, as shown in figure 1. Of course, relatively few initial positions are completely unknown, and achieving a favored position might not be possible.

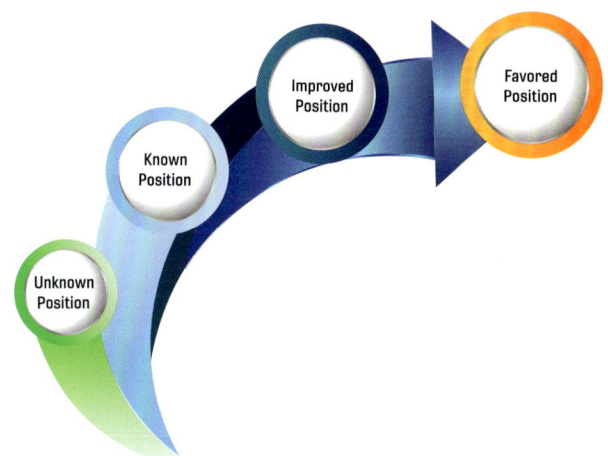

Figure 1. Capture Planning Progression. *The fundamental capture planning process is an iterative progression from an unknown to a favored position. The capture planning template is simply an orderly method to prompt research, analysis, strategy development, and tactical execution to achieve a favored position.*

To move from an unknown to a known position, research the market, interact with the customer, and analyze your findings. To move to an improved position, develop your strategy and tactics, implement, and validate them with the customer. Attain a favored position by building and strengthening customer relationships to understand their objecives.

Capture planning consists of iterative activities designed to attain a favored position with the customer.

Four potential outcomes are likely:

1. The customer opts to negotiate a contract without competition because:

   - Preparing solicitation documents, soliciting and evaluating proposals, then negotiating a contract are expensive and time consuming.

   - Implementing a solution promptly offers greater benefits than the potential cost savings from competitive bidding.

   - Finding a solution superior to yours is unlikely.

2. The customer prefers your organization and solution but opts to solicit proposals for one or more of the following reasons:

   - Purchasing regulations or guidelines mandate competitive bids.

   - Competitive bids often result in superior solutions.

   - Competitive bids often result in lower prices.

   - Competitive bids are less likely to be questioned by senior management or regulatory authorities.

   - Competitive bids give the customer additional knowledge and leverage in contract negotiations.

3. The customer opts for a full and open competition. Customers typically insist every competition is full and open. Determining whether a competition is truly full and open (or can be influenced to become so) is a key element of decision gate reviews, competitive intelligence, and capture strategy development.

4. The customer prefers another organization's solution, and you are kept in the competition as leverage or column fodder to secure a better solution or price from the preferred vendor. You should usually not pursue or bid unless you have solid evidence that staying in the competition will lead to profitable, future business.

The usual context for capture planning is within organizations pursuing complex opportunities with some or all the following characteristics:

- High value or strategic significance (for either buyer or seller)

- Buying committees or teams, rather than a single purchasing agent

- Selling committees or teams comprising many skills and disciplines

Intelligently adapt capture principles to your organization, selling environment, and the opportunity.

See WIN STRATEGY DEVELOPMENT

- Long sales cycles (months or years)

- Significant communication prior to a solicitation between buying and selling teams, often including meetings and document exchanges

- Formally structured procurement environments

A capture plan is a documented, action-oriented plan analyzing and summarizing the situation and recording tasks and steps to persuade a customer to prefer your organization's solution for a specific opportunity. While the length, complexity, and format vary, a documented plan offers reviewable evidence of the quality of thinking of the planners and the soundness of the plan. Capture plans can be developed using online collaboration tools, Microsoft Office tools, or a combination.

Capture planning is compatible with and supportive of major sales methodologies, despite minor differences in defined roles, titles, processes, and tools. Managers in many organizations opt to incorporate capture planning concepts into their sales methodologies or incorporate sales methodologies into their capture planning processes, depending on which are most mature.

In summary, capture planning is a disciplined approach to persuading customers to favor your solution. Capture planning relies heavily on research and analysis about the customer, the opportunity, and potential competitors.

What Are the Benefits of Capture Planning?

Doubling win rates, improving profitability, and predictably meeting revenue and profit forecasts are the most frequently reported benefits of capture planning. If you are not already practicing some form of capture planning, you likely will be after you learn of the quantitative, documented benefits reported by others.

Consider the potential benefits of capture planning from three perspectives:

- Qualitative justification
- Quantitative justification (ROI)
- Applicability to your selling environment

The qualitative justification for implementing a capture planning discipline is linked to improving the ability of your organization to capture competitive business opportunities. Instituting a culture with regular, structured capture planning processes can impart three major benefits:

- Increase top-line growth or total sales revenue in a competitive environment. Few organizations can grow total revenue by selling more of the same products and services to the same customers. They must expand beyond their core business to new markets with existing products or services, new products or services in existing markets, or new products or services in new markets as shown in figure 2.

- Reduce costs of capturing new business. Capture planning improves both efficiency and effectiveness of new business development, which translates to capturing more bids, larger bids, and perhaps more profitable bids at the same or reduced cost. Savings may convert directly to profit or fuel additional growth.

- Improve the predictability of quarterly and annual revenue and net profit. Capture planning puts organizations into closer contact with their markets and customers and gives management greater visibility over potential new contracts.

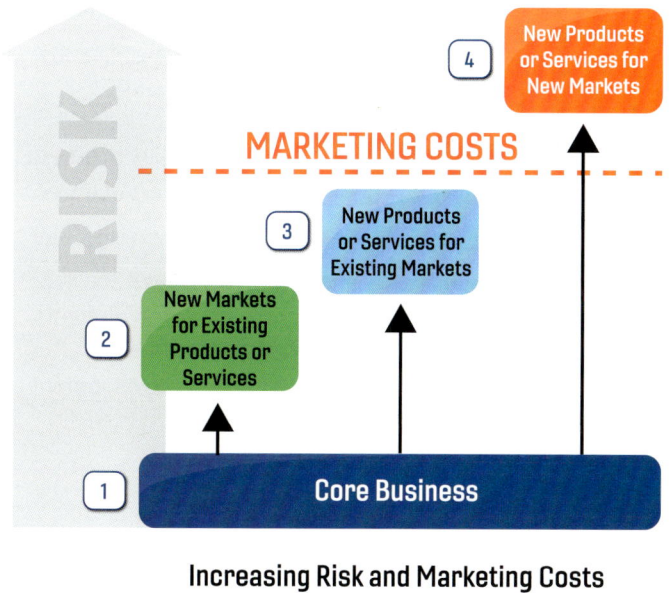

Increasing Risk and Marketing Costs

Figure 2. Measuring Risk and Marketing Costs. *To meet revenue growth goals, most organizations must expand beyond core business areas. The least risky expansion is to offer proven products or services to new markets because you can predictably price and deliver. Offering new products and services to existing markets and familiar customers might seem less risky, but a stumble threatens current revenue. Taking new products and services to new markets requires solid strategic, business, and market planning and is beyond the normal scope of capture planning.*

Quantitative, documented, and verified benefits demonstrate that capture planning principles benefit organizations in most selling environments and markets.

The quantitative justification for introducing capture discipline into your organization must be that the benefits significantly outweigh costs. Implementing new systems, training personnel to use them, and then maintaining operational discipline require investment. Perhaps the best way to assess potential quantitative benefits is to consider the experiences of other organizations.

The quantitative results are summarized in figures 3 and 4. Across varied industries, countries, and selling environments, organizations reported remarkable results after incorporating capture planning into their structured business development processes. Results often exceeded their expectations and in relatively short time frames.

A common success factor in the organizations summarized in figures 3 and 4 was that one or more senior managers embraced and championed the changes. These managers knew that process mattered and capture practices were effective. Just focusing on improving proposal quality was no longer sufficient.

Capture planning best practices have proven effective in a range of organizations, not just large contractors. While defense contractors were the first to embrace capture planning disciplines, best practices apply universally to large and small organizations, across market sectors, and in different selling environments.

Finally, consider the applicability of capture planning to your selling environment by assessing the characteristics of the opportunities you target.

COMPANY DESCRIPTION	BEFORE	TIME FRAME	AFTER IMPLEMENTING CAPTURE PLANNING
IT services (federal, state, municipal)	1,200 proposals per year Under 30% win rate $440 million annual sales	9 months	Less than 500 proposals submitted per year Over 70% win rate $1.05 billion annual sales
Engineering services	$20 million annual sales	12 months	Over $60 million annual sales
IT services	$350 million annual sales	18 months	$1 billion annual sales Doubled capture ratio
IT services and logistics	$1.2 billion annual sales	12 months	$1.8 billion annual sales Lowered costs by pursuing 40% less business
Defense contractor	$1 billion annual sales	12 months	$1.8 billion annual sales
Defense contractor	28% win rate $223 cost per proposal page 0.28 proposal pages per hour	24 months	89% win rate $109 cost per proposal page 0.65 proposal pages per hour
Telecom	55% win rate $49 million net profit	12 months	Above 70% win rate $64 million net profit
International business consulting	30% win rate	18 months	65% win rate 50% annual sales increase 50% fewer bids submitted
Legal services	Under 30% win rate	24 months	70% + win rate

Figure 3. Before-and-After Metrics Show Benefits of Capture and Process Discipline. *If you doubt the benefits of a disciplined capture and business development process, review these before-and-after metrics reported by other organizations. Each organization collected and managed different metrics, but all reported improvements. (Companies shared their stories with the understanding that their identities would remain confidential.)*

COMPANY DESCRIPTION	DIVISION WITH AD HOC PROCESSES	TIME FRAME	DIVISION FOLLOWING STRUCTURED BUSINESS DEVELOPMENT PROCESS
Global Telecom	51% win rate 33% capture ratio (percent of total amount bid)	18 months	67% win rate 80% capture ratio (percent of total amount bid)
Defense	65% re-compete win rate 50% capture ratio (percent of total amount bid)	12 months	100% re-compete win rate 67% capture ratio (percent of total amount bid)

Figure 4. Shipley Clients Show Measurable Results. *In two instances, capture and business development process disciplines were implemented in only one of two similarly performing divisions within the same organization. The benefits of practicing capture and process discipline were clear within 12–18 months. (Companies shared their results with the understanding that their identities would remain confidential.)*

BUSINESS DEVELOPMENT FRAMEWORK

A business development framework is a systematic series of sales actions or steps directed toward a specific end. Organizations that follow business development and capture planning best practices win more business.

Organizations with an effective and documented business development framework gain the following benefits:

- Reduced costs
- Increased productivity
- Improved forecasting
- Increased management visibility and control

Defining, building, and sustaining an effective business development framework require management focus and continuous effort. Barriers include corporate inertia, individual resistance to change, and constantly changing priorities that blur focus and erode commitment.

While senior business leaders or other upper management will generally establish a business development framework, understanding each phase is necessary to fulfill your role as a capture manager.

The need to reengineer an organization's business development process often stems from one of the following situations:

- Merged or reorganized organizations
- Changes in management
- Failure to meet sales or win-rate goals
- Staffing fluctuations
- Sale of the organization
- Analyst's concerns affecting stock price
- Maturing markets
- Loss of key customers or contracts

Businesses with an organized business development framework see increased capture success because proven best tactics are repeated.

BUSINESS DEVELOPMENT FRAMEWORK

1 Commit to a single, flexible, scalable business development framework based on industry best practices and championed at the executive level.

2 Align your business development framework with your customers' buying cycles.

3 Define framework phases broadly, delineated by clear decision gates with verifiable inputs and outputs.

4 Use consistent reviews at decision gates to control and add value to the process.

5 Adapt your process to individual opportunities by using flexible support tools.

6 Define business development roles, responsibilities, and levels of authority, including thresholds by types of opportunities.

7 Align your business development framework with corporate policies, strategies, practices, and other processes.

8 Document your business development framework to make it consistent and repeatable.

9 Train team members to give them the understanding and skills to follow the framework.

10 Designate a process owner to collect metrics, foster continuous improvement, and maintain tools and infrastructure.

©Shipley Associates

1　COMMIT TO A SINGLE, FLEXIBLE, SCALABLE BUSINESS DEVELOPMENT FRAMEWORK BASED ON INDUSTRY BEST PRACTICES AND CHAMPIONED AT THE EXECUTIVE LEVEL.

Organizations with a single, flexible process can conduct business more efficiently and effectively. Every opportunity follows the business development framework. Individuals assigned to capture and proposal teams can immediately focus on the opportunity rather than determining or justifying what needs to be done.

A flexible framework works for you, not against you, by including best practices based on the type of opportunity.

A scalable framework can be adapted to the size, delivery deadline, and available resources. For example, a mandatory kickoff meeting might be shortened, conducted virtually, and include fewer participants. A color team review might be serial and virtual rather than a co-located, single event.

This type of framework implies that phases, decision gates, and color team reviews are included based on the category of opportunity. Milestones might be mandatory, recommended, optional, or not applicable.

You can determine industry best practice by regularly comparing your process to other organizations, by participating in industry forums and professional associations, and by engaging with professionals that specialize in business development best practice reviews and business development process reengineering.

The Shipley Business Development Lifecycle Guide *is a useful starting point if you are revising your organization's process.*

2　ALIGN YOUR BUSINESS DEVELOPMENT FRAMEWORK WITH YOUR CUSTOMERS' BUYING CYCLES.

Customers care about their needs, not yours. Customers have different needs at different phases of the buying cycle. Design your framework to address customers' needs as their needs change. The framework outlined in figure 1 meets the single, flexible, and scalable criteria of Guideline 1.

The fixed milestones required for every opportunity establish the framework of a single process. Flexibility and scalability come from intelligently tailoring both the milestones and the steps between them. The top two bars in the figure depict customer buying phases and milestones. The bottom two bars show the alignment with selling phases and milestones.

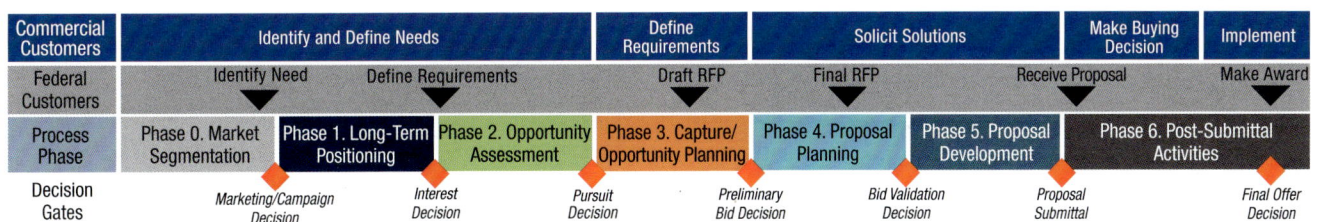

Figure 1. A Seven-Phase Business Development Framework. *The seven-phase business development process aligns with buying phases. Readily identifiable customer and selling milestones are shown. Customer milestones mark key customer decisions. Decision gates separate the selling phases.*

During the **Identify and Define Needs** phase, customers' needs become explicit. Customers usually experience or recognize a compelling event that spurs them to seriously assess their needs. A capture or opportunity manager should help customers assess the pros and cons of satisfying each need.

During the **Define Requirements** phase, customers identify services they need, then compose a solicitation for proposals. The earlier you participate in this phase, the more you can help the customer shape their requirements and prepare your organization for proposal development later on. Persuading a customer

See VALUE PROPOSITIONS.

that your organization will fulfill their needs before an RFP is released positions you favorably.

During the **Solicit Solutions** phase, customers tentatively select a solution and try to determine what could go wrong. Risk avoidance is paramount, so emphasize risk management and the value of the solution to the customer.

During the post-award **Implement** phase, customers are focused on attaining the anticipated benefits of the purchased solution. Reinforce the value delivered, and highlight the additional value of further enhancements. Begin positioning your next sale.

3   DEFINE FRAMEWORK PHASES BROADLY, DELINEATED BY CLEAR DECISION GATES WITH VERIFIABLE INPUTS AND OUTPUTS.

Define phases broadly to include the wide variety of opportunities your organization pursues. Narrow definitions encourage participants to work outside the process. The framework introduced in figure 1 is expanded in figure 2.

Phases are separated by management decision gate reviews. Clusters of potential activities are shown under each phase. Documents generated during those activities verify the output of phases and are input for subsequent phases.

See DECISION GATE REVIEWS *and* COLOR TEAM REVIEWS.

This framework is divided into seven phases. Phases 0 and 1 are iterative; Phases 2–6 are opportunity-specific.

Phase 0: Market Segmentation. Management considers potential new market niches or customers to identify possible growth paths.

Phase 1: Long-Term Positioning. Campaign plans are executed to establish your organization's presence and capabilities, aimed at identifying leads or opportunities.

Phase 2: Opportunity Assessment. Newly identified opportunities are assessed to determine your organization's interest and whether they are winnable.

Phase 3: Capture/Opportunity Planning. Individuals in customers' organizations are influenced to prefer your solution and organization.

Phase 4: Proposal Planning. The proposal effort is planned while sales efforts continue.

Phase 5: Proposal Development. The proposal is prepared, approved, and submitted.

Phase 6: Post-Submittal Activities. Customers' questions are answered, leading to contract negotiation and award.

Defining clear, mandatory decision gates with verifiable inputs and outputs establishes a solid framework for all

opportunities, large or small. Predefined quality checks at each gate minimize wasted effort and increase capture effectiveness. Each decision gate is described below:

- **Marketing/Campaign Decision.** Determine whether the market or customer fits your strategic focus.
- **Interest Decision.** Determine whether an identified opportunity fits your organization's goals, capabilities, and interests sufficiently to justify expending resources to gather more information, develop your relationship with the customer, and begin developing a solution.
- **Pursuit Decision.** Determine whether you have a realistic chance of influencing the customer to prefer your solution and your organization.
- **Preliminary Bid Decision.** Determine whether the opportunity and your success influencing the customer warrant allocating resources to begin planning the proposal and your solution before receiving the final bid request.
- **Bid Validation Decision.** Determine whether your capture activities have placed you in a position to win the job, justifying the expenditure of proposal resources, after considering any requirement changes, risks, and competitive conditions.
- **Proposal Submittal Decision.** Decide, before submitting your proposal and after taking into account all risk factors, whether your organization is satisfied with all aspects of the proposed solution and price.
- **Final Offer Decision.** Decide whether to accept offered terms and conditions or submit a proposal revised at the customer's request.

Capture managers should be actively involved in key decision gates. You will often have knowledge of the customer and pursuit status necessary to determine whether or not to advance the opportunity through the decision gate.

©Shipley Associates

4 USE CONSISTENT REVIEWS AT DECISION GATES TO CONTROL AND ADD VALUE TO THE PROCESS.

Careful tracking is the only evidence that a task has been completed. Without tracking, you cannot control and manage capture activities. The quality of a business development review reflects the quality of the work done to research, develop the lead, and collaborate with the customer. Each decision gate should incorporate standard documentation requirements, appropriately tailored for the type and size of the opportunity.

Figure 2 suggests documents or templates for each decision gate. These may need to be adapted to reflect the requirements of your organization. The availability and quality of these documents at the gate are indicators of your readiness to advance to the next phase. Poor documentation should raise serious doubt about continuing to spend resources.

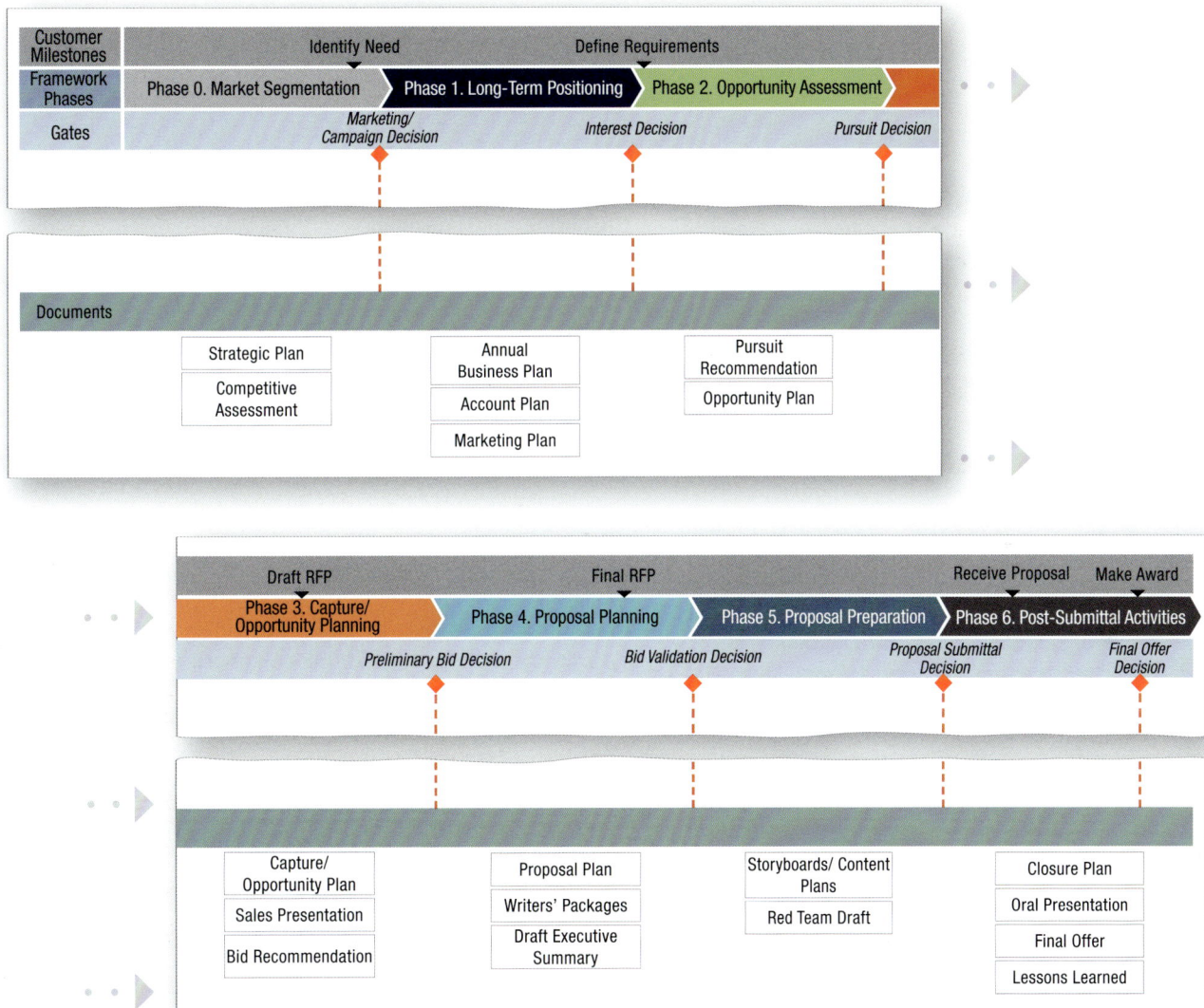

Figure 2. Sample Process Framework and Documentation for Business Capture. *This framework is aligned with the customer's buying cycle. Management decision gates apply to major opportunities. Simpler circumstances might call for fewer gates, following guidelines of your process documentation. Representative documents are shown along the bottom of the chart. Add or subtract according to your needs.*

5 ADAPT YOUR PROCESS TO INDIVIDUAL OPPORTUNITIES BY USING FLEXIBLE SUPPORT TOOLS.

No single process is right for every business organization and every opportunity. The process shown in figure 2 is widely useful but might require tailoring for your products, services, or market. The tasks completed during each phase of your business development framework may need to be adjusted based on the following considerations:

- Value of bid, both in absolute terms and in comparison to other business you have

- Knowledge of customer, especially relating to prior working relationships

- Time projected to be available during each phase of business development

- Similarity of new business to other work your organization has performed

- Knowledge of other competitors

- Expectations in the marketplace concerning sophistication of proposals and other aspects of the business development process

Likewise, the information required to support the decision gates may be different. For example, in a commodity market, knowledge of competitors may not play a large role in deciding whether to bid; instead, information about price will be more significant in each phase.

In a service industry, you may have limited potential to influence the buyer's preferred solution. Instead, focus on identifying the best personnel resources for a job early in the process.

When business development staff circumvent your process, your process may no longer fit your circumstances. Processes can be changed but should not be modified without good reason.

See PROPOSAL PREPARATION TOOLS, Proposal Guide.

Regardless of the tasks that are right for your organization or the information needed for decision making, a consistent business development framework will help you spend more of your resources pursuing better opportunities. You will typically submit fewer bids but will improve your win rate and increase total dollars won.

A high-level framework definition provides structure, but you need flexible tools to respond to shifting market demands.

Tools need to support both knowledge and process. Knowledge management includes boilerplate development, retrieval, and maintenance. It also supports collaborative solution development by giving access to previous work and products. Process tools direct the user, save time, and improve effectiveness.

The best business development tools are adaptable to a broad range of opportunities and proposals. They help collect, organize, and analyze information so better decisions can be made. Ultimately, they help your organization prepare winning proposals.

Potential tools come in many forms, from simple templates and forms to fully integrated web-based, electronic systems. To be broadly accepted, your process must do more than give direction—it must help users do their jobs effectively and efficiently. Tools that save time and improve effectiveness help users and promote acceptance and adherence to your process.

The best tools empower the user to be better organized, more customer-focused, and more responsive to the specific requirements of each business opportunity.

©Shipley Associates

6 DEFINE BUSINESS DEVELOPMENT ROLES, RESPONSIBILITIES, AND LEVELS OF AUTHORITY, INCLUDING THRESHOLDS BY TYPES OF OPPORTUNITIES.

Roles are functions of a person in business development, such as capture manager, account manager, proposal manager, proposal specialist, proposal writer, and subject matter expert. A single person can fill multiple roles. In some organizations, a person in the account manager position might assume sales, proposal manager, proposal writer, estimator, and reviewer roles.

Responsibilities are tasks that people are accountable for, whether they complete the task themselves or assign the task to another. In business development, people in roles are assigned specific responsibilities. Traditionally, an individual in the proposal manager role is responsible for the preparation of the proposal document to a defined standard.

Levels of authority delineate the power of a person to lead, direct, or decide. Levels of authority establish whether the person can make a decision and the limits of the decision. For example, the level of authority to make pursuit, bid, and bid submittal decisions usually varies with the size and risk of the opportunity.

In a similar way, authority to expend marketing or bid and proposal funds on capture activities may be assigned based on familiarity with the customer. A regional sales manager may receive opportunities with existing customers and markets, but a division manager may be assigned to handle new products or services with unfamiliar customers.

Business development frameworks are more flexible and scalable when roles, responsibilities, and levels of authority are clearly defined. Decisions are clearer, easier, and faster. Individuals know what actions are within their personal scope and when to seek involvement or approval elsewhere. Wasted efforts are reduced. Managers can keep projects on track by verifying that roles are assigned and responsibilities understood. They can steer the direction of the organization by adjusting roles and responsibilities to encourage changes in staff behavior.

See APPENDIX A: TEAM ROLES AND RESPONSIBILITIES, Business Development Lifecycle Guide.

7 ALIGN YOUR BUSINESS DEVELOPMENT FRAMEWORK WITH CORPORATE POLICIES, STRATEGIES, PRACTICES, AND OTHER PROCESSES.

Alignment is critical in all areas. A corporate strategy to "be the technology leader" is more compatible with a sales approach that emphasizes added value than one that stresses low price. For each opportunity, align your capture strategy, proposal strategy, messaging, and solution.

Align all performance metrics, incentives, and proposal development processes. Good capture management sets the company up for successful proposal development and contract execution.

An effective capture process does not provide additional business; it sets the stage for smooth transitions later in the business development framework. Aligning capture efforts and information with other corporate processes or teams allows there to be a smooth transition later in the framework.

Good capture management includes the following best practices:

- Share sales or capture team information with the proposal team.

- Streamline the proposal review process to support a short capture and proposal delivery schedule.

- Balance reviewers' rewards for preventing risk with potential cost of lost sales.

- Align capture, solution development, and project delivery processes to reduce transition risk.

8 DOCUMENT YOUR BUSINESS DEVELOPMENT FRAMEWORK TO MAKE IT CONSISTENT AND REPEATABLE.

Define all framework elements before creating process flow diagrams and documenting the process. Definitions are linked, and changes will create a ripple effect.

After framework element definitions are final, document the process. Documentation can assume many forms. Because your process must guide and help users, ask yourself the following questions:

> **?**
> - Where and when will users refer to the documentation?
> - Do users work in a central office or in remote locations?
> - How will the form and format affect availability, acceptance, and repeated use?
> - How easy will it be to update and keep users' data current?

Ideally, the tool you use to document your process disguises much of the framework. Most importantly, follow your process and use your tools. Contributors follow what you do more than what you say.

©Shipley Associates

9 TRAIN TEAM MEMBERS TO GIVE THEM THE UNDERSTANDING AND SKILLS TO FOLLOW THE FRAMEWORK.

Even users who understand and accept the process need the skills to execute and adapt it appropriately.

An initial and ongoing investment in training on best practices and tools is critical. To achieve maximum return, training must be process-specific rather than role-specific. Otherwise, people will not understand the reasons for their assigned tasks.

Business development process and tool training cannot consist of lectures and one-time demonstrations. Participants must practice the expected skills during the training and receive immediate feedback to improve their performance.

Without practice, participants usually return to their pre-training approach.

10 DESIGNATE A PROCESS OWNER TO COLLECT METRICS, FOSTER CONTINUOUS IMPROVEMENT, AND MAINTAIN TOOLS AND INFRASTRUCTURE.

Processes erode quickly without an owner. Turnover, loss of learning, and even active resistance to process discipline reduce effectiveness. Consider these all too common occurrences:

- A template with an outdated logo is used, creating an inconsistent brand image
- An electronic template incompatible with an upgraded operating system is abandoned, forcing business development staff back to inaccurate, inefficient, manual techniques
- Boilerplate graphics and text describing obsolete products and services prompt a customer to select another source
- Inadequate reviews lead to unacceptable risk or low profit margins
- Contract disputes arise because the bidder is not fully aware of the content of a proposal

Assigning an owner to implement, monitor, and improve the process keeps the benefits alive.

Metrics are a basis for continuous improvement—we manage what we measure. Using good metrics, you can monitor sales support costs, cycle times, and proposal quality. All are usually related to higher win rates.

Metrics help process owners understand which elements of their processes work well and which need to be changed. Accurate and credible metrics are the only valid way to justify requests for additional resources, to resist reductions in current resources, or to measure the value of enabling technologies and tools.

Consider the following questions when determining what metrics to collect:

- How will you use this metric? If you cannot anticipate its use, do not track it.

- Can the metric be collected with minimum impact to staff and clients? Try to capture metrics as by-products of your normal process. For example, collect labor hours from time sheets.

- Does the potential value of the data exceed the cost of collection? A relatively expensive program to obtain customers' feedback on wins and losses is often justified.

- Does the metric broaden your potential understanding of a process that you own or can influence? Keeping metrics on organizations or individuals outside your control and influence may only lead to conflict. If you have no control over your field sales force, why track data on account executives? Leave that to sales management.

Avoid tracking metrics that overlap unless you are trying to determine which metric is most representative. For example, overlapping metrics might be kept on desktop publishing (DTP). You could track pages per day of combined graphics and text, or separate measures of pages per day of text and graphics per day. The appropriate measure might depend on whether your DTP professional also does the graphics and whether the ratio of graphics per page is expected to change. Figure 3 lists potential business development process metrics.

COMMONLY COLLECTED BUSINESS DEVELOPMENT METRICS	
Proposal quality (standards)	Number of graphics per hour
Duration (start to finish)	Percent new vs. existing graphics
Staff hours	Number and value of opportunities added to pipeline
Hours by resource	Number and value of opportunities pursued
Win/Loss	Number and value of opportunities retired by customer
Dollars won/loss	Capture budget vs. actual by opportunity and phase
Production costs	Percent of budget spent pre-RFP
Page count	

Figure 3. Potential Business Development Process and Proposal Metrics. *Business development and proposal process owners track many of the listed metrics, but never track all of them. Balance the number of metrics collected and the collection cost against the potential value of the metric.*

CAPTURE PLANNING, AN OVERVIEW

Capture planning is the process of identifying opportunities, assessing the environment, and devising and implementing winning strategies oriented toward capturing a specific business opportunity. Consistently successful capture planning requires documented, action-oriented capture plans.

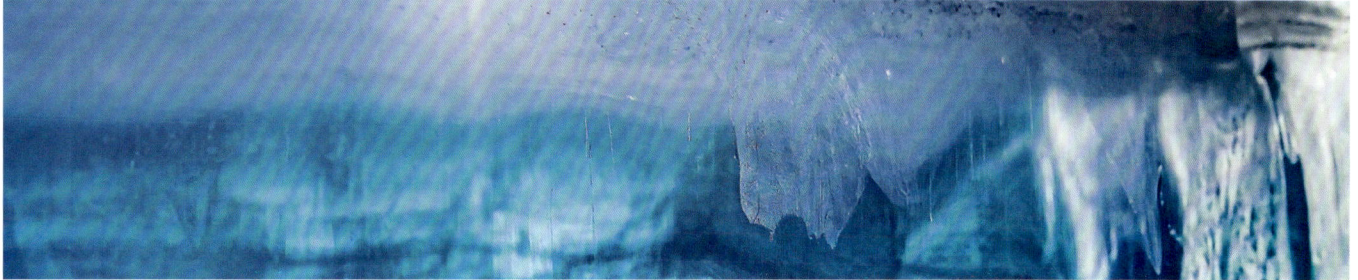

Most sales and marketing veterans agree that 40–60 percent of the time, customers decide whom they would prefer to buy from before proposals are submitted.

The aim of capture planning is to position the customer to prefer your organization and your solution to the exclusion of competitors, or to at least prefer to do business with your organization prior to proposals being submitted.

The phrase capture planning originated in the 1980s in organizations that were primarily focused on large U.S. Department of Defense opportunities.

Concurrently, commercial organizations pursuing large, complex opportunities were developing detailed account or sales planning disciplines. Both were pursuing complex opportunities with the following characteristics:

- High value
- Buying committees (multiple people influencing the purchase decision)
- Long sales cycles (months or years)

Some organizations use the terms *capture plan* and *account plan* interchangeably. However, many account plans are not opportunity specific and may merely allocate the organization's revenue objective among accounts. Capture planning is opportunity specific.

See BID DECISIONS *and* PROCESS, Proposal Guide.

CAPTURE PLANNING, AN OVERVIEW

1 Implement a capture planning discipline to capture new business more efficiently.

2 Enhance capture planning effectiveness by aligning activities.

3 Select a compatible medium—whether text, presentation, or web-based—to develop, review, share, and update capture plans.

4 Keep the process dynamic, flexible, interactive, and current.

5 Maintain a balance between planning and execution.

6 Complete the Integrated Customer Solution Worksheet and the Bidder Comparison Chart— even when time is short.

7 Gain and maintain senior management approval and support.

8 Commit the right people to the capture team.

9 Assign specific, measurable objectives, schedules, and completion dates to individuals, by name.

10 Establish regular decision gate reviews to determine whether to advance the opportunity to the next phase or end the pursuit.

11 Schedule color team reviews to improve the capture plan.

12 Use the capture plan to jump-start the proposal planning process.

A capture planning best practice is to prepare a documented, action-oriented capture plan. While the length, complexity, and format may vary, a documented plan offers reviewable evidence of the quality of thinking of the planners and soundness of the plan.

The primary audience for a capture plan is each person who will manage, approve, or execute the plan, the proposal, and the resulting contract.

A good capture plan will be realistic and specific, detailing the objective, action, responsible individual, timing, and frequency of review.

Organizations that apply a formal capture planning discipline benefit in the following ways:

- More realistic understanding of each opportunity
- Saved time, reduced capture cost, and improved win rates
- Improved bid decisions
- Improved solutions and capture strategies
- Greater consensus and information transfer among individuals pursuing each opportunity

1 IMPLEMENT A CAPTURE PLANNING DISCIPLINE TO CAPTURE NEW BUSINESS MORE EFFICIENTLY.

Disciplined capture planning offers benefits to everyone involved:

- Executives gain early and regular visibility over business development opportunities.
- Sales and business development professionals win more opportunities by efficiently specifying and managing capture activities.
- Organizations increase revenue by efficiently deploying limited business development resources.
- Participants are motivated by knowing their efforts are productive.
- Employees stay employed.

Unlike the top-down, management-driven corporate planning process, capture planning is opportunity specific. Capture plans are driven bottom-up by the opportunity and the customer, as illustrated in figure 1.

The discipline associated with best-in-class capture planning aligns organizational objectives and investment with high-win probability opportunities within approved strategic business objectives.

Capture planning nests efficiently within existing business development and planning processes, as illustrated in figure 2. Strategic business plans contain data about markets, trends, buying history, and competitors. Some organizations will prepare a strategic plan and a separate, annual business plan.

Account plans contain data about the customer's strategic direction, management, history, financial performance, issues, buying plans and patterns, competition, and suppliers. Strategic business plans and account plans are rich sources of data for the capture plan.

Much information in one plan applies in subsequent plans, such as proposal or closure plans. Business capture efficiency and effectiveness are improved when all employees have consistent information and communicate consistent messages to customers.

Business development professionals often question the emphasis on a written plan. Because a capture plan is a collaborative effort, contrast the before-and-after states.

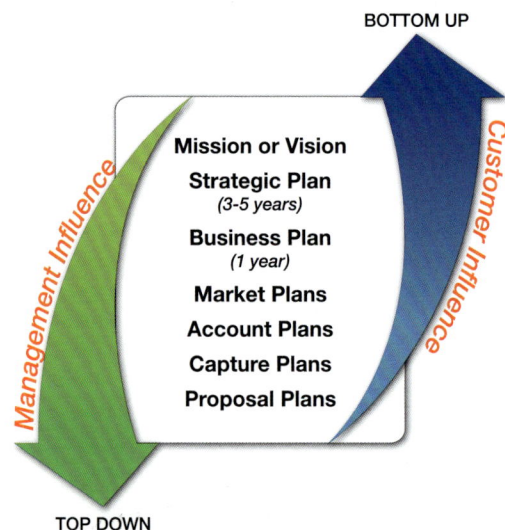

Figure 1. Planning Hierarchy. *Capture planning is driven bottom-up by the customer's opportunity-specific needs. It is also influenced top-down within the context of the overall corporate and sales planning process.*

©Shipley Associates

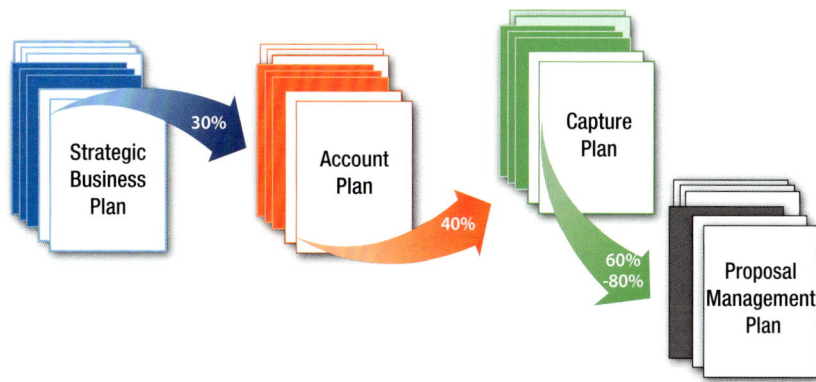

Figure 2. Capture Planning Improves New Business Efficiency. *Much of the data in each plan can be reused because it transfers or flows into the next plan. Up to 80 percent of the capture plan data is reused in the proposal plan or closure plan.*

2 ENHANCE CAPTURE PLANNING EFFECTIVENESS BY ALIGNING ACTIVITIES.

In the context of moving from an unknown to a favored position with the customer, figure 3 shows the types of activities to take and the focus of those activities.

To move from an unknown to a known position with the customer, research, analyze, and validate your data with the customer. Validation is key because the only relevant view is the customer's view.

The next step is to develop and define your solution, strategy, cost, and price to win from a known position. The listed capture plan elements often include tools and templates that help you develop and document your position.

Next, implement your action plans to influence the customer and improve your position. Change requires action.

Keep iterating to achieve and then maintain a favored position. With every action, factor newly gained information into your analysis. Fine-tune your solution, strategy, cost, and price to win. Update your action plans and implement.

Figure 3. Aligning the Capture Planning Process to the Capture Plan. *In the over-arching capture planning process, you seek to move from positions of "unknown," to "known," and then to an "improved position." Elements of the capture plan are matched to this iterative process by phase. Specific content of your capture plans will vary depending on the opportunity, your organization, and the value of the opportunity to your organization.*

3 SELECT A COMPATIBLE MEDIUM—WHETHER TEXT, PRESENTATION, OR WEB-BASED—TO DEVELOP, REVIEW, SHARE, AND UPDATE CAPTURE PLANS.

Envision a capture plan as a framework, a series of folders where you assemble and organize data by topic. Ask capture team members to add, update, share, and purge data as relevant and permitted.

The original capture plan medium and structure was a text-based document that evolved from strategic plans, annual business plans, market plans, and account plans. Given a preferred table of contents, preparers knew what was expected, information could be adapted from prior plans, and the plan could be read before a gate review—which potentially shortened the information transfer portion of the review. Text-based plans may take more time to prepare, are harder to update, and often are not kept current.

See SAMPLE TEMPLATE 1 *for a PowerPoint-based example.*

Many organizations select presentation-based plans instead of text-based plans, primarily because they are easier to prepare, review, and update collaboratively. Some business development managers use the presentation format to collaboratively construct the first draft with a less-experienced capture manager. They use the initial gate review to gain maximum participation and input, turning the review into a facilitated free-for-all. Handled diplomatically, this is an effective, constructive approach.

An additional advantage of presentation-based plans is that they are web-conference adaptable, which eases scheduling of busy executives, reduces meeting costs, and secures input from geographically dispersed experts. Presentation-based formats are easily customized, both a positive and negative aspect.

See SAMPLE TEMPLATE 2 *for a Word-based example.*

A disadvantage of presentation-based templates is the omission of supporting detail. Ask preparers to link, reference, or attach support files or folders.

Web-based collaboration tools are secure ways to collaboratively prepare and share capture information and documents. Keeping the latest data available to all authorized participants is far preferable to having multiple, outdated versions on laptops and desktops, where the capture manager and key participants cannot locate or identify the current version.

One of the best features of the online, web-based format is that senior managers can readily track progress, updates, and activity. The lack of updates suggests that nothing is happening.

Another advantage is immediate access for participants dispersed across multiple time zones. While conferencing might be inconvenient, web material is always available and can be updated while others sleep.

Many participants have a collaboration tool installed as an organizational standard. Getting business development professionals to use web-based tools takes some initial file structuring, training, and then management persistence to use it consistently. If not, participants will revert to old habits of keeping multiple, outdated files on their laptops.

Maintaining file security and access rights is a must. The person controlling access must be readily available, or participants will become frustrated and not use the tool.

©Shipley Associates

4 KEEP THE PROCESS DYNAMIC, FLEXIBLE, INTERACTIVE, AND CURRENT.

Keep your capture planning process flexible to permit adjustments depending on the importance of the opportunity to your organization, the competitive situation, and the resources you can afford to commit. Adapt to the needs and acceptable norms of your organization.

Build the plan interactively to support a fast start with reasonable effort and to encourage regular updates. Capture plans are living documents that are repeatedly updated as you gain information. Information will change and become more specific as the opportunity matures. Figure 4 reflects a practical progression: populate, validate, update, and implement.

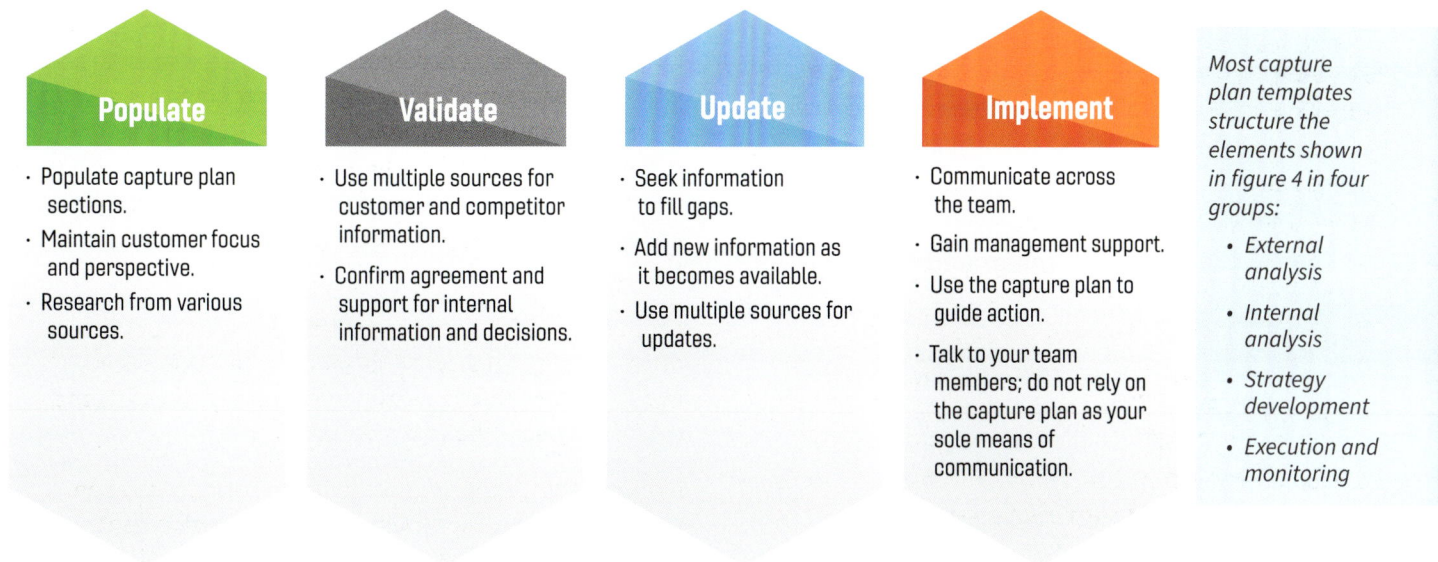

Populate

· Populate capture plan sections.
· Maintain customer focus and perspective.
· Research from various sources.

Validate

· Use multiple sources for customer and competitor information.
· Confirm agreement and support for internal information and decisions.

Update

· Seek information to fill gaps.
· Add new information as it becomes available.
· Use multiple sources for updates.

Implement

· Communicate across the team.
· Gain management support.
· Use the capture plan to guide action.
· Talk to your team members; do not rely on the capture plan as your sole means of communication.

Most capture plan templates structure the elements shown in figure 4 in four groups:

· *External analysis*
· *Internal analysis*
· *Strategy development*
· *Execution and monitoring*

Figure 4. Iteratively Develop Your Capture Plan. *Keep your capture plan current and correct by repeatedly updating the content. Populate: complete what you think you know; validate: check and confirm; update: add and correct data; and implement.*

5 MAINTAIN A BALANCE BETWEEN PLANNING AND EXECUTION.

Changing perceptions requires action. Detailed plans without action are a waste of time because they fail to influence customers' perceptions.

Limit your plans to the resources available. If more resources are needed than your organization will commit to win, reconsider your pursuit decision.

Effective capture planning requires a balance between action and planning.

Assign deadlines to each action item and enforce accountability at each milestone in the capture plan.

6   COMPLETE THE INTEGRATED SOLUTION WORKSHEET AND THE BIDDER COMPARISON CHART—EVEN WHEN TIME IS SHORT.

See WIN STRATEGY DEVELOPMENT; and DISCRIMINATORS, Proposal Guide.

The "gap" is the difference between the customer's requirement and your available solution.

The Shipley Integrated Solution Worksheet, shown in figure 5, is a powerful analysis tool that should be applied throughout the capture process. Early in the process, use it to focus collaboratively with your customer to define the issues and influence the requirements. If you discover an opportunity after requirements are defined, use it to define the underlying issues driving the customer's requirements.

Next, extend your analysis to outline your solution, outline your competitors' solutions, identify discriminators, and then develop your strategy and actions to better position your solution with the customer.

The Shipley Bidder Comparison Chart, shown in figure 6, is used to analyze the customer's current perception of how your solution compares to various competitors. Use it repeatedly throughout the capture process to measure the strength and effectiveness of your positioning. A Bidder Comparison Chart helps guide the development of your win strategy.

ShipleyAssociates®   **Integrated Solution Worksheet**

Item No.	Customer Issues	Customer Requirements	Available Solution	Gap	Competitor Solution	Discriminators	Strategy	Action Required
1	System must be available.	8 hr. response time.	2 hr. response time	1 hr	3 hr. response time	Faster response but more expensive?	Emphasize no additional cost with cellular.	Show current response time. Show photo-service with cell phone.

Figure 5. **Integrated Solution Worksheet.** *Begin by filling out the Customer Issues column when you are early in the process. If the customer has already drafted requirements, fill out the Customer Requirements column. Then complete each row horizontally, carefully evaluating each item.*

Additional uses and alternative approaches for the Integrated Solution Worksheet and Bidder Comparison Chart are discussed in EXECUTIVE SUMMARIES, WIN STRATEGY DEVELOPMENT, *and* TEAMING.

Customers have issues. Sellers have gaps. Essentially, gaps are sellers' issues.

ShipleyAssociates   **Bidder Comparison Chart**

Issues	Weight	Us		Competitor A		Competitor B		Competitor C		Competitor D		Competitor E	
		Points	Score	Points	Score	Points	Score	Points	Score	Points	Score	Points	Score
Specific Experience	10	8	80	7	70	5	50						
Low Price	10	3	30	5	50	8	80						
Familiarity with Manager Named	10	8	80	5	50	5	50						
Ability to Meet Schedule	10	8	80	7	70	5	50						
Totals			270		240		230						

Figure 6. **Bidder Comparison Chart.** *First list the customer's issues, then the relative importance of each issue as perceived by the customer in the Weight column. Then complete each row horizontally, indicating your estimate of the customer's perception of each competitor's ability to satisfy that issue. Scores can range from 0 to the total number in the Weight column.*

7   GAIN AND MAINTAIN SENIOR MANAGEMENT APPROVAL AND SUPPORT.

Top management must endorse and help communicate the plan to everyone managing and executing the plan, as well as those impacted by the reassignment of individuals to support the plan.

Management support must begin with the pursuit decision and continue through to the signed contract. If the opportunity remains worth winning, keep management sold by emphasizing the value to your organization. If contingent items change your assumptions, then revisit your pursuit or bid decision.

Recognize and avoid the bias toward happy information. Capture managers should feel free to reveal negative information to senior management. Similarly, senior management should never punish a capture manager for honestly revealing new information that might suggest a no-pursuit or no-bid decision.

8   COMMIT THE RIGHT PEOPLE TO THE CAPTURE TEAM.

Organizations pursuing competitive business should assign their best people to capture teams. Organizations that assign only the people they can spare from other activities usually lose the sale. Figure 7 summarizes the focus of the capture, program, and proposal managers.

Capture manager is often a role rather than a position. In most organizations, the sales or business development lead is assigned the capture manager role. However, in organizations focused on the largest opportunities, the capture manager role may be assigned to a person from program management, business development, or line management.

The capture manager role requires a person with customer and market knowledge, sales savvy, proposal experience, leadership skills, broad technical understanding, knowledge of the organization, and positive enthusiasm. The capture manager advocates the customer's position while focusing on winning the opportunity. The capture manager is concerned with the customer's budget, program cost, risk, competitive analysis, capture strategy, price to win, the customer's view of best value, and implementing the capture strategy.

Program manager is likely to be a position as well as a role and is responsible for delivery of proposed solution. If the solution is design oriented, then a chief engineer, systems engineer, or solution architect might support or overrule the program manager. The program manager advocates for the selling organization, focusing on profit, the seller's risk, schedule, personnel, resources, assumptions, terms and conditions, and the shape of the delivery organization.

Proposal manager as a role, while not mutually exclusive to the capture manager role, requires different skills to integrate the concerns of the capture and program managers. The proposal manager focuses on compliance, responsiveness,

keeping the proposal strategy aligned with the capture strategy, proposal strategy implementation, and managing a team to produce a persuasive document within set deadlines.

In addition to the core team leadership, capture team members' skills must be suited to their assigned action, whether direct customer contact, internal development, or assisting the proposal team.

See CAPTURE TEAM SELECTION AND MANAGEMENT.

See APPENDIX A: TEAM ROLES AND RESPONSIBILITIES, Business Development Lifecycle Guide.

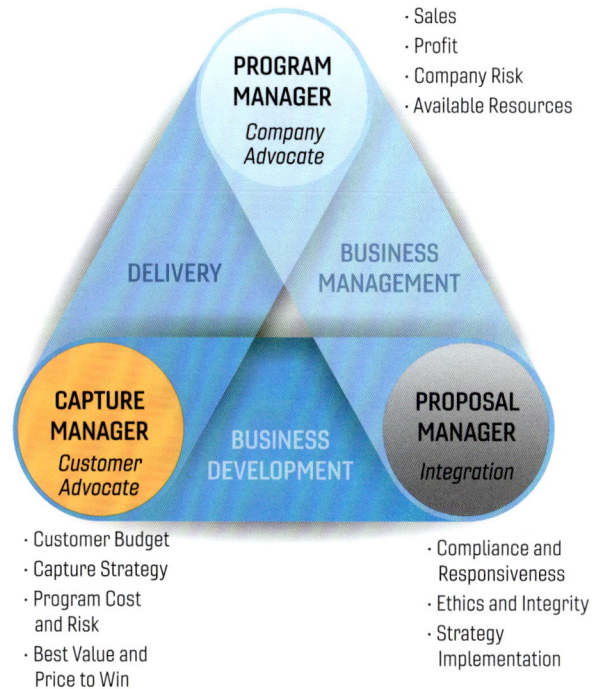

- Sales
- Profit
- Company Risk
- Available Resources

- Customer Budget
- Capture Strategy
- Program Cost and Risk
- Best Value and Price to Win

- Compliance and Responsiveness
- Ethics and Integrity
- Strategy Implementation

Figure 7. The Business Development Opportunity Team. *Win rates improve when the capture, program, and proposal manager team is balanced and integrated.*

9 ASSIGN SPECIFIC, MEASURABLE OBJECTIVES, SCHEDULES, AND COMPLETION DATES TO INDIVIDUALS, BY NAME.

Many capture team action assignments are part-time and for a limited duration. The managers of the assigned individuals should ensure task completion.

Many capture efforts fail because the individuals assigned to the task are expected to complete the task in their spare time.

Capture team members must be serious about completing the task, eliminating the task, or not bidding due to lack of resources. The single biggest reason for losing competitive business is the failure to adequately influence the customer prior to proposal submittal.

The individuals assigned to the management roles listed in figure 8 manage the capture and proposal preparation action

assignments. The chart roughly depicts typical involvement by management role throughout the opportunity lifecycle.

Set and schedule specific, measurable action objectives to simplify task management. Contrast poor and better objectives:

Poor Objective

Discuss service call procedures with the customer.

Better Objective

Demonstrate our online service call management system with Ms. Bell, Global's office manager, during the week ending May 15, 20XX.

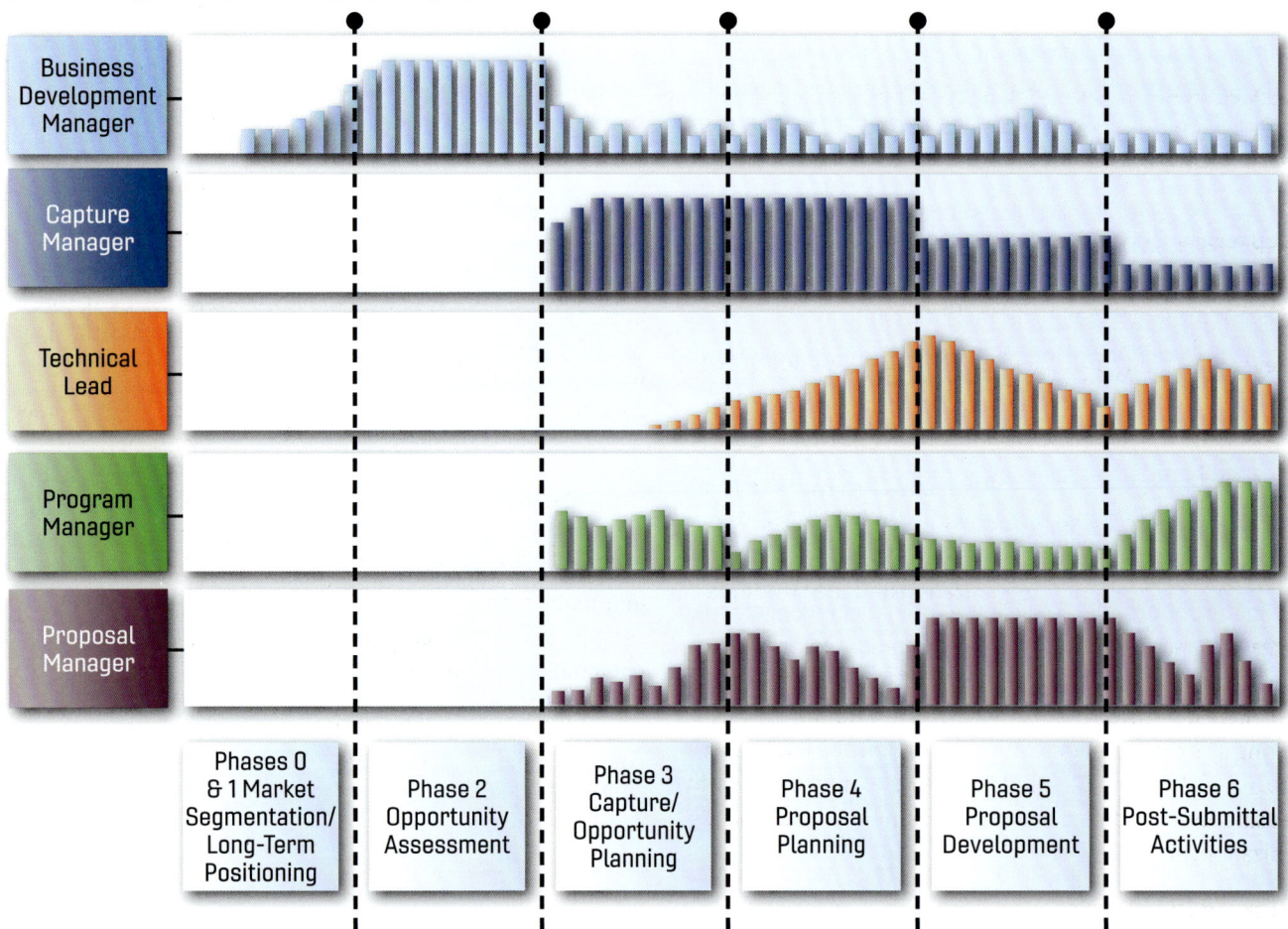

Figure 8. Capture Time Commitment by Role. *This notional representation shows how time commitments of individuals in different roles vary throughout the business development phases. A business development manager leads the process, then hands responsibility to a capture manager. The capture manager's involvement declines as the technical lead and proposal manager become more involved in proposal development. All but the proposal manager might have a spike in commitment after proposal submission in preparation for final contract negotiation and award.*

10 ESTABLISH REGULAR DECISION GATE REVIEWS TO DETERMINE WHETHER TO ADVANCE THE OPPORTUNITY TO THE NEXT PHASE OR END THE PURSUIT.

Decision gate reviews are milestones between business development process phases. The phases are shown below. Focus on four key questions:

1. Is the opportunity winnable?
2. Do the potential returns justify the expenditures?
3. Is the capture team prepared for the next phase?
4. What additional resources are required to win?

Decision gate reviews are the decision milestones between phases of the business development process, as shown in figure 9.

See DECISION GATE REVIEWS.

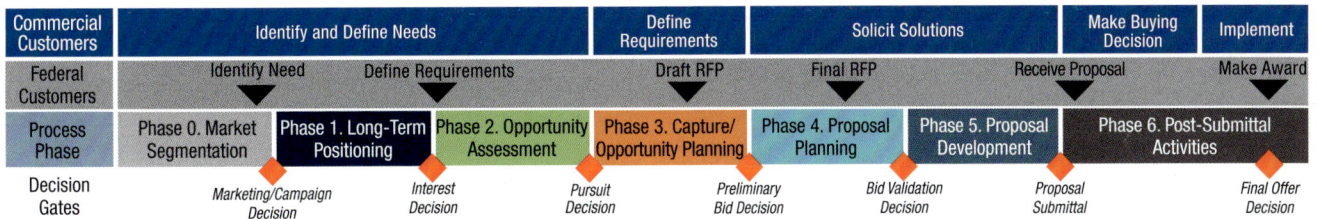

Figure 9. Relationship Among Selling Phase and Decision Gate Reviews. *Senior managers participate in decision gate reviews focusing on whether to advance, defer, or end the pursuit. The focus is on decisions.*

To keep reviews short and effective, focus on reviewing the actions taken, analyzing the results of those actions, reaching milestones, and then adjusting future actions.

Base every decision gate review on the current version of the capture plan. Keeping your capture plan updated eliminates the need to prepare for each review.

Establish organizational standards for each review. Set clear expectations by specifying review inputs and outputs linked to the value of the opportunity, selling environment, and strategic importance to your organization and the customer.

Progressively add content and detail as the opportunity matures and you advance through successive gates. Your initial interest decision gate review will likely be short, perhaps requiring less than 10 slides with information at a basic level, but successive bid and bid validation reviews might grow with increasing levels of detail, depending upon the opportunity, organization, and selling environment.

Recheck the underlying data, assumptions, and analysis only when objectives are not met or new data is uncovered. Reviewers that over-focus on the data and analysis usually under-focus on future actions. Changing a customer's perceptions requires action, not analysis.

Maintain a positive, constructive tone during reviews. Avoid penalizing contributors who raise unfavorable information that might lead to no-pursuit or no-bid decisions. Remember that the most successful organizations eventually pursue less than 30 percent of their pipeline and achieve win rates of 70 percent or greater. Seek good decisions while avoiding a bias toward go-forward decisions.

Early warning signs leading to a no-bid decision are limited information, indecision about where to obtain needed information, and limited capture team or senior management commitment. Winning competitive business requires laser-focus on winnable opportunities.

The most successful organizations eventually pursue less than 30 percent of their pipeline and achieve win rates of 70 percent or greater.

Losing bids are the most costly bids. No-bid decisions free you to shift limited resources to winnable opportunities.

11 SCHEDULE COLOR TEAM REVIEWS TO IMPROVE THE CAPTURE PLAN.

The essential quality-improvement principle is to review for the right things at the right time. Use color team reviews to solicit constructive recommendations for improvement.

See COLOR TEAM REVIEWS.

Differentiate color team reviews and decision gate reviews. Focus color teams on capture plan and proposal response quality improvement; focus decision gate reviews on whether to advance, defer, or end the pursuit.

Adapt the number and types of reviews to your organization, your business development process, selling environment, and the importance of the opportunity. While six different color reviews were shown in figure 9, most organizations conduct some variant of the following three reviews:

1. Win strategy, customer approach, and actions to influene the customer (Blue Team review)
2. Competitors, competitive assessment, and probable discriminators (Black Hat review)
3. Proposal planned content and messages before writing (Pink Team review)

4. Proposal near-final content against the customer's needs, requirements, and evaluation criteria (Red Team review)

Both the number of reviews and color designations for reviews vary widely by organization.

Align the background of the reviewers to the color team review. Seek reviewers that offer varied perspectives on the customer, competitors, selling organization or team, and solution.

Seek comprehensive and constructive recommendations for improvement. Appoint an independent, experienced facilitator to manage the color team review. Train inexperienced reviewers, and then establish clear instructions and standards before initiating the review.

Request consolidated recommendations from the review team. The capture team and executive sponsor then must decide which recommendations will be implemented, who will implement them, and debrief the team.

12 USE THE CAPTURE PLAN TO JUMP-START THE PROPOSAL PLANNING PROCESS.

Most of the information needed to prepare the proposal management plan can be extracted from a current and complete capture plan.

Relying on the capture plan to quickly prepare the initial proposal management plan saves time and maintains a consistent message. Without a capture plan, a newly assigned proposal manager starts from scratch, often with little help and under severe time constraints.

Capture plans and proposal plans have the common elements illustrated in figure 10. Information on the customer, requirements, and competitors transfers directly. The capture strategy needs to be extended or converted into a proposal strategy. Only the proposal outline, compliance checklist, proposal preparation schedule, and the writers' packages need to be created.

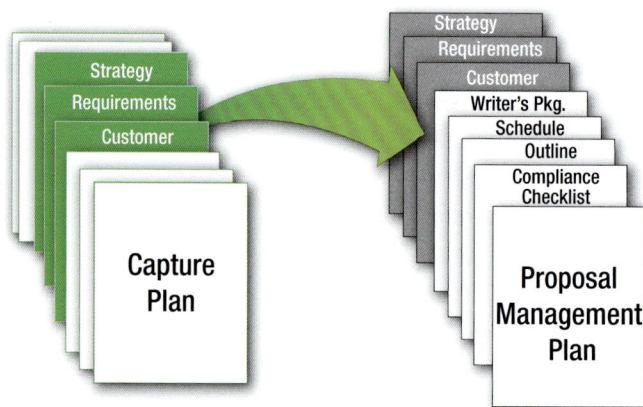

Figure 10. Capture Plans Evolve into Proposal Plans. *A current capture plan effectively front-loads the proposal plan. With approximately 60 to 80 percent of the information transferring from the capture plan, you only need to add proposal-specific material. Shortening the final proposal planning interval prior to kickoff leaves more time to develop a winning proposal.*

©Shipley Associates

CAPTURE TEAM SELECTION AND MANAGEMENT

Capture team selection and management are a matter of roles rather than positions. Capture teams range from a part-time person to a group of exclusively assigned individuals. Identify and commit individuals who have the skills, knowledge, availability, and interest to fulfill their assigned roles.

The composition of an ideal capture team varies by opportunity, depending upon customer issues and motivators, your competitive position with the customer, the technology, and individual experience with this customer. Larger, more complex opportunities usually require larger capture teams.

Assign capture team members with the right skills, knowledge, and availability. If you anticipate numerous meetings and reviews with a customer, then consider interpersonal and presentation skills. If you need to integrate or adapt new technology, consider technical knowledge.

While over-committed individuals are often the best qualified, realistically consider whether they have time within your schedule. If availability is the primary qualification, keep looking or revisit your pursuit decision.

Capture managers are made, not born. Most organizations develop capture managers internally.

CAPTURE TEAM SELECTION AND MANAGEMENT

1 Value capture management skills over technical and customer knowledge when selecting a capture manager.

2 Persuade senior leadership to commit adequate resources.

3 Define core capture team roles.

4 Identify an integrated capture team with the knowledge, skills, and experience needed to support the opportunity.

5 Train the capture team.

6 Hold a kickoff meeting to jump-start the capture effort.

7 Delegate capture work with clear expectations, schedules, target completion dates, and reporting.

8 Keep senior management informed and involved, and never surprise your management sponsor.

9 Evaluate capture success.

10 Engage with your project execution team.

1   VALUE CAPTURE MANAGEMENT SKILLS OVER TECHNICAL AND CUSTOMER KNOWLEDGE WHEN SELECTING A CAPTURE MANAGER.

The strongest and most successful capture plans are based upon detailed, intimate knowledge and understanding of the customer. The only way to develop this skill is by interacting with the customer and not by web research, no matter how sophisticated.

Capture skills are paramount when selecting a capture manager, so distinguish skills and knowledge. A person with capture skills can develop technical and customer knowledge, or team with people who offer these assets.

While sales and capture professionals must both be persuasive, the ideal capture professional demonstrates the skills summarized in figure 1. Established sales professionals usually possess most of the skills listed. If you can afford both a sales professional and capture manager, then select a capture manager with the authority to identify and commit additional resources.

Most capture efforts are lost due to poor capture intelligence.

International capture efforts need to be led by someone who is very familiar with (ideally, native to) the culture of the customer. If your organization intends to sell significant volume through international offices, consider individuals' capture capabilities by office. Enhance capture skills through training, coaching, and job aids.

In addition to direct customer interface tasks, a capture manager manages the team's capture activities:

- Intelligence collection and analysis
- Strategy development and implementation
- Customer contact and positioning
- Teaming
- Price to win
- Proposal initiation, planning, and review
- Solution development, testing, and communication
- Post-submittal negotiation and closure
- Program initiation, start-up, and extension

ESSENTIAL SKILLS	ACTIONS THAT DEMONSTRATE THE SKILL
Leadership	Builds a common vision with the internal capture team, customers, and teaming partners
Facilitation	Initiates and encourages collaborative team discussions
Strategy Development	Builds customer-focused strategies and tactics
Motivation	Creates a winning environment
Data Analysis	Turns data into useful intelligence
Management	Keeps the team focused on tasks, schedules, and standards
Persuasion	Convinces senior management to commit sufficient skills and resources

Figure 1. Essential Capture Manager Skills. *Technical knowledge is a plus, but not paramount. Assign capture managers who can demonstrate or develop these essential skills.*

©Shipley Associates

2   PERSUADE SENIOR LEADERSHIP TO COMMIT ADEQUATE RESOURCES.

Every capture manager needs a senior leadership sponsor. If one has not emerged naturally, seek and cultivate a sponsor.

Identify the team and resources needed to capture the opportunity, and persuade senior leadership that your request is necessary, appropriate, and justifiable. Your objective is to position the customer to prefer your organization and solution. You need the personnel and resources to complete specific action and contact plan tasks. Justify the capture budget based on potential revenue, profitability, and the win probability.

Place key individuals from subcontractor organizations into advisory roles for adding capture resources, reducing capture cost, and demonstrating to the customer that your subcontractors are as important and qualified as you claim.

Suggest other sources of funds. If needed, identify synergies with other programs or capture activities.

The senior leadership sponsor champions the capture effort with the executive management team and mentors the capture manager.

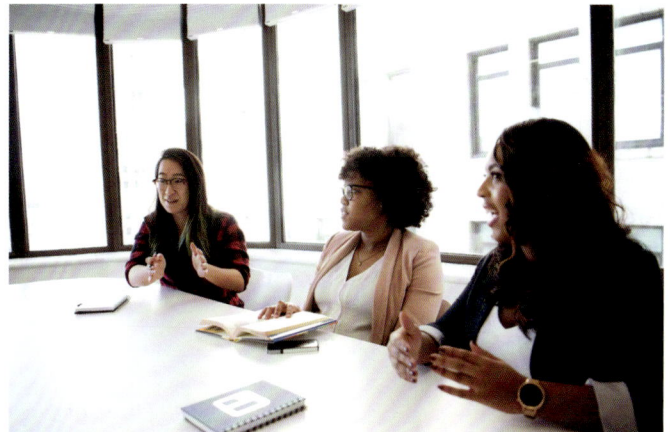

3   DEFINE CORE CAPTURE TEAM ROLES.

The four core capture roles of the capture process are the capture manager, proposal manager, program or project manager, and pricing specialist. While all four roles might be filled by a single person, they are distinct roles with specific responsibilities.

The capture manager is responsible for winning or losing. The capture manager directs customer contact before, during, and after the proposal is submitted, conforming to the customer's rules. The capture manager owns the capture strategy and aligns tactical actions with this strategy.

The proposal manager leads the proposal team and is responsible for proposal resources, planning, scheduling, development, and production of the proposal. The primary focus of proposal management is to produce a winning proposal document. The proposal manager owns the proposal strategy, derived from the capture strategy, and clearly implements that strategy in the proposal document or presentation.

The program or project manager develops a winning solution that is compliant and responsive and is acceptable to the selling organization. Generally, the program manager is responsible to the strategic business unit manager for profitability and risk management.

The pricing specialist estimates overall costs for capture efforts, partnering, and proposal preparation to determine the opportunity's price to win. The pricing specialist collaborates with other core capture team members to determine various costs.

Refine the roles and responsibilities for your organization, depending upon the size of your organization, market, value of the opportunity, and skills of the people assigned to each role. Figure 2 summarizes the potential responsibilities by role.

ROLE	KEY RESPONSIBILITIES
CAPTURE/OPPORTUNITY MANAGER Customer knowledge, marketing savvy, proposal experience, technical insight, creative casting experience, leadership skills, enthusiasm, organization knowledge, project management ability	• Manages opportunity from pursuit decision through program start-up • Develops capture plan and capture strategy • Gathers and updates intelligence on competitive positioning • Develops and owns capture strategy throughout opportunity lifecycle • Builds and sustains customer relationships • Plans and manages customer interface • Defines and manages capture budget • Leads competitive analysis, price-to-win analysis, and establishes team cost targets • Oversees transition of capture plan into the proposal management plan • Mentors proposal core team on win strategy and solution • Develops the first draft of the proposal executive summary • Instigates and schedules decision gate reviews. Drives or contributes to gate reviews • Supports color team reviews • Briefs senior management at decision gate/milestone reviews
PROPOSAL MANAGER Proposal management expertise, strong corporate knowledge, writing skills, ability to manage and coach writers, ability to present information orally, research skills, management savvy, strong work ethic	• Develops proposal strategy, proposal themes, and proposal discriminators that align with the capture strategy • Completes the executive summary initially drafted by the capture manager • Develops and implements the proposal management plan • Focuses on producing a winning document or presentation
PROGRAM MANAGER Program management expertise, technically capable and knowledgeable, schedule discipline, organization skills, customer relations expertise, written and oral communication skills, basic knowledge of contracting processes, negotiation skills	• Participates in or guides solution development, including technical issues, trade-off analysis, and costing approach • Positions organization and solution with customer in coordination with the capture manager • Develops conceptual program team and management approach and resolves program issues • Leads program planning: Defines delivery team organization, skills, and staffing levels, and timing; Work Breakdown Structure (WBS); program schedule; preliminary teaming, subcontracting, and vendor selection • Supports intelligence collection and analysis, strategy development, and implementation • Validates capture/proposal solution for practical execution in managing the program
PRICING SPECIALIST Costing experience, should-cost estimating skills, fiscal accounting and management ability, collaboration and research skills	• Collaborates with core capture team to determine should-cost estimates • Develops WBS and Contractor Statement of Work (SOW) • Defines estimating guidelines • Develops price to win and provides documentation that clearly explains to the customer that costs are reasonable and realistic

Figure 2. Key Capture Roles and Responsibilities. *Adapt the potential roles and responsibilities to the nuances of your organization and opportunities.*

©Shipley Associates

4 IDENTIFY AN INTEGRATED CAPTURE TEAM WITH THE KNOWLEDGE, SKILLS, AND EXPERIENCE NEEDED TO SUPPORT THE OPPORTUNITY.

Working with your core capture team, identify the key resources needed to form an integrated team of functional experts, such as those listed in figure 3.

Strive to build the best team possible from across your organization.

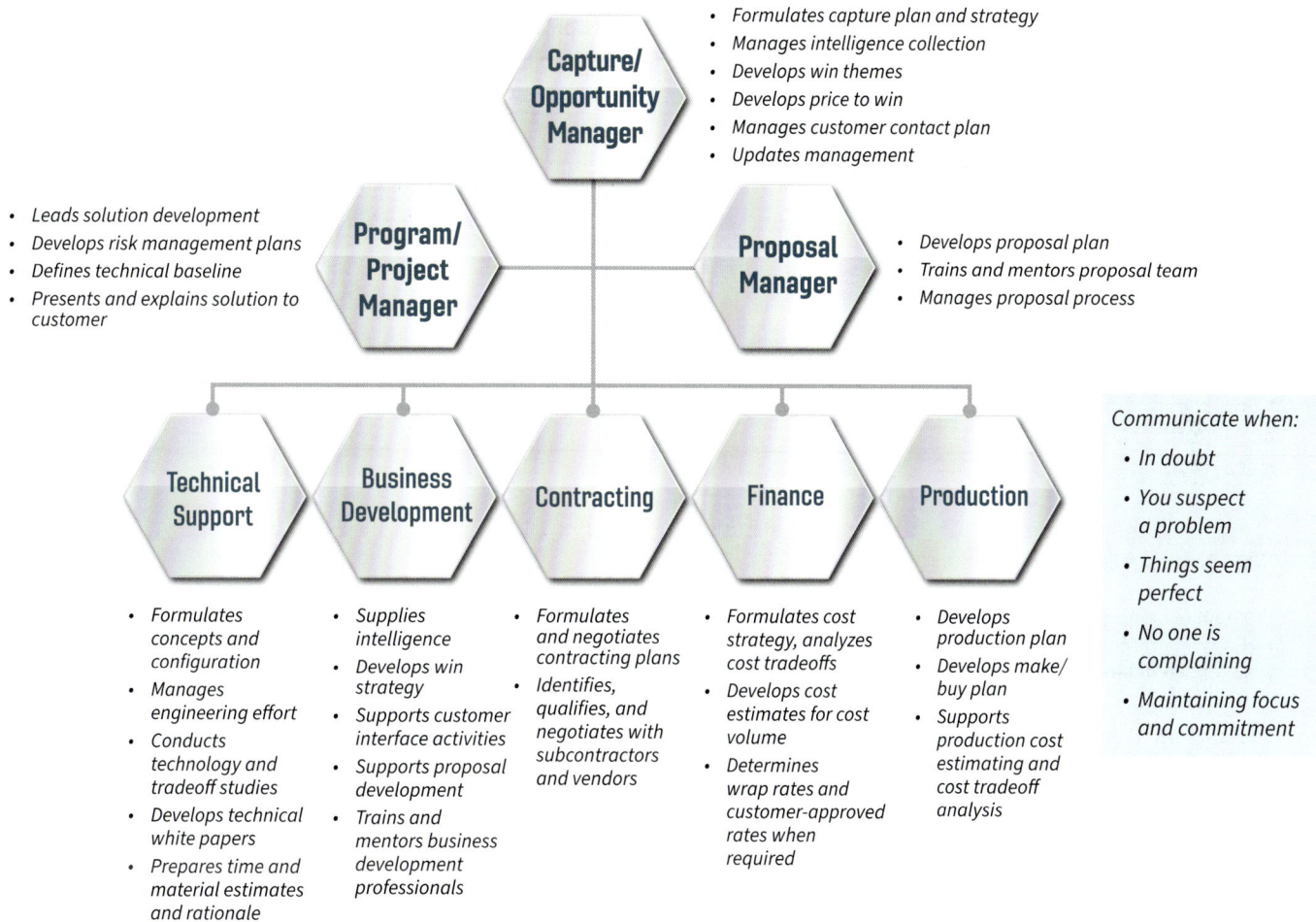

Capture/Opportunity Manager
- Formulates capture plan and strategy
- Manages intelligence collection
- Develops win themes
- Develops price to win
- Manages customer contact plan
- Updates management

Program/Project Manager
- Leads solution development
- Develops risk management plans
- Defines technical baseline
- Presents and explains solution to customer

Proposal Manager
- Develops proposal plan
- Trains and mentors proposal team
- Manages proposal process

Technical Support
- Formulates concepts and configuration
- Manages engineering effort
- Conducts technology and tradeoff studies
- Develops technical white papers
- Prepares time and material estimates and rationale

Business Development
- Supplies intelligence
- Develops win strategy
- Supports customer interface activities
- Supports proposal development
- Trains and mentors business development professionals

Contracting
- Formulates and negotiates contracting plans
- Identifies, qualifies, and negotiates with subcontractors and vendors

Finance
- Formulates cost strategy, analyzes cost tradeoffs
- Develops cost estimates for cost volume
- Determines wrap rates and customer-approved rates when required

Production
- Develops production plan
- Develops make/buy plan
- Supports production cost estimating and cost tradeoff analysis

Communicate when:
- In doubt
- You suspect a problem
- Things seem perfect
- No one is complaining
- Maintaining focus and commitment

Figure 3. Involve Relevant Functional Departments. *Capture efforts are not a solo undertaking. Seek broad participation, incorporating functional departments whose expertise is needed to address evolving customer interests or concerns. While your organization might not look the same as the one illustrated, involve departments that support similar roles.*

5 TRAIN THE CAPTURE TEAM.

Trained, licensed MDs practice medicine. Similarly, trained capture professionals practice capturing business, further developing their skills.

Train capture team members based on their roles and level of experience. Consider the role of senior management, capture team management, and capture team contributors. To be effective, members need to understand their roles and responsibilities and develop the skills to complete assigned tasks.

Opportunity-specific capture training fosters broad input, understanding of the opportunity, and acceptance of the capture strategy by team members.

Capture training focuses on developing different skill sets:

- Understanding the organization's process and individuals' roles within that process
- Developing interpersonal and collaborative skills in oral and written communication
- Using capture and proposal tools within a process framework
- Developing senior leadership's understanding of capture planning, their capture roles, and the impact of best practices on their organization

Differentiate generic and opportunity-specific capture training. Generic training familiarizes individuals with the purpose, principles, and concepts of capture planning. Opportunity–specific training focuses on the strategies and actions needed to win this opportunity. Team members who understand the concept can subsequently commit to their assigned role, task, and the need to integrate their efforts with the team.

See CUSTOMER INTERFACE.

In a complex sale, interactions with the customer must be aligned. If not, customers doubt what you say. Training helps align the team's actions.

Involve your senior leadership sponsor in opportunity-specific training to signal the importance of this capture effort and foster continued member buy-in. If sponsors cannot attend the entire session, ask them to endorse the process, emphasize the importance of the opportunity, contribute to the strategy, and conduct an out-brief at the conclusion or immediately after the training.

Training alone is insufficient to develop competent capture, program, and proposal managers. They also need coaching and mentoring.

Adapt how you train contributors based on their assigned roles and experience. Assess contributors' interpersonal communication and collaboration skills before asking them to interact with customers.

6   HOLD A KICKOFF MEETING TO JUMP-START THE CAPTURE EFFORT.

Hold a capture kickoff meeting, empower the capture manager, and motivate the team to win the opportunity.

When planning a capture kickoff, consider the following points:

- Invite key contributors, their immediate managers, and teaming partners if your teaming agreement is complete.

- Establish a competent, professional tone that inspires confidence in the capture manager and the entire core team.

- Ask your senior management sponsor to open the kickoff meeting, validate the importance of the opportunity, and state what the win means to the participants and their managers.

- Review and clarify roles, authority, and responsibilities

- Be realistic about problems and challenges. Be proactive in finding solutions, defining actions, and establishing responsibilities.

- Collaboratively solve problems. Encourage participants to raise issues and recommend solutions.

- Include vital contributors virtually if they cannot attend in person. Observe the additional ground rules for virtual meetings.

A basic capture kickoff agenda is shown in figure 4.

See VIRTUAL TEAM MANAGEMENT, Proposal Guide.

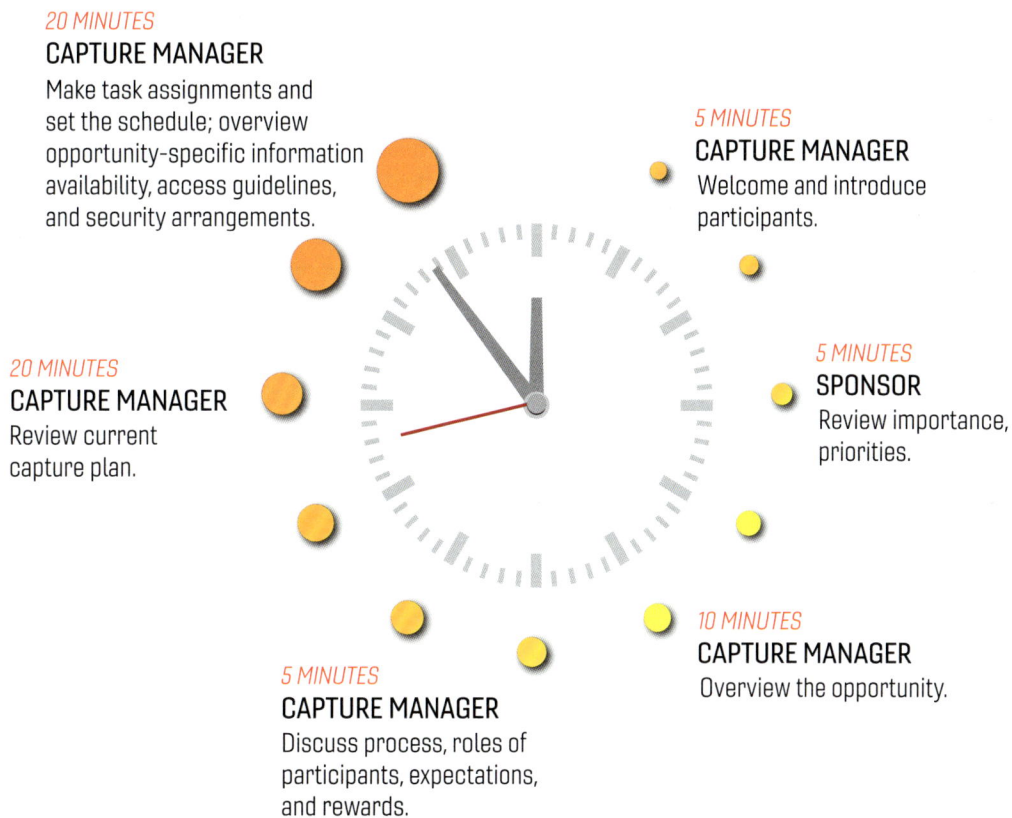

20 MINUTES
CAPTURE MANAGER
Make task assignments and set the schedule; overview opportunity-specific information availability, access guidelines, and security arrangements.

20 MINUTES
CAPTURE MANAGER
Review current capture plan.

5 MINUTES
CAPTURE MANAGER
Discuss process, roles of participants, expectations, and rewards.

5 MINUTES
CAPTURE MANAGER
Welcome and introduce participants.

5 MINUTES
SPONSOR
Review importance, priorities.

10 MINUTES
CAPTURE MANAGER
Overview the opportunity.

Figure 4. Sample Capture Kickoff Agenda. *Incorporate these topics and approximate time allocations when developing your capture kickoff agenda. As the complexity of the opportunity increases, extend the time to overview the opportunity, review the capture plan, and discuss assignments.*

7 DELEGATE CAPTURE WORK WITH CLEAR EXPECTATIONS, SCHEDULES, TARGET COMPLETION DATES, AND REPORTING.

On major capture efforts, individual team members complete most tasks, not the capture manager. On smaller efforts, capture managers complete more of the tasks, and their role increasingly resembles the role of a sales or account manager.

For each assignment, define and clarify the following:

- Objective
- Assigned individual(s)
- Deliverable, charge number, time allocation, and expected outcome
- Expected detail
- Key issues
- Due date

See SCHEDULE AND ACTION PLAN DEVELOPMENT.

- Interim checkpoints/milestones
- Linked tasks requiring coordination
- Dependent tasks

Set completion dates for every task. Schedule gate reviews to communicate progress, seek management input, and gain management support. Schedule color team reviews, such as a Black Hat review, to improve the quality of your capture efforts. Update task schedules as the opportunity progresses.

Synchronize capture efforts with the customer's buying process and schedule. Stay current on updates or changes to the customer's plans and schedules—good intelligence is vital. Decide how new information will be promptly and accurately shared within the capture team.

8 KEEP SENIOR MANAGEMENT INFORMED AND INVOLVED, AND NEVER SURPRISE YOUR MANAGEMENT SPONSOR.

Capture managers are an extension of management and are expected to keep management informed. Follow accepted protocol when addressing sensitive issues.

Discuss sensitive issues with your management sponsor. Discuss if and how sensitive issues will be addressed in gate reviews or other meetings. Many issues are best handled in one-on-one discussions.

Consider the authority, accessibility, schedule constraints, and individual concerns of senior management. Identify and discuss tasks that will require hands-on management assistance.

Task senior managers to meet with customers and potential teaming partners. Seek management help to secure resources, compel indirect reports to complete tasks, and approve budgets.

9 EVALUATE CAPTURE SUCCESS.

The primary measure of capture success is the number and value of quality contracts won. Measuring interim success is more difficult.

Balance the effort to prepare a capture plan, and keep it current.

Define which elements will be reviewed at each gate review and the expected degree of completion of that element. Always hold a lessons learned review.

10 ENGAGE WITH YOUR PROJECT EXECUTION TEAM.

Best-in-class organizations appoint program/project managers early to ensure they are engaged and feel that they own every facet of the solution from start to finish.

The program manager stays involved from this point forward, contributing to capture strategy, proposal planning and preparation, and post-submittal activities.

Figure 5 summarizes typical program manager tasks by business development phase.

CAPTURE PLANNING	PROPOSAL PLANNING	PROPOSAL PREPARATION	POST-SUBMITTAL ACTIVITIES
• Develop program management and execution approach. • Prepare the baseline program management solution. • Participate in teaming and subcontracting discussions. • Help define program management requirements. • Draft preliminary WBS/ Contractor Work Breakdown Structure (CWBS). • Contribute to make/buy and teaming discussions.	• Draft management approach, organization, and key personnel matrix for executive summary. • Complete the annotated outline and first draft of the program management plan. • Prepare preliminary WBS/ CWBS. • Support proposal evaluation and negotiation activities. • Initiate and guide transition planning. • Prepare baseline solution.	• Present baseline solution at proposal kickoff. • Lead management volume and preparation of related plans required with the proposal. • Review alignment of management volume and plans with the technical, past performance, and cost sections. • Check Basis Of Estimates (BOEs) and task descriptions for adherence to cost targets. • Incorporate color team review recommendations. • Prepare and present management plan at orals.	• Support final proposal revisions. • Update transition and program management plans. • Support negotiations. • Present management plan at orals. • Coordinate availability of proposed program personnel, facilities, and systems. • Lead/attend customer debrief, win or lose. • Conduct delivery team kickoff meeting.

Figure 5. Program Manager's Capture Tasks by Phase. *The program manager is an integral part of successful capture efforts from the Pursuit Decision Gate through contract award and start-up. The program manager either leads or collaboratively supports listed tasks.*

The named program manager is the individual who will manage the program upon award. Customers regard the program manager as a key position, even when not stated in the bid request.

The discriminating features of most proposed programs are the individuals assigned to key positions. One of the most important capture strategies is to position the customer to prefer or, at minimum, accept these key personnel.

Carefully tailor the program manager's resume. Specifically address recent experience and performance on similar programs with this client and similar clients. Emphasize the program manager's role in risk management and reduction. Quantify the program manager's performance results, if available.

Showcase and vet the program manager with the customer. Introduce key program personnel early and repeatedly in the capture process by assigning them a prominent role in presentations to customers, bidders' conferences, site

visits, and industry day events. Showcase their skills as knowledgeable, customer-focused communicators. Convince customer personnel that your key program personnel, starting with the program manager, are capable and compatible.

Delegate select tasks to the program manager during the capture effort. When delivering services, the program manager must understand the roles and requirements for every key position and the number of people required. Assign the program manager the following tasks:

- When attempting to unseat an incumbent:
  - Identify and assess the candidates working for the incumbent.
  - Determine candidates' availability and cost.
  - Prepare an incumbent employee recruiting plan.
  - Determine which vacancies can be filled by internal candidates.
  - Prepare to recruit remaining vacancies.

- When you are the incumbent:
    - Evaluate the customer's opinion of key individuals.
    - Determine who will be retained, promoted, lateralled, or dismissed.
    - Recruit replacements and new personnel.
    - Secure recruits' commitments to accept positions, if offered.
- If a new program:
    - Identify and assess availability of internal candidates.
    - Develop recruiting plan.
    - Determine candidates' availability and cost.
    - Secure recruits' commitments to accept positions, if offered.

Formally transition program responsibility from the capture manager to the program manager. Generally, the formal transition point is at contract signing when a prospective customer becomes a new or renewed customer. However, the transition timing varies depending upon the capabilities of the individuals, organizational demands on their time, and duration of post-submittal activities.

Capture managers are often asked to manage multiple opportunities, so the program manager might formally assume responsibility to manage ongoing, post-submittal activities that largely focus on contracting details. When bidding as an incumbent, the program manager is already in place and is best positioned to handle post-submittal activity.

On new contracts, make the transition a formal event that includes key customer representatives. Ask a senior manager from your organization to attend to demonstrate the importance of the contract.

Ask the program manager to lead or support the development of the following items:

- *Solution*
- *Performance Work Statements*
- *Make/buy and work share plans*
- *Work Breakdown Structure*
- *Program plan*
- *Transition plan*
- *Program schedules*
- *Costing*
- *Price-to-win analysis*

Expand the contract during execution by identifying, positioning, proposing, and closing additional tasks. In addition to managing the quality delivery of contracted services, ask program managers to grow the contract by identifying, positioning, proposing, and closing additional tasks. Program managers report spending as much as 60 percent of their time proposing and closing added tasks.

Program managers are in a unique position with unfettered access to the customer organization. Customers increasingly view contractor personnel as fellow employees or as an extension of their work force. Hence, contractor personnel are viewed as collaborators, and these contractor recommendations are accepted as the constructive recommendations of experts.

Ask program managers to devote a small portion of each internal program management meeting to discuss potential new business opportunities. In each meeting, remind employees to ask customers about their needs, review indicators of future or additional needs, and to report these needs to their program manager. Reward employees for their efforts, whether by recognition or remuneration.

Prepare for contract renewal or contract re-competition. Schedule an internal, mid-term program review to summarize customer perceptions and recommend actions to position your organization to renew this contract. If the existing contract has renewal options, persuade the customer to extend the current contract as the best course of action.

Contract renewals are the single most efficient use of business development resources. No other opportunity offers a higher win probability at a lower risk and cost. If you have performance issues, correct them years—not months—before the contract expires.

Following the mid-term contract review, appoint a capture manager, prepare the capture plan, schedule the Blue Team review, and implement the capture plan.

©Shipley Associates

COLOR TEAM REVIEWS

Color team reviews are key milestones where pursuit contributors and managers collaborate to improve the probability of winning (Pwin) a pursuit. Flexibility to adapt to the size and complexity of each pursuit is important.

Use color team reviews to enhance your probability of winning (Pwin) and the effectiveness of your business development process. Conduct or participate in color team reviews to gain unbiased assessments of strategy, progress, quality, and constructive recommendations for improvement.

Differentiate color team reviews from pursuit decision gates. While decision gates determine whether to advance an opportunity to the next business development phase or end the pursuit, color teams strengthen capture planning and proposal development efforts between gates.

Color team reviews can be tactical or strategic. Decision gates often reflect executives' strategies, directions, goals, and priorities. In contrast, color teams help you move forward with the greatest chance of success.

Select color team reviewers with balanced customer, seller, management, technical, and cost perspectives. Align their backgrounds to the review. Select reviewers capable of offering constructive recommendations, independent of their seniority. Train reviewers if necessary.

Make color team reviews constructive by defining and following a consistent approach. Institutionalize key reviews for all opportunities, but be flexible based on the sizes and complexity of the opportunity and your organizational resources.. Add other reviews when they will benefit your organization.

See DECISION GATES REVIEWS; and DECISION GATES, Business Development Lifecycle Guide.

Color team reviews, color teams, and color reviews all refer to the same type of event.

Color team members, color reviewers, and review teams all refer to people performing the color team review.

COLOR TEAM REVIEWS

1 Define your organization's color team review points.

2 Follow a consistent validate cost information for each color team review.

3 Hold a Blue Team to review your capture plan and validate your win strategy.

4 Conduct a Black Hat review to anticipate competitors' likely strategies and solutions and determine gaps in your strategy or solution.

5 Participate in a Pink Team to verify compliance and execution of your win strategy in the proposal.

6 Participate in a Red Team to predict how your proposal will be scored and make improvements to it.

7 Participate in a Green Team to validate cost information and approve pricing.

8 Participate in a Gold Team to confirm your proposal incorporates changes from Red and Green Teams and is ready for submittal.

9 Conduct a White Hat review to record lessons learned and recommend improvements.

10 Select appropriate reviewers and methods for each color team review.

1 DEFINE YOUR ORGANIZATION'S COLOR TEAM REVIEW POINTS.

Most effective business development organizations are successful partly because they follow defined and repeatable processes tailored to each opportunity. While some organizations succeed in spite of or without a defined approach, their probability of success could be increased by following known best practices.

See BUSINESS DEVELOPMENT FRAMEWORK.

Divide business development tasks into phases. The number of phases might vary with the size of your business, organizational culture, and types of opportunities you pursue.

Figure 1 lists seven industry-recognized reviews and their positions within Shipley's seven-phase business development framework. Several early phases have no reviews, either because individual opportunities have not been identified, or they are still being researched. Later phases have several reviews, particularly during proposal development.

Tailor reviews to the size and complexity of each pursuit.

NO.	PHASE	COLOR TEAM REVIEWS
0	Market Segmentation	
1	Long-Term Positioning	
2	Opportunity Assessment	Qualification gates are often part of the opportunity assessment in this phase. Determining capture readiness is a key milestone at this phase of a pursuit.
3	Capture/Opportunity Planning	**Blue Team:** Reviews initial capture planning, focusing on development of win strategy. A second blue team review often takes place after the Black Hat review to confirm win strategy. **Black Hat:** Predicts competitors' solutions to support strategy development and infuse proposal with competitive focus.
4	Proposal Planning	
5	Proposal Development	**Pink Team:** Reviews content plans for compliance and execution of win strategy. **Red Team:** Reviews proposal to predict scoring and improve effectiveness. **Green Team:** Reviews pricing, consistency across volumes. **Gold Team:** Reviews final proposal and price.
6	Post-Submittal Activities	**White Hat:** Documents lessons learned to improve capture and proposal processes.

Figure 1. Each Review Has a Purpose. *Color teams' purposes are based on the status of an opportunity. Blue Team and Black Hat help develop strategy during Capture/Opportunity Planning. Pink, Red, Green, and Gold Teams may occur in rapid sequence during proposal development and focus on creating a compliant, responsive, competitive sales document. White Hat reviews take place after proposals are submitted and help improve future efforts. Agility and flexibility are important to applying color team best practices.*

As a minimum, require reviews that focus on three items:

- Competitors' probable offerings, to identify discriminators (Black Hat review)
- Proposal strategy and messages before drafting text (Pink Team)
- Proposal near-final content compared against the customer's needs and evaluation approach (Red Team)

Some organizations use functional names instead of color identifiers to avoid confusion: win strategy review instead of Blue Team or proposal strategy review rather than Pink Team. Consistency in a naming convention helps maintain quality during each pursuit.

Your goal for the review is more important than the name. Additional reviews usually point to a few situations:

- Customer adjusts their acquisition schedule or plan.
- Your resources are constrained.
- The competitive landscape or teaming arrangements have changed.

At any point, consider ending the pursuit at a decision gate if the probability of winning diminishes significantly.

2   FOLLOW A CONSISTENT APPROACH FOR EACH COLOR TEAM REVIEW.

Each color team review serves a different purpose, prompting a somewhat different form. Some emphasize review, discussion, improvement, or approval of capture or proposal team work. Others are hands-on working sessions that contribute directly to successful pursuit of the opportunity. Regardless of their nature, follow the general methodology outlined in figure 2.

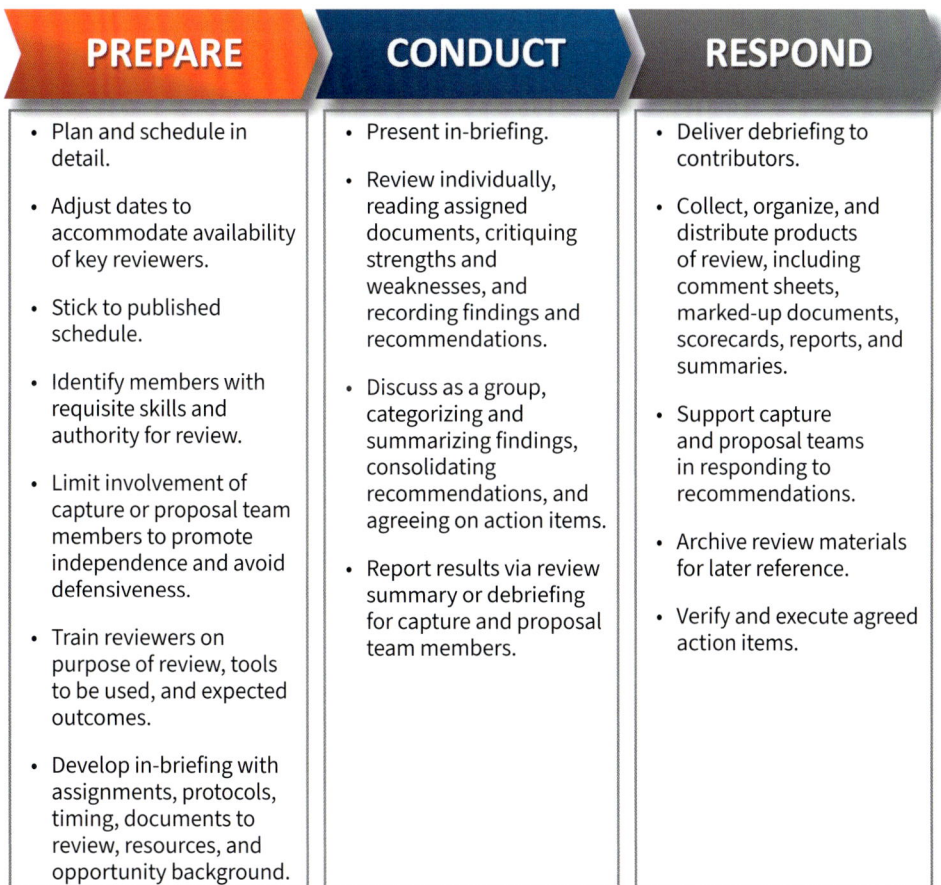

PREPARE	CONDUCT	RESPOND
• Plan and schedule in detail.	• Present in-briefing.	• Deliver debriefing to contributors.
• Adjust dates to accommodate availability of key reviewers.	• Review individually, reading assigned documents, critiquing strengths and weaknesses, and recording findings and recommendations.	• Collect, organize, and distribute products of review, including comment sheets, marked-up documents, scorecards, reports, and summaries.
• Stick to published schedule.		
• Identify members with requisite skills and authority for review.	• Discuss as a group, categorizing and summarizing findings, consolidating recommendations, and agreeing on action items.	• Support capture and proposal teams in responding to recommendations.
• Limit involvement of capture or proposal team members to promote independence and avoid defensiveness.		• Archive review materials for later reference.
• Train reviewers on purpose of review, tools to be used, and expected outcomes.	• Report results via review summary or debriefing for capture and proposal team members.	• Verify and execute agreed action items.
• Develop in-briefing with assignments, protocols, timing, documents to review, resources, and opportunity background.		

Establish consistent standards for color team reviews. Insist that reviewers tell you how to improve, not what is wrong.

Make your reviews:

Comprehensive. *Review all elements of any reviewed document using defined criteria. Consider all the facts, not just favorable ones.*

Positive. *Maintain a collaborative tone aimed at improving your chances, not demoralizing contributors.*

Constructive. *Require reviewers to recommend improvements and eliminate vague, negative comments.*

Figure 2. Approach for Color Team Reviews. *Take a consistent approach to all reviews. No matter the color of the review, follow the same process: prepare, conduct, and respond. At each step, follow the guidelines listed above.*

3 HOLD A BLUE TEAM TO REVIEW YOUR CAPTURE PLAN AND VALIDATE WIN STRATEGY.

The Blue Team review, often referred to as a win strategy review, is the first review of your evolving capture plan. Blue Team members are often independent of the capture team and knowledgeable about the customer, your offerings and capabilities, and competitors' offerings and capabilities.

From Blue Team onward, the capture team should follow the agreed win strategy unless evidence surfaces that it is not making you competitive.

With inputs and outputs as shown in figure 3, the Blue Team's major objectives are to:

- Review your knowledge of the customer and the opportunity
- Review your potential technical and management solutions, verifying their compliance and responsiveness to customer needs
- Agree on strategic actions you can take to position your organization as the customer's preferred choice

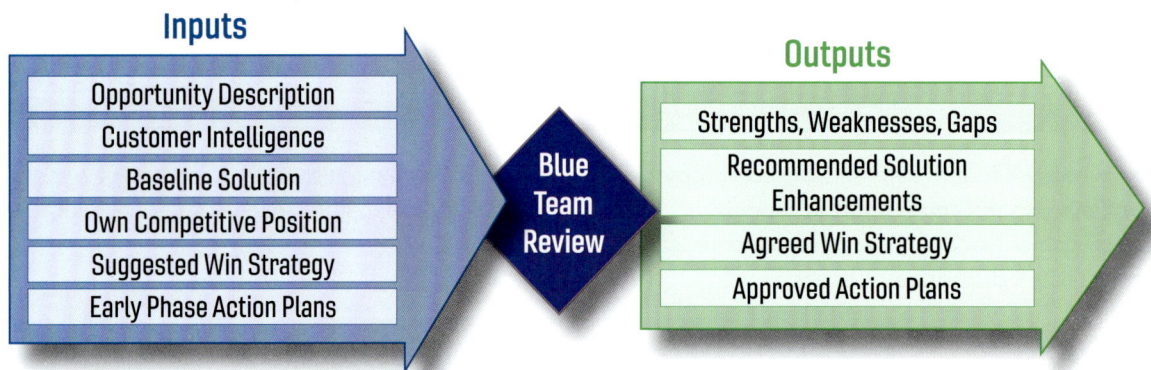

Inputs

- Opportunity Description
- Customer Intelligence
- Baseline Solution
- Own Competitive Position
- Suggested Win Strategy
- Early Phase Action Plans

Blue Team Review

Outputs

- Strengths, Weaknesses, Gaps
- Recommended Solution Enhancements
- Agreed Win Strategy
- Approved Action Plans

Figure 3. **Blue Team Inputs and Outputs.** *The Blue Team analyzes concepts represented by the initial capture plan. Members identify strengths, weaknesses, and gaps, and then recommend improvements. They affirm early capture team actions or recommend modifications. They do not allocate or withdraw resources; the capture manager and executive team will make those decisions at decision gates.*

Blue Team reviews often include both strategy development and approval. In large organizations, the capture team usually develops the win strategy. Blue Team then confirms or adjusts. In smaller organizations where roles overlap, Blue Team might be the working session where the winning approach is crafted. Without Blue Team approval, the capture team will be second-guessed on succeeding activity.

As pursuit cycles lengthen, multiple Blue Teams might be constructive. Where Blue Team #1 would look at a very preliminary capture plan and solution set, Blue Team #2 might assess a more complete plan, review a formal proposal management plan, and confirm a more advanced proposal strategy.

See SAMPLE TEMPLATE 6.

4   CONDUCT A BLACK HAT REVIEW TO ANTICIPATE COMPETITORS' LIKELY STRATEGIES AND SOLUTIONS AND DETERMINE GAPS IN YOUR STRATEGY OR SOLUTION.

The Capture or Opportunity Manager drives the Black Hat reviews. This Review assesses relative positions of known competitors, including your own organization, providing a basis for improving your strategy and competitive posture. As shown in figure 4, the team predicts competitors' solutions and strategies so you can counter them during both Capture/ Opportunity Planning and Proposal Development.

Schedule your Black Hat review once competitive information has been gathered. Feedback from the Black Hat review will help the capture team further refine their efforts, leading to the Preliminary Bid Decision. Designate an unbiased facilitator to lead or co-lead the review.

The best Black Hats include separate groups, each knowledgeable about a different competitor and charged to create a capture plan for that competitor. Each group does advanced research prior to the Black Hat review. This best-practice approach involves key resources and is time consuming.

When separate groups are not feasible or affordable, have one team prepare mini-capture plans for two or three major competitors (or competitor types).

See SAMPLE TEMPLATE 7.

At a minimum, have the capture team prepare the competitive analysis, construct or update a bidder comparison chart, and develop a win strategy based on relative strengths and weaknesses revealed.

Black Hat reviews might be conducted multiple times in major competitions. Subsequent reviews are prompted by major changes in requirements, competition, or competitors' probable solutions.

While ideal reviewers are independent of the capture team, embrace experts on your competitors wherever you find them.

Consider outside consultants as sources of knowledge about competitors.

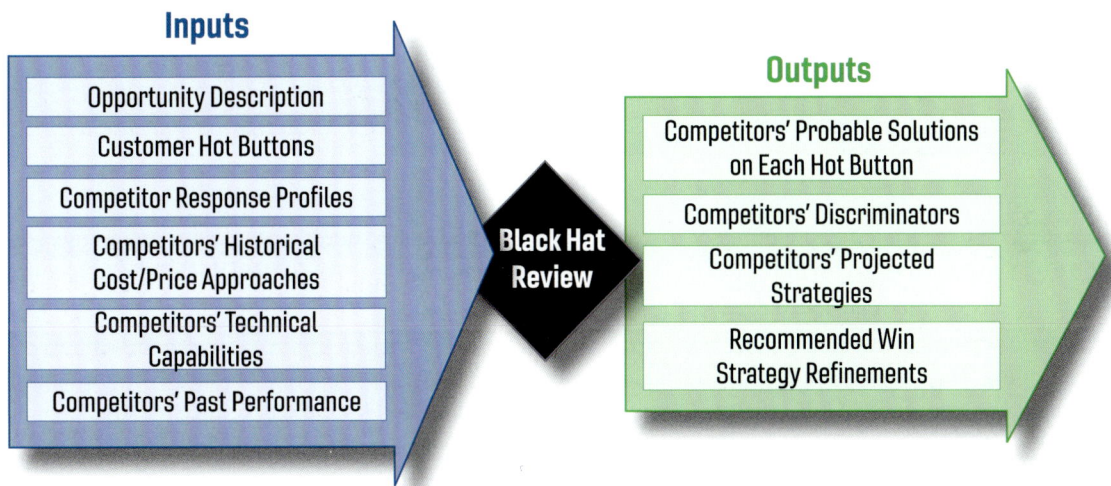

Figure 4. Black Hat Inputs and Outputs. *The Black Hat reviews require competitor research and a partial capture plan, which is somewhat more developed than the initial capture plan presented to the Blue Team. Depending on knowledge and sophistication of Black Hat reviewers, they either develop or critique the competitor analysis, construct or update a bidder comparison chart, and refine win strategy.*

5   PARTICIPATE IN A PINK TEAM TO VERIFY COMPLIANCE AND EXECUTION OF YOUR WIN STRATEGY IN THE PROPOSAL.

The Pink Team reviews proposal strategies, storyboards, mockups, or writing plans before text is drafted. Top business development professionals consider Pink Team the most important review. More proposals fail because of poorly executed or nonexistent Pink Teams than any other cause.

Team members, including the sales or capture lead, review inputs listed in figure 5 to verify compliance and responsiveness. They verify how well the proposal team is executing the approved win strategy and recommend necessary changes. This powerful influence over how the proposal will be completed dictates knowledgeable and empowered Pink Team members.

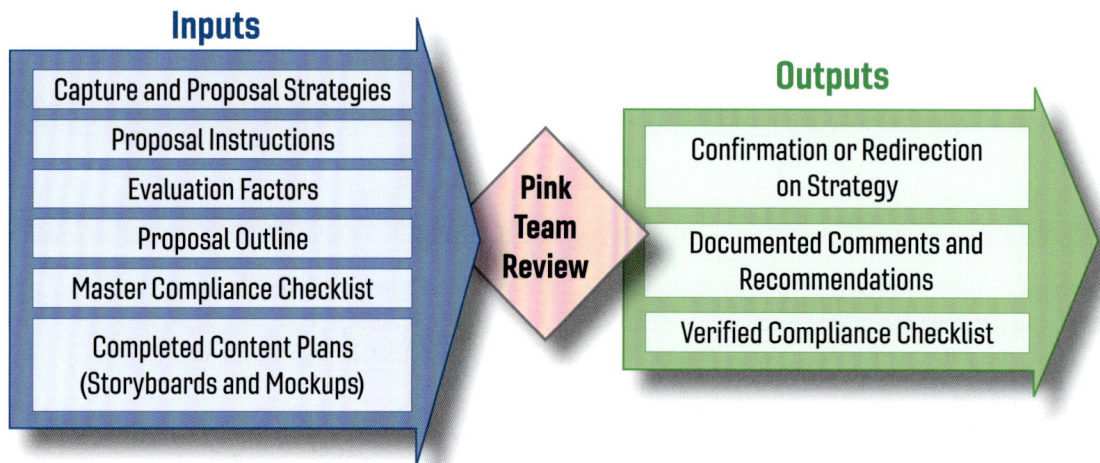

Inputs

- Capture and Proposal Strategies
- Proposal Instructions
- Evaluation Factors
- Proposal Outline
- Master Compliance Checklist
- Completed Content Plans (Storyboards and Mockups)

Pink Team Review

Outputs

- Confirmation or Redirection on Strategy
- Documented Comments and Recommendations
- Verified Compliance Checklist

Figure 5. Pink Team Inputs and Outputs. *The Pink Team reviews the entire planned proposal—in the form of content plans—against the customer's proposal instructions and evaluation factors. It verifies total compliance with requirements of the solicitation, responsiveness to unstated customer issues, and satisfactory expression of the approved capture and proposal strategies. The Pink Team also reviews the effectiveness of theme statements, visuals, and action captions.*

The Pink Team is usually scheduled approximately 20–25 percent of the way between the receipt of the RFP and submission. Consider two Pink Teams, especially if the customer issues a good draft solicitation. The first reviews early content planning. The second comes after the final solicitation and reviews updates and late changes in the customer's acquisition plans. You cannot verify compliance until the customer's final request is released.

The Pink Team should consolidate its findings and either brief the proposal team or furnish documented recommendations to the proposal manager for action. Present recommendations constructively to authors as suggestions for improvements rather than negative criticism of their work. Emphasize that early changes eliminate or reduce inconvenient, frantic, last-minute rewrites.

6   PARTICIPATE IN A RED TEAM TO PREDICT HOW YOUR PROPOSAL WILL BE SCORED AND MAKE IMPROVEMENTS TO IT.

The Red Team review predicts how well your near-final proposal would be scored by the customer. This team recommends improvements to customer focus, completeness, and clear communication of your solution and win strategy.

Avoid exploring new solutions, new themes, or major changes in direction. Strategy changes should have been directed by the Pink Team. Best practice is to arrange about one-third overlap between Pink and Red Team members to avoid conflicting suggestions.

Red Team members should be independent of the proposal team and offer different perspectives. Effective teams include experts on the customer; the customer's industry; competitors; your organization, technology, and approach; and on preparing and presenting winning proposals. To prevent Red Teams from degenerating into editing sessions, follow guidance in figure 6.

While much of this advice is aimed at proposal managers, your success as a capture manager often hinges on the effectiveness of your Red Team review. Stay involved before, during, and after the Red Team review. Help identify, recruit, brief, and debrief reviewers.

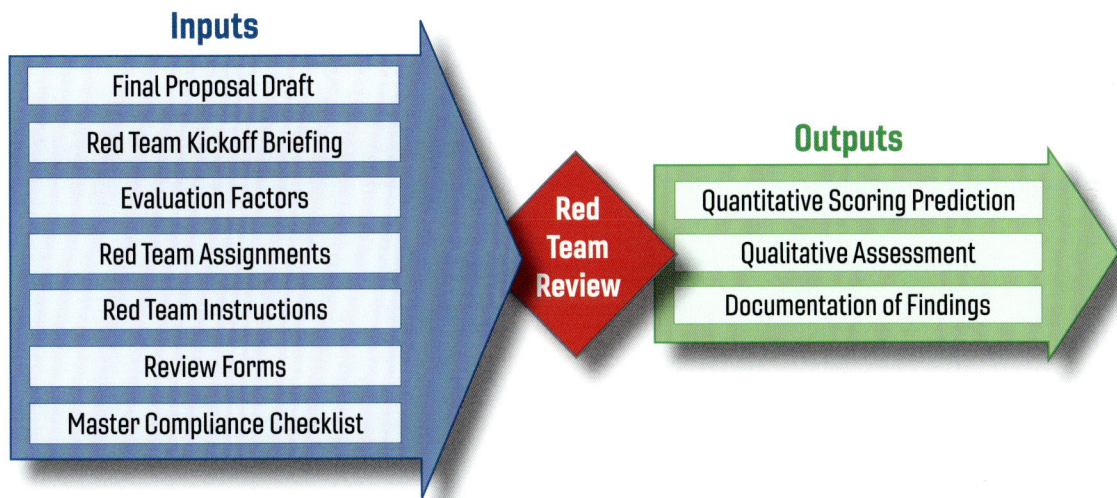

Figure 6. Red Team Inputs and Outputs. *The Red Team reviews the near-final proposal. Just as the customer's evaluation team will review your entire proposal, the Red Team must review every word, number, and visual. Thorough in-briefings are essential. Arm the Red Team with the customer's evaluation factors, detailed assignments, instructions, methods for recording review comments and results, and the master compliance checklist.*

The proposal manager should schedule Red Team about two-thirds to three-fourths of the way through Proposal Development, early enough that when changes are made to one part of the proposal, coordinating adjustments can be made to others.

Include the price volume in your Red Team review. You may not have final numbers, but verify that required contents will have a place when available.

Ask reviewers to consolidate findings to minimize conflicting recommendations. Complicated reviews of larger proposals need to be controlled using a standard set of feedback tools. Train reviewers to use these tools.

Use vertical and horizontal reviews of customer-bound documents. Vertical reviews focus on a single topic or section. Horizontal reviews focus on the consistency, continuity, and quality of a single element across the entire proposal.

7   PARTICIPATE IN A GREEN TEAM TO VALIDATE COST INFORMATION AND APPROVE PRICING.

Some organizations use a Green Team review for near-final pricing. It compares your pricing against documentation of your technical, management, and other non-price solution elements to confirm everything is included in the estimate, helps prevent discrepancies, and maintains alignment with your price to win. This team may also examine financial risk, cash flow projections, and return on investment.

Major objectives of the Green Team review are advance knowledge and approval of proposed pricing by relevant executives before the final Proposal Submittal Decision. Hasty, last-minute price cuts lead to frequent proposal errors. Exact estimating and approval procedures within your organization will dictate when it is scheduled.

See PRICING TO WIN.   Some organizations combine Green Team with Red Team, but in many cases, full

pricing information takes longer to develop than the rest of the proposal, delaying review of the final price. In those cases, the Red Team can still review the price proposal narrative and graphics, subject to numerical updates. Other organizations prefer holding the Green Team first, allowing the Red Team to verify that changes caused by price modifications have been correctly folded into the proposal.

Because price influences competitiveness, Green Teams consider information from customer, capture team, and proposal team sources, as shown in figure 7. This information is often in spreadsheets, tables, bases of estimates, and raw calculations. Green Team members are seldom disposed toward detailed price volume review, focusing on the deal rather than the documents.

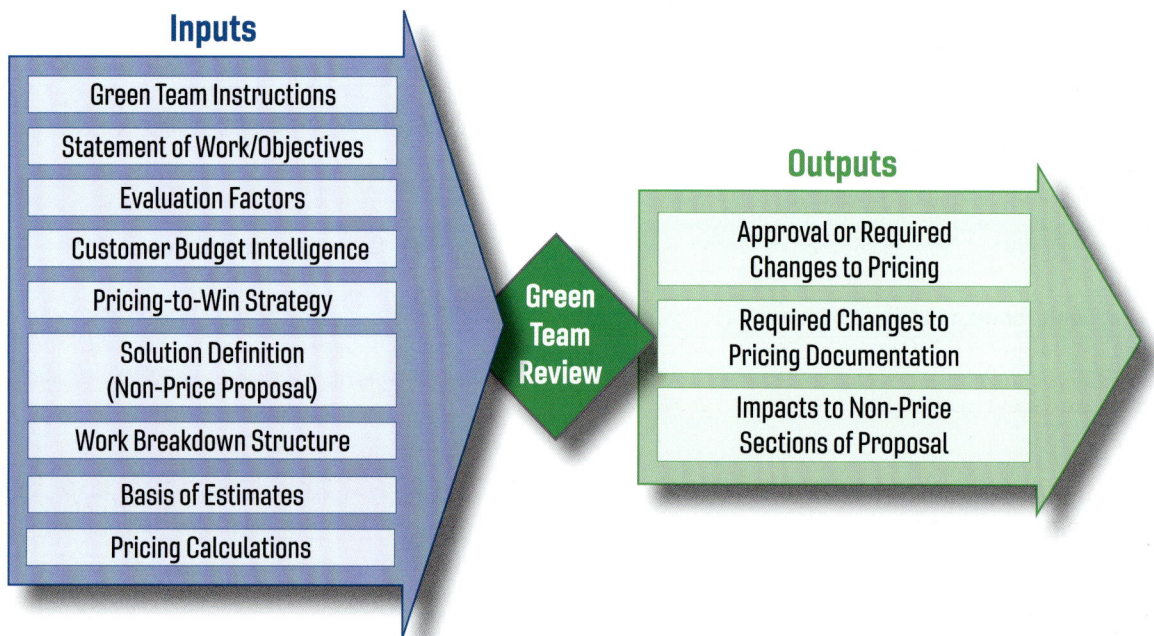

Inputs

- Green Team Instructions
- Statement of Work/Objectives
- Evaluation Factors
- Customer Budget Intelligence
- Pricing-to-Win Strategy
- Solution Definition (Non-Price Proposal)
- Work Breakdown Structure
- Basis of Estimates
- Pricing Calculations

Green Team Review

Outputs

- Approval or Required Changes to Pricing
- Required Changes to Pricing Documentation
- Impacts to Non-Price Sections of Proposal

Figure 7. Green Team Inputs and Outputs. *Price both derives from and influences every other aspect of your proposal, so Green Teams use inputs from many sources. Outputs are fewer, including either approval or required changes to pricing and associated portions of the proposal.*

If multiple Green Teams are held, the first generally occurs during capture planning, and reviews your price to win—that targeted combination of capability and price thought to appeal

to the customer's values. The second is the actual pricing review near the Red Team.

8 PARTICIPATE IN A GOLD TEAM TO CONFIRM YOUR PROPOSAL INCORPORATES CHANGES FROM RED AND GREEN TEAMS AND IS READY FOR SUBMITTAL.

The Gold Team reviews the final version of the proposal. It confirms improvements recommended by Red and Green Teams have been incorporated. This team also verifies proposal document quality and conformance to organizational standards, as shown in figure 8.

The Gold Team is not the time to modify your price, change your solution, or improve grammar. The Gold Team finds errors in the submission. In summary, Gold Team determines if the sales document is ready for the Proposal Submittal Decision—the final authorization to deliver it to the customer.

Inputs

- Completed Proposal
- Red Team Action Items
- Green Team Action Items

Gold Team Review

Outputs

- Approved Proposal Documents
- OR
- List of Required Changes

Figure 8. Gold Team Inputs and Outputs. *The Gold Team, including the capture or opportunity manager, reviews the fully completed proposal, including all volumes, letters, electronic files, and other material requested by the customer. This version is checked against Red and Green Team recommendations. Two outputs are possible: approved proposal documents and files, ready for the Proposal Submittal Decision gate, or a list of required changes.*

9 CONDUCT A WHITE HAT REVIEW TO RECORD LESSONS LEARNED AND RECOMMEND IMPROVEMENTS.

The White Hat review is a lessons-learned or after-action review conducted shortly after you submit your proposal. It helps improve your organization's business development operations. The White Hat's objectives are:

- Assess the effectiveness of your capture and proposal strategies
- Determine the quality of your competitive intelligence
- Critique your capture and proposal processes
- Evaluate management decisions

Unlike other reviews that focus on improving your chances of winning a specific opportunity, the White Hat focuses on improving your chances of winning future opportunities.

The first part of the review focuses on your internal successes, problems, and improvements. Conduct it while memories are fresh. The second part looks at the pursuit from the customer's perspective. Incorporate customer feedback about why you won or lost, if available. If not, delay the second part of the review until customer feedback is available, likely following the award decision.

Conclusions from both portions of the White Hat are documented and used to improve processes. Remember, lessons recorded are not lessons learned unless they motivate change.

Figure 9 shows inputs and outputs of the White Hat review.

Your business development process should be owned by someone charged with constantly looking for ways to improve it. Include that person as a White Hat observer, but do not let them defend the process or you will receive less valuable feedback.

Inputs

Internal Successes

Internal Problems and Workarounds

Customer's Formal Debriefing

Customer's Informal Comments

White Hat Review

Outputs

Documentation of Successes

Documentation of Problem Resolutions

Recommendations for Process Improvements

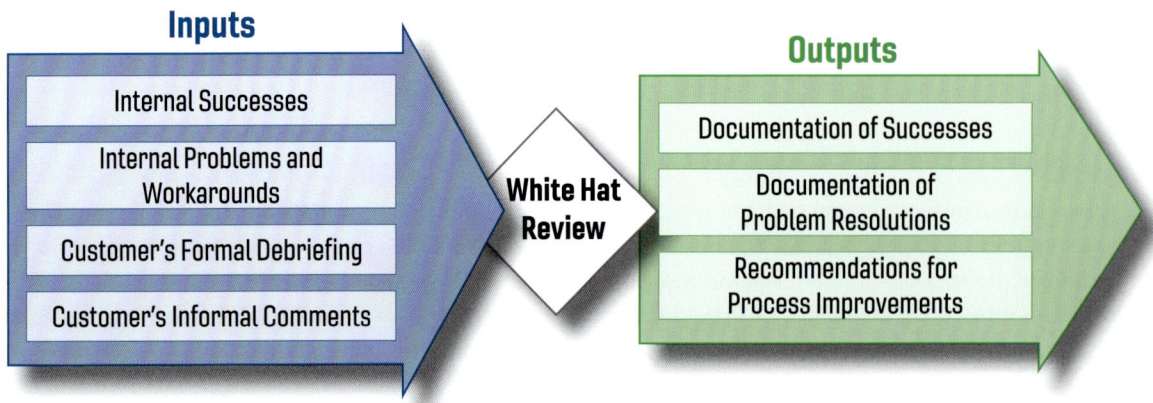

Figure 9. White Hat Inputs and Outputs. *Internal inputs on both successes and problems and their workarounds come from members of the capture and proposal teams after their efforts are complete. External feedback, both formal and informal, comes from customers. Document and archive what worked well and what did not. Recommend steps and activities to continue and methods or approaches to change.*

10 SELECT APPROPRIATE REVIEWERS AND METHODS FOR EACH COLOR TEAM REVIEW.

Color team reviewers are managers, staff, subject matter experts, and sometimes outside consultants. Staff reviews with personnel who have the expertise to contribute to the particular team. Increase the breadth of each review by increasing the diversity of reviewers. Minimize reviewers who have been contributors. They seldom maintain clear perspectives. Once a review is complete, reviewers can often help implement recommendations.

If your organization values checks and balances, top executives should contribute primarily to decision gates, not color teams. When executives become too invested in the work of a color team, they can lose objectivity for subsequent decision gates. And the color team recommendations are biased by executive input.

The following pages list suggestions for who should lead and attend each color team review and documents and methods to prepare. Smaller organizations will adjust the scope and composition of the reviews and review teams.

BLUE TEAM

ORGANIZER

- Capture/opportunity manager

CANDIDATE TEAM MEMBERS

- Independent, respected Blue Team leader
- Business development management
- Operational management
- Experts on customer
- Product/service experts

OTHER POTENTIAL ATTENDEES

- Capture/opportunity manager
- Capture or sales team

PRIMARY DOCUMENTS

- Pursuit Decision package
- Initial capture plan

METHODS TO CONSIDER

- Structured presentation
- Individual review
- Facilitated discussion
- Brainstorming

©Shipley Associates

BLACK HAT

ORGANIZER

- Capture/opportunity manager

CANDIDATE TEAM MEMBERS

- Independent Black Hat leader
- Business development management
- Experts on competitors
- Product/service experts (subject matter experts)

OTHER POTENTIAL ATTENDEES

- Capture/opportunity manager
- Capture/sales team

PRIMARY DOCUMENTS

- Blue Team summary report
- Partial capture plan
- Black Hat summary report

METHODS TO CONSIDER

- Competitor simulation by teams
- Group discussion of key competitors or competitor type
- Consultant analyses
- Capture team analysis
- Bidder comparison chart
- Walking the wall
- Sequential presentation
- Virtual review of planning documents
- Independent compliance verification

PINK TEAM

ORGANIZER

- Proposal manager

CANDIDATE TEAM MEMBERS

- Independent, respected Pink Team leader
- Line managers
- Subcontractor executives
- Business development managers
- Subject matter experts

OTHER POTENTIAL ATTENDEES

- Capture/opportunity manager
- Program manager
- Sales executive
- Account manager

PRIMARY DOCUMENTS

- Competitive assessment
- Capture/opportunity plan
- Request for Proposals/Request for Tender
- Compliance checklist and proposal outline
- Storyboards, content plans, and mockups

METHODS TO CONSIDER

- Sequential presentation
- Virtual review of planning documents
- Independent compliance verification
- Walking the wall

RED TEAM

ORGANIZER

- Proposal manager

CANDIDATE TEAM MEMBERS

- Red Team preparation leader
- Independent Red Team leader
- Executives
- Teammate executives
- Operations personnel
- Subject matter experts
- Customer experts
- Pink Team members
- Capture manager

PRIMARY DOCUMENTS

- Final proposal draft
- Customer's evaluation factors

METHODS TO CONSIDER

- Mirror of customer's evaluation process
- Detailed in-briefing
- Vertical section reviews
- Horizontal reviews of headings, theme statements, graphics and captions, and callouts
- Independent compliance check
- Gadfly review to check for consistency
- Proposal team debriefing
- Core team recovery to minimize personnel involved

GREEN TEAM

ORGANIZER

- Proposal manager

CANDIDATE TEAM MEMBERS

- Executive who must approve price
- Operations personnel
- Pricing manager
- Capture/opportunity manager

OTHER POTENTIAL ATTENDEES

- Proposal manager
- Price volume manager

PRIMARY DOCUMENTS

- Request for proposals
- Capture/opportunity plan
- Complete solution definition, non-price proposal
- Pricing documents and worksheets

METHODS TO CONSIDER

- Pricing spreadsheet review
- Cross-volume comparison
- Closed-door meetings due to closely held information

©Shipley Associates

GOLD TEAM

ORGANIZER

- Proposal manager

CANDIDATE TEAM MEMBERS

- Proposal manager
- Proposal volume managers (if assigned)
- Capture/opportunity manager
- Pricing manager
- Red Team/Green Team leader

OTHER POTENTIAL ATTENDEES

- Publication and/or production manager
- Proposal coordinator

PRIMARY DOCUMENTS

- Completed proposal, with all letters, documents, electronic files, attachments, other required material
- Red and Green Team action item lists

METHODS TO CONSIDER

- Action item check-off
- Horizontal spot checks
- Delivery media evaluation

WHITE HAT TEAM

ORGANIZER

- Proposal manager
- Capture/opportunity manager
- Sales executive

CANDIDATE TEAM MEMBERS

- Proposal team
- Capture/opportunity team
- Business development management
- Technical lead

OTHER POTENTIAL ATTENDEES

- Business development process custodian

PRIMARY DOCUMENTS

- Internal survey results
- Customer debriefing

METHODS TO CONSIDER

- Well-documented team discussions
- Customer debriefing analysis in context of business development lifecycle
- Competitor success/failure analysis
- Standardized survey to compare effort to other pursuits
- Direct, tailored questions about the pursuit

COSTING

Costing requirements vary by market and are unique to every organization. In some markets with only one customer and few sellers, sellers might be required to base their prices on a defined set of costing rules plus an allowable profit margin.

In open markets with many customers and sellers, cost is one of many factors used to set the price. In proposals to governments, costs often must be disclosed, profit margins must follow prescribed guidelines, assumptions and rationales are questioned, and the final price is usually negotiated.

Consider this paradox:

- Most sellers say customers in their market select the solution with the lowest price.
- Most customers say they seldom select the solution with the lowest price.

The reality is that most customers try to select the best-value solution within their budget.

This Costing section focuses on developing the cost of your solution and then supporting and presenting that cost credibly to the customer. Determining the winning price (i.e., estimating the customer's tradeoff between capability and purchase price) is the focus of the Pricing to Win topic section.

COSTING

1 Differentiate cost, price, and value.

2 Develop should-cost estimates early.

3 Define a costing strategy that supports your sales strategy.

4 Base cost-estimating rationale on the assumption that nothing is new; everything has been done before.

5 Prepare or tailor written estimating guidelines for each competition.

6 Minimize negotiated price decrements by using the most credible rationale.

©Shipley Associates

1   DIFFERENTIATE COST, PRICE, AND VALUE.

Begin with common definitions:

COST

What it costs you to deliver the solution, not the cost to the customer.

PRICE

What you charge for a product or service.

VALUE

Your customer's perception of what the product or service is worth.

ADDED VALUE

Difference between the customer's perception of the total value of the solution and what it costs them to fully implement the solution.

Value is both tangible and intangible. Tangible value is the quantified improvement in a customer's profit or a decreased loss. Intangible value is by definition not easily quantified and is often undervalued.

Even for government procurements, price is rarely the single factor that determines a buying decision. Other, less tangible factors influence the buying decision, contributing to the customer's perception of value. This is true even for commodity items. When buying a gallon of fuel, a driver will value the relative safety, cleanliness, convenience, and courtesy of a service station to justify or rationalize a higher vs. lower fuel price.

2   DEVELOP SHOULD-COST ESTIMATES EARLY.

In early meetings with customers, try to understand the approximate cost of their needs and the potential budget to eliminate their problem or meet their need. Note that most customers have some idea of what a reasonable estimate should be but are reluctant to disclose it.

Avoid giving your initial solution development and costing team a broad description of the customer's requirements without an estimate or a target. Without a target, the first cost roll-up often reveals that the cost of your solution far exceeds the customer's budget.

Develop a "should-cost" estimate using top-down and bottom-up approaches until they converge.

Top-down costing begins with each customer's perception of value, the customer's budget, and comparisons with other similar projects, adjusted as appropriate. The overall target price is broken into target costs or should-cost estimates by task, service, and hardware.

Establishing early should-cost estimates reduces the number of cost and design iterations. Accurate, top-down estimates assume similar methods, materials, and processes.

Bottom-up costing is simply a cost roll-up of time and material estimates with appropriate overheads added. The inherent weakness of bottom-up costing is that estimators tend to incorporate safety factors at each cost level to avoid subsequent blame for cost overruns.

Seven alternative approaches to costing are summarized in figure 1, along with the advantages and disadvantages of each approach.

APPROACH	ADVANTAGE	DISADVANTAGES
Research: Collect information on customer budgets and program funding.	Rough target for bid price can be developed by deleting customer administrative costs from funding.	Does not consider competitive approaches; funding estimates are usually based on outdated historical data and poor understanding of technology.
Expert judgment: Consult with one or more experts.	Little or no historical data needed; good for new or unique projects.	Experts tend to be biased; knowledge level can be questionable.
Parametric models: Use design parameters and mathematical algorithms.	Fast and easy to use; useful early in program; objective, repeatable; often used by customer early in funding development.	Can be inaccurate if not properly calibrated and validated; expensive to maintain models; historical data used for calibration may not be valid for new project.
Analogy techniques: Compare with similar programs.	Based on actual experience.	Often, no truly similar program exists; not used alone; better used to check estimates.
Competitive analysis: Examine competitor history and technology to determine likely offering.	Provides understanding of strengths and weaknesses of competitors; can better target proposal at competition; investigates technology tradeoffs.	May not know teaming and vendor solutions; cannot be sure of pricing/profit decisions by competitor management; competitors may not share same understanding of program; historical data may not fit current opportunity.
Bottom-up techniques: Unit costs are totaled to determine cost and effort.	Provides a detailed basis for cost estimating; promotes individual accountability; useful mainly for cost tracking after award.	Time- and cost-intensive; sometimes results in double dipping on estimates and usually results in higher costs; historical data not always available to support estimates; may not capture costs of integration; focuses on individual requirements, not overall program.
Top-down techniques: Unit costs are based on customer budget and historical data.	Begins with customer budget information and results in customer-focused solution; helps enforce traceability between cost and technical; uses historical actuals.	Requires good information on customer and competition; requires significant amount of work and adherence to a pricing process; often is erroneously based on conjecture rather than supported with validated information.

Figure 1. Various Costing Approaches. *Organizations tend to select costing approaches based upon tradition, history, or convenience. If alternative approaches converge on a common cost, our confidence increases. Consider the customers' views; customers seriously question estimates based upon expert judgment.*

©Shipley Associates

3 DEFINE A COSTING STRATEGY THAT SUPPORTS YOUR SALES STRATEGY.

A sales strategy that emphasizes leading-edge performance is inconsistent with a costing strategy that emphasizes selecting the lowest cost components, methods, suppliers, and subcontractors. Similarly, a sales strategy that emphasizes the efficiency and productivity of the seller is inconsistent with a high cost. When technical and cost teams are physically separate without an agreed costing strategy, the solution is usually technically superior and high-cost.

Influence—or at least determine—whether the customer is seeking lowest total added value, maximum technical performance, market image, minimum acquisition cost, or total cost of ownership. Next, determine competitors' probable approaches. Finally, adopt a discriminating position aligned with the customer's needs.

Develop your solution based on what the customer values:

- Add low-cost features that the customer values highly.
- Eliminate costly features that the customer does not value.

Try to persuade the customer to require a solution that is better matched to your capabilities than to your competitors'. The key is influencing the bid request early. Your aim is to establish requirements that are expensive for competitors to meet.

If you are late in the competition and trying to find a solution for a bid request influenced by a competitor, try to reengineer the customer's vision. Persuade the customer to value your discriminators more highly than competitors' discriminators. The success of this strategy hinges on whether the customer has the latitude to change the requirements or to select a noncompliant solution.

See WIN STRATEGY DEVELOPMENT.

Do all you can to influence the requirements favorably. For example, when competing for a cost-driven services contract, brainstorm ways to reduce your cost by asking the following questions:

See SERVICE PROPOSALS Guideline 7, Proposal Guide.

- How can we reduce management layers?
- Can we increase management's span of control?
- Where should we place people within grades?

Incumbents often have less latitude to suggest changes in how services are delivered. Customers wonder why the incumbent's cost-saving proposals have not already been implemented.

4 BASE COST-ESTIMATING RATIONALE ON THE ASSUMPTION THAT NOTHING IS NEW; EVERYTHING HAS BEEN DONE BEFORE.

Cost analysts in many market sectors assume everything has been done before. Base your estimating rationale on the same assumption.

In any selling environment, few customers want to purchase serial #001. The risk of being the first is often too great. Base

estimates on the most similar historic tasks. Break down the project until you can identify subtasks that are similar to subtasks from prior projects.

5 PREPARE OR TAILOR WRITTEN ESTIMATING GUIDELINES FOR EACH COMPETITION.

Unique, complex programs require new estimating guidelines for each competition. For services or products that are similar from bid to bid, consider whether your current guidelines warrant tailoring.

Estimating guidelines cover the following types of assumptions:

- Program schedule and milestones to determine when costs occur
- A Work Breakdown Structure (WBS) to indicate what work will be done by which cost centers
- A make versus buy subcontracting determination
- A Statement of Work (SOW) and WBS dictionary to define the services and products to be delivered
- Relevant financial ground rules regarding escalation, facility capitalization, facilities and locations of work, direct labor and overhead rates, preapproved rates, etc.
- A deliverables list, including all hardware, services, and data
- The level at which costs will be estimated, disclosed, and reported, if required

Estimating ground rules should be written for the following reasons:

- Only written ground rules are auditable and defensible, both externally and internally.
- Estimators working in teams must be consistent.
- When costs must be disclosed, include the ground rules in the proposal cost volume introduction to increase your credibility.
- Partners, vendors, and subcontractors need ground rules to give accurate and competitive estimates.
- Written ground rules reduce both schedule and cost risk.

6 MINIMIZE NEGOTIATED PRICE DECREMENTS BY USING THE MOST CREDIBLE RATIONALE.

Many evaluators require full disclosure of all task descriptions, cost estimates, and rationale. The soundness of the rationale determines their subsequent price negotiating position. A poor rationale leads to larger price decrements during negotiations.

Some auditors rank estimating rationale in the following order, from most to least reliable:

01 Firm, negotiated, forward price agreement.

02 Actual historic cost with appropriate escalation.

03 Quotation from vendor (internal or external).

04 Engineering estimate.

CUSTOMER INTERFACE

Customer interface skills and tactics require an aligned team of individuals with the interface skills to listen actively, establish rapport, build trust, assess situations accurately, collaborate effectively, and communicate persuasively. Invest your time and attention helping customers meet their goals and objectives, and they are more likely to invest their time and money with you.

Selling and capture planning are similar disciplines and both require professional customer interface skills.

Both disciplines emphasize engaging customers early in the business development process by establishing productive working relationships, thus improving win probability.

Selling is often referenced in business-to-business market environments. Capture planning was originally focused on business-to-government interactions. Recently, the two terms are often interchangeable depending on organizational cultures and preferences.

Consider the following:

- Organizations selling to governments have historically been more likely to embrace capture concepts and less likely to train capture participants to interact with customers. They often select people for marketing and capture roles because they previously worked for the customer or have broad service and product expertise, but they assume adequate interface skills.

  For example, a high-ranking government civilian employee is often hired by a large contractor because of customer connections rather than strong customer interface skills.

- Organizations in the business-to-business (B2B) sector employ sales professionals and invest more heavily in their training and development than any other group of employees.

Three familiar quotes reinforce the importance of connecting with customers:

The aim of marketing is to know and understand the customer so well that the product or service fits him or her and sells itself.

—*Peter Drucker*

The fact is, everyone is in sales. Whatever area you work in, you do have clients and you do need to sell.

—*Jay Abraham*

This may seem simple, but you need to give customers what they want, not what you think they want. And, if you do this, people will keep coming back.

—*John Ilhan*

Few organizations offer services or products that sell themselves. Develop the interface skills of your capture team members so they discern what each customer wants, and jointly create the preferred solution. Then deliver the solution effectively so customers become repeat customers.

See CAPTURE PLANNING, AN OVERVIEW.

The most overlooked aspect of capture planning is developing the ability of capture team members to interact persuasively with members of the buying team.

CUSTOMER INTERFACE

1 Recognize how customers buy, and then employ varied sales activities.

2 Help customers discover potential benefits.

3 Accord uniqueness to every individual and organization.

4 Never assume. Ask.

5 Actively listen during every customer interaction.

6 Establish rapport and build trust by becoming a credible advisor.

7 Interact effectively with groups. Facilitate your meetings with confidence.

8 Anticipate and handle concerns during customer interactions.

9 Test your potential solution with the customer early and often.

10 Develop a logical business case for buying.

11 Seek agreement on next steps.

1 RECOGNIZE HOW CUSTOMERS BUY, AND THEN EMPLOY VARIED SALES ACTIVITIES.

How private and public sector customers buy is affected internally by their vision, objectives, and immediate needs; externally by the economy, technology, laws, regulations, and customs; and by the personal issues, needs, and experiences of the individuals involved. In general, these principles apply:

1. Customers buy from people they trust. Schmoozing is likely to turn off rather than motivate the customer to buy, especially in a government environment. Schmoozers are viewed as time wasters and superficial people. Customers want to buy from those who will treat them right.

2. Customers frequently buy from people who know their business and will not waste their time or have patience with anyone who is less knowledgeable or less skilled.

3. Customers want the best deal. That means value (perceived worth). Sellers who offer real value are most likely to win the contract.

4. Capture/sales team members who have the ability to listen and understand what customers want and need have the competitive edge. You must learn quickly what your customers need and how they buy.

5. Capture/sales team members who know how to sell the way their customers prefer to buy have the competitive edge.

6. Capture/sales team members who can demonstrate that they offer the best solution at a low risk have the advantage.

Learning to interface with customers based on these principles will advance the relationship and improve your competitive position. Consider how many members of your capture/sales team participate in these customer interaction activities and tactics:

- Industry days are an excellent forum to meet potential decision makers, stakeholders, and influencers. Your attendance and participation are important; equally important is establishing credibility, rapport, and trust.

- Bidders' conferences are opportunities to gather competitor information and details about customer issues, requirements, evaluation criteria, and restrictions or limitations. Potential one-on-one connections, when allowed, are invaluable if you are prepared.

©Shipley Associates

- Trade shows offer a showcase for personnel, services, and products. Decision makers and influencers are often more accessible than at their base location. Seize the opportunity to meet potential teaming partners, decision makers, program personnel, and competitors.

- Web conferences and other multi-media virtual interactions.

- Email is a frequently underestimated and overlooked opportunity to interact with customers. The frequency, tone, and content of your email messages say a lot about you, your selling style, and your organization. Actively manage email traffic and strategies to maintain consistent content and tone.

- Telephone conversations and conference calls advance the relationship. Leave detailed, concise, and relevant voicemail messages. Rambling, disorganized messages hurt the relationship.

- Face-to-face meetings require active listeners. Probe for information that is not publicly available. Proposing your solution before customer needs and issues are clearly identified and a business case can be established is unproductive at best and potentially arrogant and off-putting at worst.

- Site visits offer relatively unguarded opportunities for multiple one-on-one interactions among members of the buying and selling teams. Capture/sales team members must understand their role, listen carefully, and stay on message.

- Social media visibility and activity can significantly impact a customer's perception of the capture sales professional and the organization.

2   HELP CUSTOMERS DISCOVER POTENTIAL BENEFITS.

Plan, initiate, and maintain the focus of customer interactions on the customer, not on you or your organization. Help them discover, analyze, and quantify, if possible, the potential benefits to them and their organization. Discover the potential benefits the customer envisions before focusing on the benefits of your solution.

In complex sales with complex solutions, discover, explore, and analyze the breadth of customer issues and concerns. Hidden issues often turn into objections.

Establishing trust with the customer is essential. Foster a relationship where you are collaborating to solve a customer problem. In most situations, your collaborative discussion will expose underlying issues and deepen your customer's and your own understanding of the potential benefits derived from reducing or eliminating the customer's problem.

Helping the customer discover how your solution will solve their problem(s) is critical.

You cannot fake sincerity or integrity. Being honest and up-front with your customer is your only option. Credibility is difficult to gain and easy to lose.

3   ACCORD UNIQUENESS TO EVERY INDIVIDUAL AND ORGANIZATION.

Every customer has different issues and concerns that are important to that customer to achieve his or her objectives. Whether buying commodities, complex services, or products, each customer, organization, and situation is unique. Capture activities must align with the unique needs of the customer.

- **Commodities:** Commodities are assumed to be items with no perceived differences other than price. How many commodities meet this definition? For example, assume that you are purchasing flour in a market. Choices among just the wheat flours are whole, unbleached, bleached, all-purpose, bread, and pastry flour. Sources of the flours include store brand, national brand, specialty, and certified organic. Consider these options and as a unique buyer: do you select the same flour every time?

- **Complex services:** Your choices include: 1) buy exactly what you bought last time, 2) buy something completely new, 3) purchase internally, 4) delay, or 5) decide not

to purchase anything. If you do purchase, additional variables include service levels, warranties, terms, mix of services, and delivery schedules.

Think of every customer as a new friend you are trying to help. As with new friends, you cannot sound or appear to be overly familiar, or you will appear insincere.

- **Products:** Many organizations, such as car dealers, sell the same product. However the terms, conditions, warranties, services surrounding the sale, and post-sale support services are customized to address the unique issues of individual and organizational buyers.

If you agree that customers and their organizations are unique, why go into customer meetings with pre-set presentations? Prepare an agenda, but also expect to adapt your agenda to customer requests and actions.

4 NEVER ASSUME. ASK.

Many customer issues and needs are not obvious based on publicly available information on websites, at bidders' conferences, industry days, or trade shows. Capture/sales team members must not assume they know and understand all of the issues, needs, or requirements. They have to ask.

As illustrated in figure 1, uncovering needs is much like measuring an iceberg—what shows above the waterline is a poor indicator of the real size or shape of the issue. Knowing what lies below the waterline is critical when selling in any market sector.

Get below the metaphorical waterline with your customers by asking good questions and developing trust.

Figure 1. Probe to Discover Hidden Issues. *Like an iceberg where 90 percent of the ice is hidden below the waterline, many customer issues are hidden or poorly understood by both the buyer and seller. Ask, explore, and collaborate.*

Asking a customer to answer all of your questions in a single sitting is unlikely. Instead, ask questions by phone, email, and other means. Record questions and responses for future reference as you shape your win strategy and proposal.

Gain perspective, and confirm the breadth of issues by asking different people similar questions. Customer issues evolve over time, so reconfirm issues without exasperating the customer.

Shape questions to discover and clarify issues, motivators, and hot buttons.

Validate issues and assess their impact:

- Validate: Is the problem, issue, or requirement real? Is it still a problem?
- Assess impact: How much is the problem or issue costing customers in lost time, inefficiency, or waste?

Observe three guidelines:

- Ask questions that help validate a need or requirement. Seek evidence that a need really exists. Identify motivators and issues.
- Explore the quantifiable impact of the problem, issue, or requirement. Identify who is being impacted and how.
- Listen actively by clarifying customer positions and concerns. Never assume. Ask.

Apply these three guidelines to your internal capture strategy sessions and planning activities. The more willing capture team members are to ask good questions, the better your plan, strategy, and solution.

©Shipley Associates

5   ACTIVELY LISTEN DURING EVERY CUSTOMER INTERACTION.

Capture/sales team members who interface with the customer must apply sound, active listening skills to establish rapport and trust.

The key to active listening is clarifying—asking the customer to clarify key requirements, issues, and needs as they arise. Clarifying is neutral. Your aim is to learn more about the customer, not to persuade the customer to change his or her position.

When talking to a customer, remember these points:

- Confirm your interpretation of what they have told you by asking, "What exactly does that mean? Why is that important to your organization?"
- Signal that you are listening by taking notes, nodding your head, and acknowledging what they are saying.

- Make your clarification statements or questions conversational, not overly rehearsed.
- Avoid the impulse to insert your opinion about a specific need, issue, or requirement. Listen, seek clarification, and confirm the intent and content of what the customer is saying.

Customers do not like to be sold to, but everyone likes to buy. Customers want a business partner that listens, understands, and responds based on active listening and clarification. Guidelines for active listening are summarized in figure 2.

Active listening engages you in addressing the customer's issues and needs. Active listeners accord uniqueness to the customer.

Judge a man by his questions, not his answers.

—Voltaire

GUIDELINE	RATIONALE FOR BUILDING RELATIONSHIP
Clarify when you want your customer to feel understood.	If you want to build rapport, cooperation, and trust, clarify what is significant to your customer.
Clarify when you need to make sure that you understand.	If you do not clarify, you will not know for certain if your interpretation is right. You might be guessing or assuming.
Clarify what is appropriate; be selective and empathetic.	You cannot clarify every statement in your discussions. Consider what is appropriate and what is not. Focus on the key points or details, and exclude the extras.
Lead with clarifying phrases.	Clarification phrases signal your willingness to listen and confirm the message. "Help me understand…", "So, what you're saying is…", "You mean if you could implement this by March…"
Change the wording, not the content of the customer's statement.	If you vary the wording, you will sound more natural and not parrot your customer, which is annoying.
Converse; avoid canned phrases.	Clarification should sound as natural as conversation. Avoid clichés, jargon, or repeated clarifying phrases.
Keep questions short and simple.	Ask one question about one topic at a time. Do not use compound questions with multiple subparts.
Do not add your thoughts or opinions.	Clarification is neutral; no opinions or advice are allowed. Clarify before you refine.
Avoid questions when you should be clarifying.	Questions are fine for learning, discovering, and building respect with your customer. They do not build understanding and should not be used as a substitute for clarifying. Put a question mark in your voice, not your content.
Clarify concerns; do not ignore or bypass them.	If you fail to build understanding on a customer concern or issue, you will have a terrible time resolving it. Customers do not forget important concerns. Clarifying concerns positions you to move the relationship forward.
Clarify answers to your questions.	Whenever you ask a question, clarify the response as a sign of respect. Without the clarifier, you might be perceived as being interrogative or probing.

Figure 2. Improve Your Active Listening Skills. *Apply active listening guidelines to your customer conversations to demonstrate that you are interested, want to understand, and are fully engaged.*

6 ESTABLISH RAPPORT AND BUILD TRUST BY BECOMING A CREDIBLE ADVISOR.

When building rapport and trust as a capture/sales team member, consider how you approach individuals in the customer organization, their working environment, and how you align multiple interactions with the same individuals.

Alignment might be one of the most overlooked concepts in capture management, selling, or persuasion.

To maintain trust in a complex sales or capture environment, both an individual's action and the actions of capture team members must be aligned.

Maintaining alignment might be the most important justification for preparing capture or opportunity plans in a complex selling environment. The capture/opportunity plan documents your messages. Then the capture/sales lead focuses on keeping team members on message at every customer interface.

The goal of capture team members is to become trusted advisors to individuals in the customer organization instead of a vendor. Establish and reinforce trust at every customer interface, whether face-to-face, voice, electronic, or in writing.

Today's customers and customer team members exhibit these characteristics:

- **Demanding.** They expect more, expect it faster, and expect it better. Customers demand better products, services, sales skill, and knowledge.
- **Sophisticated.** They are more aware of products, costs, and ways to negotiate terms. Most know how to investigate you, your organization, your products and services, and competitors' products and services.
- **Skeptical.** They are skeptical and suspicious of sales people. They instantly recognize and detest hype, hard

selling, and trick selling. Clichéd phrases, jargon, and generic language signal muddled thinking, minimal benefit, and potential arrogance. Their trust is hard to gain and easy to lose.

- **Conditional.** They are less loyal than ever before. They will buy from you if they believe you have the best value to offer. Each sale is new and conditional.
- **Cautious.** They are more hesitant and cautious. Many have been impacted by economic challenges and tough times.
- **Valuative.** They are more judgmental. They are more likely to test and debate the value they think they are receiving.
- **Open.** They are open to consider new vendors and other localities. This openness includes worldwide competition.
- **Pressured.** They feel pressured to make the right decisions, to be efficient, and to be productive. Stressed-out customers say they have less time to do more.

Because most capture team members interface with the customer in some manner, they must be aware of these environmental and customer issues to become a trusted, credible advisor. Trust between a buyer and a seller takes time to establish. However, customers will lose trust in a vendor, supplier, or partner whenever they feel misled or misunderstood.

Consider the general and personal working environment of your customers. The general working environment encompasses the guidelines that govern their interactions with contractors. Customer working environments differ by market sector, organization, and situation.

7 INTERACT EFFECTIVELY WITH GROUPS. FACILITATE YOUR MEETINGS WITH CONFIDENCE.

Previous guidelines in this section focused mainly on one-on-one interactions. But many capture/sales interactions are group events. No one interacts with a group; you interact with

individuals that comprise a group. Consider group dynamics and modify your approach. Guidelines and rationale for dealing with groups are summarized in figure 3.

To be most effective in group presentations, persuade individuals one at a time.

©Shipley Associates

GUIDELINE	RATIONALE FOR DEALING WITH GROUPS
Understand the roles and personalities of individuals within the group.	Someone may appear or profess to be the leader, to be managing the meeting. Direct much of the conversation to the leader, but also address the others. The other people often have a huge influence on the outcome.
Assess the personalities of individuals within the group.	Include everyone in the conversation. Observe body language. Practice active listening skills, and ask clarifying questions to expose hidden agendas.
Determine the group's decision-making process.	Begin by asking, and then clarify until you have agreement. Here are some common group structures and coping suggestions: – Strong leader and weak followers: Persuade the leader to champion your approach. – Strong leader and strong peers: Persuade everyone. One holdout can ruin the deal. – Weak leader and weak peers: Establish rapport with everyone individually, move slowly, and educate without arrogance. – Weak leader and strong peers: Address everyone's questions. The leader will seek consensus and look to others to make decisions. – Information collector for an absent decision maker: Educate and rehearse immediate participants to convince the decision maker.
Control the meeting and agenda.	Establish immediate group roles, individual issues, and individuals' expectations for the meeting. Invite participants to briefly state their roles, issues, and objectives from a personal perspective.
Address each person's individual objectives during the meeting.	If you do not uncover each person's issues and then address them in the course of your presentation, you will be interrupted with questions from all angles and lose control of the meeting. As you address each issue, link it to the person who raised the issue, and then confirm that you have understood and addressed that issue. Unaddressed issues lead to subsequent objections.
Adapt to ad hoc groups with no leader.	Cross-functional teams, including many Integrated Product/Project Teams (IPTs), are often appointed to address an issue, but they lack an appointed leader. Ask: "Who is the leader?" You need to determine if the group does make the decision or if it will take the analysis and recommendation to an absent decision maker. If the committee decides, ask about the time frame, what they need to know, and how you can help.
Use best-practices when fielding questions.	1. Respond to one question at a time. 2. Listen to the full questions carefully. 3. Focus on the questioner: 　– Face the questioner. 　– Lean forward or move toward him or her. 　– Establish eye contact. 　– Do not interrupt. 　– Listen for content (words) and intent (ultimate purpose). 4. If you do not know the answer, admit it. 5. Answer questions in the following steps: 　– Restate the question. 　– State a summary answer. 　– Support your answer. 　– Summarize or restate your summary answer. 6. Ask if the questioner is satisfied. Following these guidelines helps you respond to the question asked, answer it logically and persuasively, and demonstrate respect for the questioner.
Do not restate negative questions. Agree with the questioner, if possible. Admit challenges, cite positive elements, and then bridge to two or three specific points.	Following these guidelines demonstrates your willingness to acknowledge unfavorable information, and then turn the discussion to more positive aspects.

Figure 3. Observe Common Guidelines when Meeting with Groups. *Adapt your approach to group dynamics. Learn and practice a consistent process when responding to various types of questions. While presentations to groups are much more difficult to facilitate than one-on-one meetings, the rewards can be much greater.*

The person talking is the focus of the presentation. Visual aids should aid the presenter but must not be the focus of the presentation or a crutch for the presenter.

When presenting to groups, do not lose sight of the individuals in the group. Focus on meeting the individual agendas of everyone present and often the agendas of others represented by those individuals.

When faced with conflicting issues among group members, attempt to facilitate a constructive discussion. Avoid taking sides.

8   ANTICIPATE AND HANDLE CONCERNS DURING CUSTOMER INTERACTIONS.

Concerns are a normal part of every sales opportunity. Anticipate concerns, but do not treat them like a ping-pong match where you supply a brilliant response to every issue.

Customers will raise one concern after another if they are not completely comfortable with your solution and organization.

Differentiate by how you sell as well as by what you sell.

Seeking to overcome concerns without exploring ideas with the customer can create a rift and undermine trust.

Treat concerns positively. Concerns show the customer is still considering your solution, is not yet ready to buy, but is also not ready to end the process.

Concerns that are stated often conceal an underlying issue. Look beyond the words. Figure 4 summarizes some common concerns, the underlying issue, and how you might treat the concern as a request.

CONCERN	UNDERLYING CUSTOMER ISSUE	RESPONSE
Your price is too high.	Perceived benefits do not justify the cost.	Substantiate the value, supported by credible references.
I would like to talk to my partner, management, or a trusted advisor.	Worried about owning and justifying the decision.	Seek ways to reduce the perceived risk.
I need to get additional quotes.	Unsure if you are meeting their needs. Concerned that they have not considered all alternatives or that the high benefits might permit you to earn inordinately high profit margins.	Emphasize your customized, targeted solution. Review or introduce your trade analysis. Some government buyers will require you to disclose your costs and margins.
We are all set with our current vendor.	They do not see your solution as sufficiently better to justify making the switch.	Review your discriminators. Offer to offset selected transition costs.
We had a poor experience with your organization or a similar organization.	They see minimal difference between your proposed solution and prior or familiar solutions.	Offer specific proof of performance linked to specific personnel proposed. Highlight lessons learned and improvements made compared to your solution or other solutions that they cited.

Figure 4. Handling Concerns Is a Process. *Listen, acknowledge, and empathize. Ask questions in your conversations with customers to demonstrate that you are interested, want to understand, and are fully engaged.*

©Shipley Associates

9 TEST YOUR POTENTIAL SOLUTION WITH THE CUSTOMER EARLY AND OFTEN.

Envision helping customers buy rather than selling to customers. Customers make buying decisions in a series of steps, and you are helping them advance step-by-step.

As you step through this process, test potential solutions to get feedback about what you will propose. Determine if you are in sync with customer expectations. A collaboratively developed solution is more difficult to reject.

Use discussions, white papers, site visits, presentations, documentation reviews, and other means to test your solution with the customer. Assess their readiness to purchase and the alignment of your solution to customer needs.

Test potential solutions using one of the following approaches:

Exploratory Approach

Ask customers what they want to do next. Help customers buy instead of trying to convince them to buy. For example:

"Are you interested in learning more about…?"

"What do you see as the next step?"

Clarification Approach

Confirm what you have heard or sensed from customer words or body language. For example:

You seem to be ready to wrap this up.

You seem to be saying that you want to meet our project manager and get the project moving.

> Everyone likes to buy. No one likes to be sold to.

Recommendation Approach

Suggest or advise your customer on next steps. Make a recommendation to measure the result or to quantify the improved outcome. For example:

"I recommend that you give us the go-ahead so that we can get your project started before the end of the quarter."

"Based on our discussion today, I think it's time for you to move to the next step, which is to execute an agreement and…"

The more often you ask the customer about alignment and expectations, the more trusted you become.

10 DEVELOP A LOGICAL BUSINESS CASE FOR BUYING.

Most customers seek positive results by improving their business approach and processes. As a capture/sales lead with customer interface assignments, help customers establish a business case for your solution.

Sales and capture professionals are notorious for falling into the trap of showcasing features of their product or service. They thrive on talking about the speed of their technology, the accuracy of their weapon system, or their world-class people rather than benefits to the customer.

A logical business case might range from a series of statements that describe the benefits and features of your solution, to a fully developed value proposition based on collaboratively developed quantitative analysis. Consider both approaches.

Informal business case

Your objective is to position your services and products as the solution to this customer's needs, a means to alleviate issues. Specifically address each issue. Imagine these two linked scenarios.

Ineffective General Positioning Approach

Seller: Here is our understanding of your requirements. You need…(followed by a summary of the customers issues and requirements).

Our solution comprises…(followed by a description of the solution).

> One thing we've discovered with certainty is that anything we do that makes the customer more successful inevitably results in a financial return for us.
>
> —Jack Welch

The problem with this approach is that the link is general. Specific issues are not directly linked to features of your solution that deliver the benefits, so some features of your solution might appear to be extraneous. The customer is forced to accept or reject your entire solution. They feel trapped and manipulated.

> The model dialogue suggested is identical in content and structure to theme statements used in proposals. See WIN STRATEGY DEVELOPMENT; and THEME STATEMENTS, Proposal Guide.

Effective Issue-Specific Approach

Seller: From what you have said, you are concerned about the cost, you want to avoid service interruptions, and you need to reduce customer inquiry response time. Correct?

Customer: Yes, that's right.

Seller: To minimize your cost, we will retain your current employee workstations, saving you $2200 per customer service representative. To avoid service interruptions, we plan to install the new server and software and run preliminary tests in advance. Then we can cut over during a 3-day weekend when you said that inquiries would be minimal. The live tests that we ran last week showed that CRM cut representatives' total response time by 28 percent.

Note how each customer issue is directly linked to a feature of the solution. If you cannot link a feature to a customer issue, do not mention that feature. Customers buy benefits, not features. If they could get the benefit without the feature, they would.

Repeatedly cite a benefit when discussing a feature of your solution throughout the capture process, not just in your proposal. Benefit statements in discussions and correspondence repeatedly remind customers that you understand their needs and requirements.

Business case as a formal value proposition

Value propositions establish the quantified value basis for the business relationship. The best value propositions go beyond traditional theme statements by incorporating as many of the following elements as possible:

- Quantifies the anticipated business improvement
- Specifies the timing of the benefits
- Specifies the timing of the costs
- States the payback period
- Specifies how the results will be measured and tracked

Executives, users, and technical buyers have different issues and values. Model your written value propositions around the template shown in figure 5.

See VALUE PROPOSITIONS.

<Customer Name> will realize <quantified business improvement> by purchasing <our solution> for <total investment cost>.

Beginning <implementation date>, the improvement in <specific business process or function> will achieve an economic payback in <timeframe>.

We have agreed to document the delivered value by <results measurement and tracking approach>.

Figure 5. Use a Template to Develop Value Propositions. *The best value propositions are developed collaboratively with the customer and contain the elements listed. Value propositions sound stronger if the benefits are placed at the beginning.*

Value propositions, as shown, summarize the business case. Perhaps the greatest benefit of a value proposition is as a collaborative capture tool. You cannot build a value proposition without customer participation. By collaboratively focusing on the quantified and unquantifiable benefits of potential, alternative solutions, the customer will come to understand the business case for selecting your solution.

This business case is the heart of the win strategy and your win strategy sessions. Unless the customer can articulate the business case within his or her organization, your solution is not credible and validated.

11   SEEK AGREEMENT ON NEXT STEPS.

Gaining agreement on next steps when interfacing with the customer should not be a traumatic event for either party. You are helping customers acquire something that they want and need; gaining agreement is the next logical step.

Some guidelines for suggesting and agreeing on next steps include the following:

- If you sense that the customer is reluctant to discuss the next steps (could simply be an RFP or Tender), step back. Assess what is missing. Did you miss an issue? Is something distracting the customer, such that your timing is wrong?

- Be candid and direct. If the timing of their next step concerns you based on your potential delivery, say so.

- When you ask about next steps, wait for an answer.

- Outline and document next steps.

Gain agreement through collaboration, not tactics. Proceeding is the next, natural, logical step. Remember, you are looking for a successful outcome for both organizations to establish trust and position follow-on business.

DECISION GATE REVIEWS

Decision gate reviews are critical milestones in the business development process at which leadership decides whether to advance an opportunity to the next phase or end the pursuit.

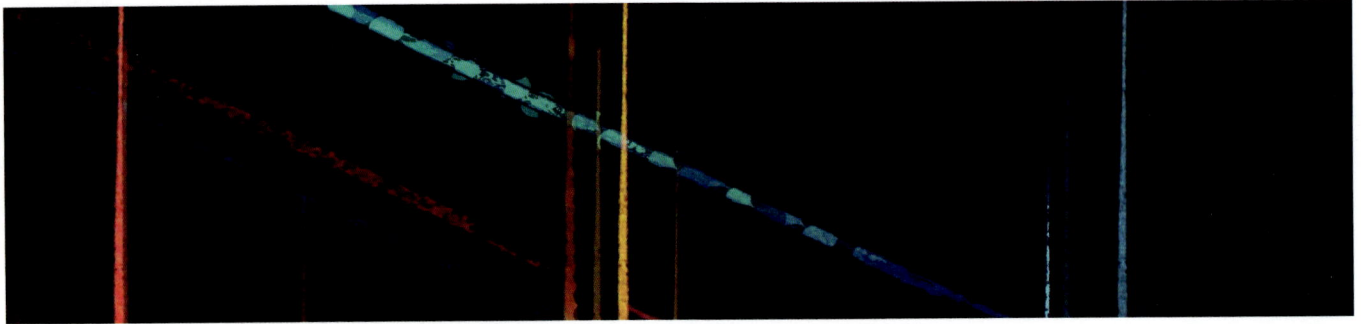

See BUSINESS DEVELOPMENT FRAMEWORK.

Organizations that repeatedly win new business in complex markets typically approach business development tasks in phases. They win more business at lower cost by aligning their activities in each phase with customers' buying cycles. This alignment improves customer focus, promoting better solution development and greater competitive differentiation.

Decision gate, decision milestone, and gate review are synonymous phrases, used interchangeably.

Business opportunities are qualified as they pass through a series of decision gates. At these gates, leaders advance and allocate resources to opportunities the organization has the greatest chance of winning and that best match their organization's objectives. Typical objectives are to capture revenue, increase profit, enter new markets, or extend current market positions.

Effective leadership ends the pursuit and withdraws resources from less promising opportunities. This winnowing creates an opportunity funnel as shown in figure 1. Applying decision gate discipline improves win rates because resources not spent on poor candidates can be redirected toward better

See COLOR TEAM REVIEWS.

opportunities. Organizations that eventually bid on fewer opportunities in their pipeline due to smart decisions have historically achieved sustained improved win rates.

Business development professionals sometimes use decision gates poorly and confuse them with color team reviews. These critical milestones have starkly different objectives:

- Decision gates are to determine whether to advance or end business opportunities.
- Color team reviews are to improve the probability of winning of those opportunities remaining in the funnel.

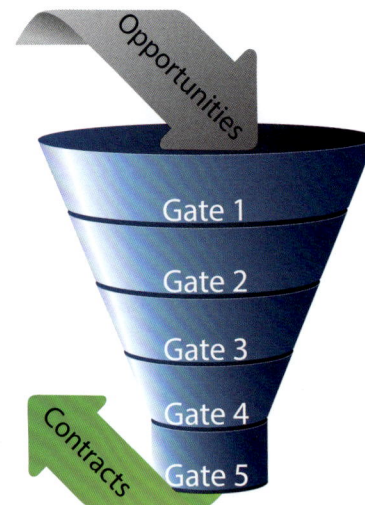

Figure 1. Opportunity Funnel. *Use decision gates to progressively limit pursuits to the most winnable opportunities that serve your organizational objectives. Descriptions of each gate are in the following guidelines.*

DECISION GATE REVIEWS

1 Use decision gates to control progression through the business development lifecycle.

2 Include relevant roles and limit non-essential participants.

3 Hold decision gates at the right level.

4 Plan decision gates carefully.

5 Specify inputs and outputs for each decision gate.

6 Consider using a facilitator.

7 Eliminate personal opinion, bias, and ego.

8 Avoid over-focus on the technical solution.

9 Continue the decision gate review until management reaches a decision.

10 Be prepared to end the pursuit.

11 Record the decision, update the capture plan, archive information, and document lessons learned.

1   USE DECISION GATES TO CONTROL PROGRESSION THROUGH THE BUSINESS DEVELOPMENT LIFECYCLE.

Conserve resources and improve your probabilty of winning by using decision gates to control progression of opportunities through the opportunity pipeline. Organizations normally establish from four to seven process phases, depending on these parameters:

- Company characteristics
- Size and complexity of customary opportunities
- Market nature, particularly speed at which opportunities develop

- Number and behavior of competitors
- Leadership decision-making preferences
- Interest, willingness, and availability of senior management to participate in decision gates

Frame decision gates separating phases, as summarized in figure 2.

NO.	PHASE	GATE	QUESTIONS
0	Market Segmentation	Campaign/ Marketing	Is the market niche congruent with goals in our strategic plan?
1	Long-Term Positioning	Interest	Does the opportunity merit expending resources to research and assess it?
2	Opportunity Assessment	Pursuit	Should we commit resources to developing a capture plan and influencing our customer to prefer our solution?
3	Capture/Opportunity Planning	Preliminary Bid	Have capture activities positioned us favorably enough with the customer to justify planning a proposal?
4	Proposal Planning	Bid Validation	Is the opportunity still worth pursuing and the proposal worth preparing, considering final details of the solicitation?
5	Proposal Development	Proposal Submittal	Should we submit our completed proposal? Is programmatic risk justified by the probable financial reward?
6	Post-Submittal Activities	Final Offer	After negotiations, is programmatic risk still justified by the financial reward considering terms of contract?

Figure 2. Fundamental Decision Gates and Questions. *Use questions like these to qualify your opportunities. Note that Phase 0, leading to the Campaign/Marketing Decision, is not opportunity-specific.*

Determining the number of phases and gates in your lifecycle is less important than defining, documenting, and following that process. Organizations that commit to a single, flexible, scalable business development process cite several benefits:

- Reduced business capture costs
- Increased productivity
- Better forecasting
- Improved management visibility and control

Ideally, seek one of only two outcomes at each decision gate:

1 Advance the pursuit, obligating sufficient resources for successful pursuit

2 End the pursuit, redirecting resources to other, more winnable opportunities

If the decision is deferred pending sufficient information, define what and when additional information is needed. Allowing poorly executed pursuits to drag on wastes resources and reduces your win probability.

Some organizations find their win rate on deferrals is higher than average because leadership demanded better information and then made better-informed decisions. Ideally, executives use deferrals as teaching opportunities to improve subsequent pursuits.

Avoid being trapped by overly complex processes. Define categories according to opportunity characteristics, such as:

- Strategic importance
- New or existing customer
- Expected contract value
- Contract type
- Financial and programmatic risks
- Investment requirements
- Alignment with corporate authority levels

Specify required decision gates, participants, inputs, and outputs by category. If your organization has not already defined such categories, work with senior management to establish them.

2   INCLUDE RELEVANT ROLES AND LIMIT NON-ESSENTIAL PARTICIPANTS.

Include personnel with relevant roles at decision gates to reduce second-guessing, reconsideration of decisions, poor commitment, wasted resources, and poor win rates. Limit non-essential participants.

Roles are temporary functions only loosely related to positions or job titles. The person filling a role often varies by opportunity category or business development phase. For each business opportunity category, determine which roles are relevant and who within your organization will fill them. One person might fill multiple roles. Define responsibilities by role and hold individuals accountable for fulfilling them, whether they perform tasks themselves or delegate to others.

Assign the following generic roles, using role names acceptable within your organization. Adapt the principal responsibilities suggested in figure 3 to your needs.

ROLE	EXECUTIVE	OPERATIONS	BUSINESS DEVELOPMENT MANAGER	CAPTURE MANAGER	BUSINESS DEVELOPER
PRIMARY DUTIES	• Define • Decide • Lead	• Advise • Support	• Assign • Monitor • Collaborate	• Engage • Inform • Execute	• Identify • Qualify

Figure 3. Primary Roles and Duties. *Business development roles are characterized by a set of primary duties. The executive role is relevant at all decision gates, though the person filling it may change.*

Executive. The executive often defines strategic direction and business criteria for the organization. He or she makes specific decisions to advance or end pursuits. Consider the decision gate as being held for this person, so the executive leads the group. The executive is obligated to formulate and disseminate expectations before decision gates.

Many organizations assign executive or leadership authority based on their predefined opportunity categories. For example, a small contract to support an existing customer might be assigned to a department head. A large contract with a new customer might be assigned to a business unit vice president. And a major, strategic opportunity requiring corporate investment or exposing the organization to high risk might go to the president. Assign the executive role to a level sufficient to minimize superiors' second-guessing and micro-managing.

Operations. Operations personnel advise and support the executive, contributing critical information. They will eventually oversee and execute the contract. They manage personnel resources, direct manufacturing, schedule development and delivery of products and services, and have product or service expertise. Operations also includes functional support organizations, such as contracts and pricing.

Business Development Manager. The business development manager is responsible for starting, growing, and maintaining the revenue stream of a business segment. Generally, he or she allocates time and money across opportunities, assigning and monitoring capture and proposal professionals to maximize success. The business development manager also collaborates with capture and proposal staff to mentor and lend perspective.

Capture Manager. The capture manager leads the team that engages directly with the customer to determine needs and craft an acceptable solution. He or she develops and executes a capture plan, guides positioning activities to improve win probability, oversees proposal strategy creation, and supports proposal development where needed.

Business Developer. The business developer is the front-line representative of the company, presenting products, services, and capabilities in the market and identifying and qualifying new bid opportunities. Business developers often are called account managers, sales executives, marketers, or sales directors, depending upon the market, organization, and industry.

If an opportunity is sufficiently mature to have teaming partners, consider whether members of those organizations need to participate as advisors, contributors, or executives.

Avoid filling the room with minimally connected managers or participants. Larger groups tend to be less constructive, with more time spent informing people instead of discussing the positives and negatives of continuing or ending the pursuit. Larger groups typically require more time to reach a decision, but the quality of the decision seldom improves as the group grows.

3   HOLD DECISION GATES AT THE RIGHT LEVEL.

Strike a balance between remaining nimble in your market and ensuring that various levels of management have the knowledge to constructively direct and advise on new business pursuits. Make decisions too low in your organization, and critical oversight will be lacking. Make them too high, and top executives will be micromanaging day-to-day operations rather than focusing on strategic planning and growth.

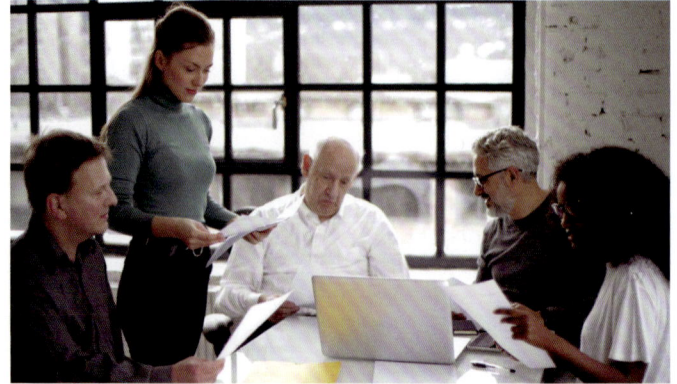

Define who fills which roles at each decision gate for each opportunity category. For example, Interest Decisions are best made informally and low in the organization to encourage a wide opportunity funnel. A business developer could feasibly make the executive's decision on most leads with acceptable risk.

4   PLAN DECISION GATES CAREFULLY.

Decision gates are planned, structured events, not ad hoc gatherings. Figure 4 is a summary of tips for the sales lead or capture manager.

Invite the right people. Omit people if you cannot define their role. Set clear expectations and standards for all attendees. Attendees must understand the purpose of the meeting and their roles.

Schedule decision gates early to improve the attendance of key participants. If key participants are unable to attend in person, add them virtually using web teleconferencing. If their time is limited, ask them to join for the summary discussion, wrap-up, and recommendations.

Confirm that all inputs are complete and available. Inputs typically vary by opportunity size and complexity. Executives frequently set minimum information thresholds and presentation templates for gate meetings. For example, they might require signed teaming agreements before Bid Validation Decision gates but eliminate capture plans for task order proposals under master ordering agreements.

Avoid developing a culture where elaborate information packets substitute for the difficult and essential work of interacting with the customer and developing solid competitive intelligence. Your objective is to use gates to narrow your range of pursuits to the most winnable few.

Offer an honest recommendation on what decision is in the best interests of your company. Avoid the common trap of capture managers seeking approval for the next phase regardless of the pursuit's status. Sometimes your best approach is to convince management to redirect precious resources to more winnable opportunities.

01	Categorize the opportunity.
02	Invite the right people for the category.
03	Schedule decision gates early to improve the attendance of key participants.
04	Confirm prescribed inputs are complete and available.
05	Avoid developing a culture where elaborate information packets substitute for interacting with the customer.
06	Offer an honest recommendation.

Figure 4. Tips for Effective Decision Gates. *To maximize decision gates, incorporate the tips listed above. When the right people attend and the recommendations are incorporated, capture and proposal efforts are strengthened.*

 ©Shipley Associates

5   SPECIFY INPUTS AND OUTPUTS FOR EACH DECISION GATE.

Define mandatory and optional inputs and outputs for each decision gate by opportunity category. Adapt these by market, prospect, and strategic importance of the lead. When presenters' and participants' expectations are aligned, everyone can focus on making sound decisions rather than debating what information is missing or who is at fault.

For large, complex opportunities, most decision gate inputs come from your capture plan. Capture plans should evolve as opportunities progress, minimizing effort on early-stage pursuits that might not continue. Predetermine which capture plan elements will be required for each decision gate.

For smaller, simpler pursuits, less comprehensive tools and inputs suffice. Your process may also require additional documentation at various decision gates:

• Opportunity assessments
• Competitive intelligence summaries
• Pricing-to-win analyses

• Solution descriptions
• Financial analyses
• Teaming agreements
• Color team review summaries

Decision gate outputs record the decisions made. To continually improve your capture process, consider including critiques of the capture team's work, instructions for future actions, or conditions attached to approvals in the opportunity file.

6   CONSIDER USING A FACILITATOR.

Decision gate reviews should be crisp, professional, and productive. Minimize defensive behaviors, blaming, and nonproductive discussions. Consider assigning a facilitator to help maintain a positive tone, keep participants focused on the competitive situation, and steer the group away from ad hominem attacks.

A skilled facilitator will have a number of methods to lead the review, ranging from a courteous redirect, to the meeting agenda, to adjusting team personnel throughout the meeting.

Facilitators can reduce the possibility of participants applying personal agendas by establishing the following ground rule:

"Please respect the professional role of each member of the team. As your facilitator, I will ask all of you to support your statements with validation. I am not suggesting that your personal opinions lack merit, but others need to understand the basis for your position."

Facilitators should resist injecting personal opinions and limit themselves to the following activities:

• Introducing and stating the roles of the facilitator, executive decision maker, advisors, and presenters
• Emphasizing the objective for the decision gate as decision making rather than problem solving
• Explaining the decision options: advancing or ending the pursuit
• Stressing the negative aspects of deferral
• Presenting review guidelines
• Conducting the review according to a published agenda
• Bringing out conflicting opinion, while keeping things constructive
• Eliciting a decision from leadership, announcing it to the group, and having it signed off

7 ELIMINATE PERSONAL OPINION, BIAS, AND EGO.

Some participants in gate reviews approach decision gates as opportunities to display their expertise, knowledge, or political savvy. Others seek to impress management, settle old scores, bolster their egos, or embarrass other participants.

Avoid decisions based on conjecture. Examine estimates for reasonableness and coherence with facts; challenge unsupported assertions, including those from powerful individuals.

Establish a positive, collaborative tone. Remind the team to focus on explaining and clarifying required information, not just reading from the capture plan or debating reviewers.

Encourage individuals with alternative perspectives to voice their opinions; they can be invaluable resources at decision gates.

Avoid a culture in which decisions to end pursuit are viewed as failures and blamed on capture managers. Such shortsightedness dissuades business developers from considering innovative growth opportunities, discourages honesty, and focuses capture managers on short-term management approval rather than long-term corporate success.

8 AVOID OVER-FOCUS ON THE TECHNICAL SOLUTION.

Conduct a comprehensive appraisal of your full offer before making a gate decision. Consider not only your technical solution, but also your management approach, price, quality assurance plan, transition plan, and the relevant experience and past performance by which you will bolster credibility with your customer. Senior managers often rise from technical backgrounds and are tempted to return to familiar territory.

Reduce reviewers' focus on the technical solution by adopting some or all of these approaches:

- Review and seek acceptance of the ground rules before beginning the meeting.
- Remind participants that they agreed to the ground rules.

- Suggest a separate review of the technical solution, identify who should participate, then set the time and place.
- If leadership refuses to continue without resolution of technical issues, your team was ill-prepared for the decision gate. Reschedule when better, more complete information is available.

9 CONTINUE THE DECISION GATE REVIEW UNTIL MANAGEMENT REACHES A DECISION.

When a decision gate is scheduled, push to a definite conclusion—advance or end the pursuit. Defer as a last resort, recognizing that deferral usually means you or other participants were ill-prepared.

Before deciding to advance, realistically scope the people, activities, and funding needed to position your organization to win.

Do not defer a decision because the answer seems unclear. Lack of clarity is a no-bid indicator. If you must defer, set a firm schedule for reconsideration. List events or intelligence on which a decision will depend. Then follow your agreed conditions.

Deferred decisions often have negative consequences:

- Subsequent activities are postponed, compressed, or eliminated.
- Leadership remembers capture managers as unprepared due to information gaps.
- Capture teams lose momentum when members delay completing assigned tasks.
- Managers returning to an unfinished review retain negative biases.

10 BE PREPARED TO END THE PURSUIT.

Ending a pursuit is often an excellent decision. If your organization lacks the resources, commitment, or capabilities to win, you are likely to lose to a hungrier, more resourceful, or more committed competitor. Redirect your time, energy, and resources to more winnable opportunities.

End the pursuit if the management team, the executive sponsor, or the capture manager is only moderately committed to winning. Strong indicators you should end a pursuit include vague decision-making information or a capture team that does not know if, how, where, or when better information can be obtained.

Submitting a poor solution or response to a customer tarnishes your image. Customers assume your proposals accurately represent your capability. If they do not, do not submit them.

Before ending a pursuit, however, consider the availability of other opportunities, your market position, and the most productive alternative assignments for your business development team. Ask yourself whether business development skills or resources will be lost by not going forward.

Sometimes, realities of the market dictate moving ahead under less-than-ideal conditions. Think about both positive and negative impacts before making your decision.

11 RECORD THE DECISION, UPDATE THE CAPTURE PLAN, ARCHIVE INFORMATION, AND DOCUMENT LESSONS LEARNED.

Promptly record and disseminate decisions. To support subsequent analysis of gate decisions and foster familiarity, develop a standard decision record for your organization. Include these key elements:

- Date
- Participants
- Decisions
- Recommendations
- Commitments
- Approved process deviations and extraordinary exceptions
- Lessons learned

Tailor the record or entry to the complexity of the opportunity. A separate record for each decision gate is appropriate for complex opportunities or business development protocols. Simpler situations can be handled with a single form covering all gates.

Have leadership approve the decision record or entry. Good practice generally confers decision authority on a single individual, not a committee.

Add the decision gate record to your database. Note the decision and date on the capture plan title page.

Continue this practice to collect and record lessons learned after each decision gate.

EXECUTIVE SUMMARIES

Executive summaries are often the most important pages in a proposal. They set the tone for individual evaluators and are often the only pages read by the decision makers. A draft should be developed during capture planning.

A draft executive summary should be developed early during the capture/opportunity planning phase. It provides a roadmap for the rest of the capture plan, and later the proposal.

The capture manager should prepare the first draft of the proposal executive summary and present it at the Preliminary Bid Decision gate review and later in the proposal kickoff meeting.

Readers of your executive summary must clearly understand your solution and its unique benefits and be able to justify recommending your solution over competing solutions.

Effective executive summaries meet the following criteria:

- Connect your solution to the customer's buying vision.
- Identify the customer's needs.
- Connect your solution directly to the customer's needs.
- Offer clear proof of your claims.
- Show how you offer greater value than the competition.
- Present the value proposition.
- Be brief, but comprehensive, by eliminating confusing technical details that are better explained in the body of the proposal.
- Indicate the next step, usually by previewing how your proposal is organized.

See SUPPORTING
THE PROPOSAL.

Executive summaries also:

- Help refine your bidding strategy
- Become a vehicle to gain senior management endorsement for pursuing the opportunity
- Communicate your strategy in-house to all contributors
- Drive proposal development
- Become a model for the complete proposal

Evolve the content, form, and detail in the executive summary until the proposal is submitted. The capture manager's first draft usually lacks the following executive summary information:

- Technical solution
- Program management structure and team members
- High-level deliverables schedule
- Teaming relationships
- Substantiating experience and performance examples/references

Assign the person with the best perspective, writing skills, and availability to complete the executive summary.

©Shipley Associates

EXECUTIVE SUMMARIES

1 Always include an executive summary in a proposal.

2 Maintain customer focus throughout.

3 Build on your existing sales process and strategy.

4 Organize the content to be clear and persuasive.

5 Expand the Executive Summary Organizer into a draft.

6 Further develop your executive summary based on proven best practices.

7 Follow sound writing guidelines.

1 ALWAYS INCLUDE AN EXECUTIVE SUMMARY IN A PROPOSAL.

If the customer asks for an executive summary, submit one. If not, do so anyway.

Call it whatever the customer calls it. Common alternatives are management summary and management overview.

Independent of what the customer calls it, understand the difference between a summary and an introduction. A summary condenses the essential content of your proposal. An introduction indicates how your proposal is organized. Other terms for introduction are preview, roadmap, and informal table of contents.

To include an executive summary when the proposal outline is strictly defined in the bid request, you have several compliant alternatives. One is to include a separately bound executive summary. Another is to place a copy in every volume submitted, either in a pocket in the front or in the binder or as a separate attachment to online submissions.

Note that in page-limited proposals, the executive summary is considered part of your technical proposal and is included in the page count.

Even when preparing a response to a short notice request, include an executive summary. It need not be long, but follow the same best practices to address benefits, customer focus, and your solution.

See ORGANIZATION, Proposal Guide.

Three model executive summaries are included in MODEL DOCUMENTS 2–4 *in the* Proposal Guide.

2 MAINTAIN CUSTOMER FOCUS THROUGHOUT.

The executive summary should focus on customer needs, issues, and motivators (hot buttons) and explain how your solution meets those needs.

Check every executive summary against the following customer focus criteria:

See CUSTOMER INTERFACE.

- States the customer's buying or acquisition vision
- Connects the vision to the immediate opportunity
- Cites the customer's hot buttons in order of importance or the order listed in their bid request. A hot button is a customer's need or motivator
- Makes the customer's ownership of the hot buttons explicit, when possible
- Addresses each hot button in the order introduced
- Names the customer more than the seller
- Names the customer before the seller in the document, paragraphs, and sentences
- Cites benefits before features
- Validates all claims

3 BUILD ON YOUR EXISTING SALES PROCESS AND STRATEGY.

To maintain a consistent message with your customers and to save time, exploit your existing internal information sources as much as possible.

Many organizations have embraced a strategic and/or tactical sales process. Exploit it to develop your executive summary rather than starting over. With a little effort, you can map the information from existing sales tools into your executive summary.

See CAPTURE PLANNING, AN OVERVIEW; PROPOSAL MANAGEMENT PLAN *in the* Proposal Guide.

When business development people are asked to draft the executive summary, too many still pull the last one they prepared, do a Search and Replace for customer and product names, add one or two sentences, and submit. They continue to tailor their last executive summary for subsequent opportunities until the executive summary completely unravels.

Most of the information needed to prepare the executive summary is contained in the capture plan. The template summarized in figure 1 is recommended to help assemble and organize the information needed for an executive summary.

ShipleyAssociates

EXECUTIVE SUMMARY
PLANNING WORKSHEET

Plan Around the Hot Buttons

If you have more than 4 hot buttons, use additional worksheets and renumber hot buttons.

Hot Buttons

Hot buttons are an amalgam of issues, needs, requirements, and evaluation criteria. List hot buttons in order of importance unless you are mirroring the order stated by the customer.

#1	#2	#3	#4

Solution

Identify key technical, management, support, and cost aspects of your solution. To be more competitive and responsive, consider eliminating aspects that do not align with any hot button.

Benefits or Value Propositions

List the benefits of your solution to the customer or provide details of a value proposition (which is a form of benefit). Customers buy benefits that resolve issues, especially hot buttons.

Discriminators

Discriminators are aspects of your solution that differ from at least one competitor's solution and that the customer cares about. If a competitor could make the same claim, make your discriminator more specific.

Proof, Experience, and Past Performance

Enter information to substantiate your ability to provide the solution, including relevant experience in similar situations and how well you performed.

Key Visual(s)

Briefly describe a visual that illustrates an aspect of your solution, a benefit, a discriminator, or some element of your substantiation. Consider what visual impact you can make on your reader in this important document summary.

Copyright Shipley Associates   For individual use only. Do not distribute.

Figure 1. Executive Summary Planning Worksheet. *Complete the worksheet by listing customer hot buttons in priority order across the first row. Across the second row, list aspects of your solution under the hot buttons they most closely address. If a feature doesn't fit a hot button, consider leaving it out of the executive summary. For the remainder of the planning worksheet, list benefits your solution provides, discriminators, and proofs under the corresponding hot button. Note visuals that illustrate any of those points.*

4   ORGANIZE THE CONTENT TO BE CLEAR AND PERSUASIVE.

Transfer the content that you developed in the Planning Worksheet into the Executive Summary Organizer, shown in figure 2.

See MODEL DOCUMENTS 2–4 *in the* PROPOSAL GUIDE *for examples of executive summaries in the four-box organization style.*

The Organizer is based on fundamental principles for creating persuasive documents using what is called four-box organization.

Four-box organization is nearly always more customer focused than the narrative or mirror approach. The mirror approach is a mini-version of your proposal, most often used when the proposal is formally solicited and the structure is rigidly defined in the bid request.

The draft executive summary becomes a working document for the capture team as strategies and solutions evolve during the capture process. Teams should regularly review the draft to update and refresh content and win strategies.

CONTENT

Box 1–SUMMARY:

Recognize customer's vision, challenges, and objectives, and introduce your solution.

Box 2–INTRODUCTION:

Establish and prioritize customer's needs (current needs and desired status). This is a preview of what's to come—key points, customer issues, challenges, etc.

Box 3–BODY:

Present solutions to the customer's needs, emphasizing benefits and results. Identify your proof. Maintain the same organizational scheme introduced in Box 2.

Box 4–REVIEW:

State why the customer should select you. Summarize the unique contribution your solution makes to your customer's success. Indicate the next step.

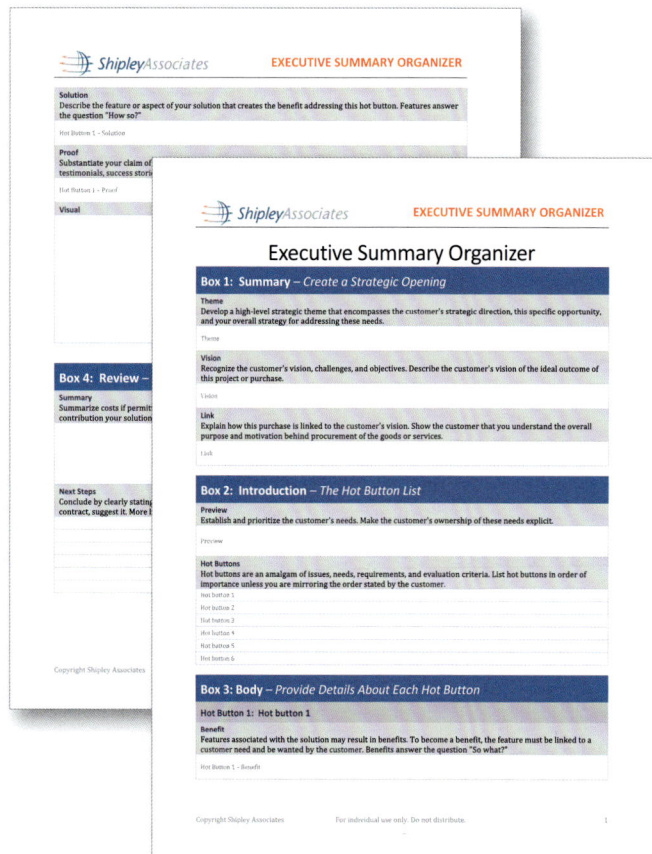

PROCESS

1. Brainstorm a high-level strategic theme that encompasses the customer's strategic direction, this specific opportunity, and your overall strategy to address needs. Write the theme and introduction to the executive summary in Box 1.

2. Copy the customer's top hot buttons from the Executive Summary Planning Worksheet into Box 2. These customer hot buttons will be the basis for the bullet points.

3. Copy the hot buttons from Box 2 into Box 3 as subtitles.

4. Under each subtitle in Box 3, list the paragraphs that you plan to write to communicate your organization's solution, including:

    – The benefits and features of the solution, emphasizing any applicable discriminators.

    – The visuals of any type that will be included. Think of visuals before text.

    – Proof of claims to be included. Most should be visual.

    – Alternatives and justification of your approach.

5. Restate your overall strategy and summarize your solution and discriminators in Box 4. Suggest the next step as appropriate.

Figure 2. Using the Executive Summary Organizer. *Rearrange material planned with the Executive Summary Planning Worksheet into a persuasive order with the four-box method used in the Executive Summary Organizer. The template assures a high degree of customer focus and helps produce an executive summary intuitively appealing to the customer. When proposal instructions are restrictive, an executive summary organized this way may be the only place you can tell a coherent story.*

5   EXPAND THE EXECUTIVE SUMMARY ORGANIZER INTO A DRAFT.

The Executive Summary Organizer helps you identify key selling points within a customer-focused, clear framework. Expand the framework into a first draft:

- Develop the visuals.
- Determine customer hot buttons.
- Draft action captions for the visuals.
- Draft text describing your benefits and solutions.
- Draft text describing your experience and proof of performance.
- Summarize your costs/pricing, if permitted by purchasing rules.
- Draft text summarizing how your proposal is organized.

Figure 3 illustrates how the Executive Summary Organizer is expanded into the executive summary. Allocate space in the executive summary according to the relative importance of the topic to the customer, tempered somewhat by the relative competitive strength of this feature or aspect of your offer. Determining the total length of your executive summary is discussed in Guideline 6.

See VALUE PROPOSITIONS; *and* RELEVANT EXPERIENCE/PAST PERFORMANCE, Proposal Guide.

If you develop a value proposition as an integral part of your sales approach, summarize it in your executive summary. Present your summary value proposition in Box 1. Introduce individual value propositions in Box 2. Discuss each value proposition against your solution in Box 3. Summarize in Box 4. Align the value proposition with customer hot button issues.

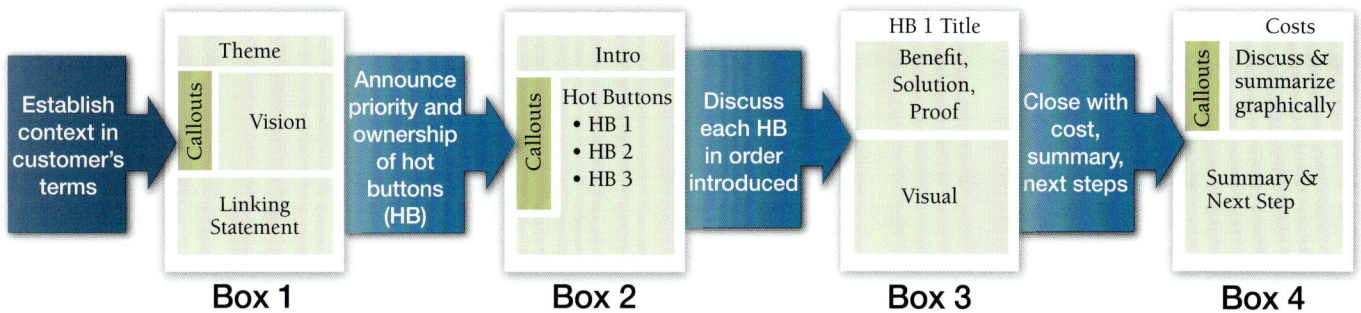

Figure 3. Expanding the Executive Summary Organizer into a Draft Executive Summary with a Focus on Hot Buttons (HBs). *A four-box structure helps you quickly draft highly effective, customer-focused executive summaries. Build out the Executive Summary Organizer content as depicted here to develop and evolve the draft.*

6 FURTHER DEVELOP YOUR EXECUTIVE SUMMARY BASED ON PROVEN BEST-IN-CLASS PRACTICES.

See PRESENTATIONS TO CUSTOMERS.

The following guidelines are based on years of application observation in organizations with a proven ability to cost-effectively win business:

- Direct the sales/capture team to complete the first draft of the executive summary prior to the proposal kickoff meeting.
- Direct the proposal manager or sales support to review the draft, add detail on the solution, and complete it early enough to permit review by sales and management.

- Review your draft executive summary with your customer, if possible.
- Generally, limit the total length to 2–5 pages.
- Use a key visual or two to help tell the story.
- Use your executive summary as the basis for your oral briefing. Update it if needed and distribute copies to the customer at the end.
- Maintain customer focus from start to finish.

7 FOLLOW SOUND WRITING GUIDELINES.

Follow these writing guidelines to write consistent, effective executive summaries. If you are a reviewer, use it as a checklist.

- Except in small proposals (under 20 pages), write the executive summary as a stand-alone document.
- Write executive summaries for upper-level, nontechnical decision makers.
- Make the executive summary brief but comprehensive.
- Include key visuals and other graphics in the executive summary.
- Do not assume that readers of the executive summary have been privy to information given during earlier discussions.
- Organize the executive summary using a customer-focused framework.

See PROOFREADING, EDITING, AND REVISING, Proposal Guide.

- Clearly state what you are offering and how it benefits the customer.
- Align solutions to customer hot buttons.
- Offer clear proof of your claims.
- Link major discriminators prominently and explicitly to a customer issue.
- Organize information within the paragraph from general to specific, from benefits to features, and from familiar to unfamiliar. Such obvious relationships require less explanation and will produce more concise paragraphs.
- Begin with a sentence that states the main idea.

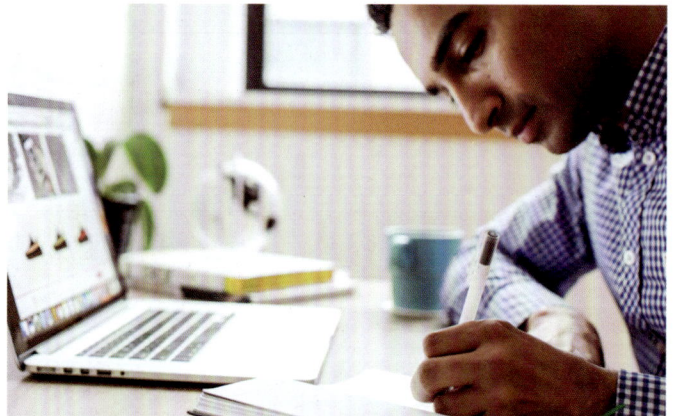

©Shipley Associates

OPPORTUNITY QUALIFICATION

Opportunity qualification involves a careful and unbiased analysis of a given opportunity to ensure that you invest only in opportunities with a reasonable chance of winning. Execution of pursuit decision gates is part of the opportunity qualification process.

Business development teams that apply consistent standards when qualifying business opportunities see the greatest Return on Investment (ROI) of their marketing, bid, and proposal budgets. The qualification process is often compared to a funnel that only allows opportunities that meet certain criteria through to the next business development phase.

Many effective organizations also refer to opportunity qualification as "pipeline management," which involves

careful oversight of each sales opportunity as it progresses through the sales cycle. Often, a Probability of Winning (Pwin) is assigned to opportunities as they advance toward the proposal phase or presentation to the customer.

As opportunities are qualified, there should be a decision to advance, defer, or end the pursuit, as shown in figure 1.

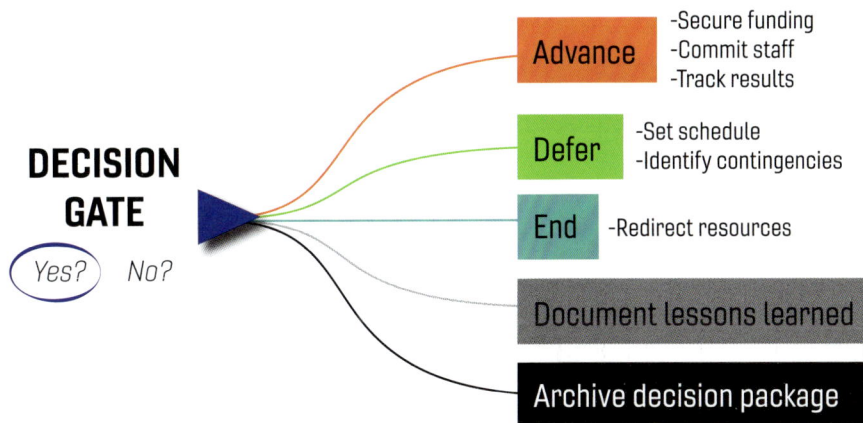

Figure 1. Use Decision Gates to Qualify Opportunities. *No matter what the final decision is, all decision gates require action once they are finalized. You should only advance an opportunity if you have a high Pwin and adequate resources to fulfill the contract if awarded. If Pwin is low for an opportunity, save resources and time by ending the pursuit and redirecting capture efforts on other opportunities.*

OPPORTUNITY QUALIFICATION

1 Qualify early and often.

2 Be consistent in your analysis of opportunities.

3 Use rigorous checklists and decision gate tools to advance each opportunity.

4 Qualify based on customer assessment, competitive intelligence, your capability to deliver, and cost and price.

1   QUALIFY EARLY AND OFTEN.

A one-time assessment of a potential sales opportunity is insufficient. Qualification is an iterative process. Carefully review all aspects of the opportunity on a regular basis. Many effective organizations use a formal capture plan template or structure to continuously track and update opportunity details. The "opportunity owner" has the responsibility to adjust the Pwin based on any updates to the customer's need, timing, or requirements.

As opportunities are qualified, the number of pursuits is often reduced since some opportunities will be eliminated from the pipeline. Figure 2 shows how the number of active opportunities decreases over time as opportunities are qualified.

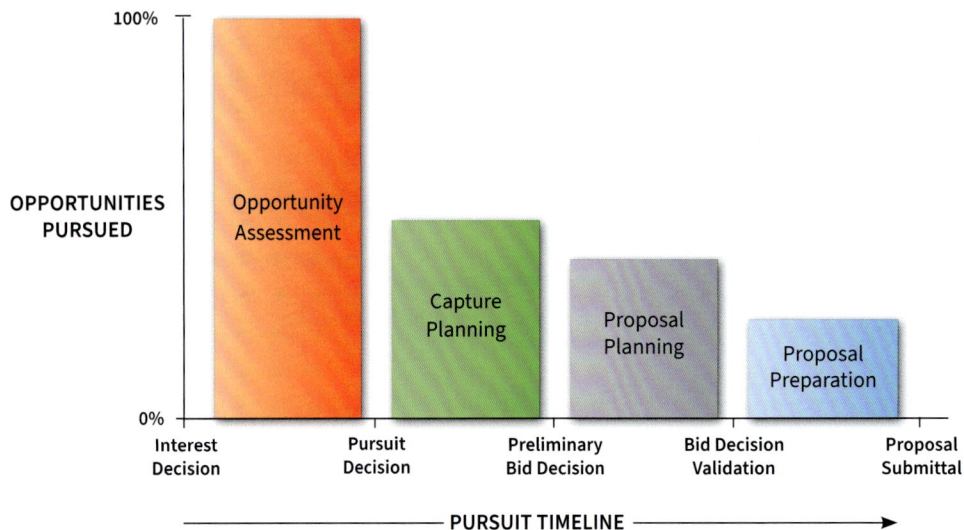

Figure 2. Selecting the Best Opportunities. *After the initial opportunity assessment, reassess whether to continue to pursue each opportunity at successive decision gate reviews. Establish criteria for each decision gate review in advance to improve the quality of the feedback from reviewers.*

2   BE CONSISTENT IN YOUR ANALYSIS OF OPPORTUNITIES.

Consistency in how and when to qualify and assess pursuits is important. Often, bias or opinion carries too much weight when deciding whether or not to pursue or continue pursuing an opportunity. Leaving opportunity qualification to "chance" or bias can be a finance and resource drain by allowing for

opportunities with very low win probability to advance through the pipeline.

Figure 3 shows factors that can impact the qualification process.

©Shipley Associates

Figure 3. Avoid Potentially Incorrect Qualification Fodder. *Evaluation influences like speculation, bias, outdated research, guessing, or "gut feelings" are not effective factors to base your opportunity analysis on. If you include these types of factors in your opportunity qualification process, you will likely lose the deal.*

GUESSING

Too often business development professionals resort to guessing on customer requirements, needs, or issues. Avoid guessing by asking the customer effective questions and researching their answers.

BIAS

Biases in opportunity qualification come in various forms and from various sources. Hopeful capture managers or sales executives are often financially motivated to bid on as many opportunities as possible. They can be swayed toward a bid decision based on perceived biases or financial incentives. Leadership and management can also sway an opportunity toward a positive bid decision based on personal bias.

SPECULATION

Allowing an opportunity to continue through the sales cycle based on someone's speculation or assumptions can lead to poor win rates and wasted resources.

INCUMBENT STATUS

Being an incumbent on a contract can either be an advantage or a disadvantage depending on many factors, including past performance. Sometimes business development professionals assume they will win a re-compete and fail to adequately re-qualify the opportunity. Competing for incumbent projects should involve the same opportunity qualification rigor as for new projects.

GUT FEEL

Trusting someone's gut feel that an opportunity will be a win without going through the qualification process is a bad idea. In competitive markets, relying on research, data, and facts offers the best qualification safeguard.

OUTDATED RESEARCH

Because so much information is at our fingertips, you should never rely on opportunity, competitor, or customer research that is more than a few months old. Even on re-compete opportunities, current research is a must in today's competitive markets. Research should also come from a variety of sources as opportunity qualification proceeds.

3   USE RIGOROUS CHECKLISTS AND DECISION GATE TOOLS TO ADVANCE EACH OPPORTUNITY.

See DECISION GATE REVIEWS *for more detail.*

See COLOR TEAM REVIEWS *for checklists that can also be applied.*

Organizations that maximize their marketing, sales, and bid and proposal funds apply rigor to opportunity qualification using checklists at each key milestone of qualification.

Effective organizations also manage the decision gate stages and allow for an "off ramp" if an opportunity no longer fits the necessary Pwin percentage or target.

Common qualification decision gates for opportunity qualification are shown in figure 4 below.

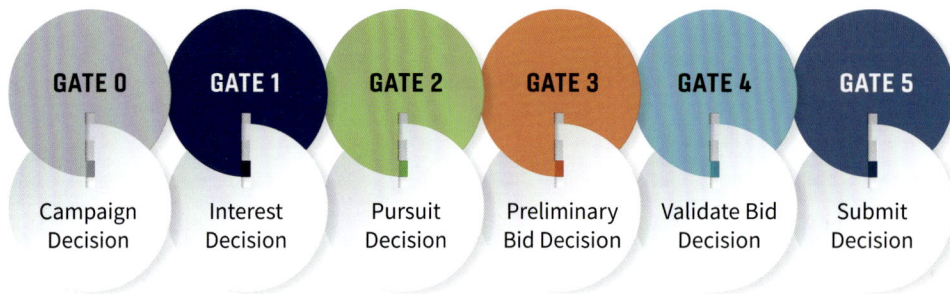

GATE 0	GATE 1	GATE 2	GATE 3	GATE 4	GATE 5
Campaign Decision	Interest Decision	Pursuit Decision	Preliminary Bid Decision	Validate Bid Decision	Submit Decision

Figure 4. Qualification Decision Gates Help Focus on the Best Opportunities. *The ultimate goal of decision gates is to qualify the opportunities you have the best chance of winning. Decision gates allow you to allocate resources to the most "winnable" opportunities and prevent you from wasting resources on opportunities with a low Pwin.*

When you come across customer concerns about your solution or organization's ability to meet their needs, address those concerns immediately. Ignoring or "passing over" customer concerns during opportunity qualification leads to potentially bidding on unwinnable projects or work. By applying checklists and decision gate tools, you can be sure customer concerns are addressed before advancing the opportunity.

4   QUALIFY BASED ON CUSTOMER ASSESSMENT, COMPETITIVE INTELLIGENCE, YOUR CAPABILITY TO DELIVER, AND COST AND PRICE.

Opportunity qualification must be done from various perspectives. Too often, business development professionals focus on opportunities only from their perspective, not taking into consideration the customer's view.

- **Customer Assessment.** You must try to understand how the customer perceives you—what are your strengths, weaknesses, and gaps in the eyes of the customer. Look at potential solutions to their needs and issues from their perspective. Opportunity qualification is only valid if you consider the opportunity based on an assessment from the customer's perception.

- **Competitive Intelligence.** When qualifying an opportunity, assess each competitor to determine how well you stand up to their potential solutions and strengths. Look for competitor weaknesses that you can exploit when positioning your solution.

- **Capability to Perform.** As opportunities are being qualified, continuously confirm your ability to execute on the deliverables being proposed. Qualifying an opportunity on which you cannot perform does no good. Careful consideration about your ability to deliver on the solution is a key aspect of opportunity qualification.

These criteria are all included in an effective capture plan.

PRESENTATIONS TO CUSTOMERS

Presentations to customers are usually related to written proposals. Both are planned and structured to advance the opportunity. Any disconnect or conflict between what you say and what you submit in writing creates dissonance and confusion, reducing your credibility.

Customer presentations usually have one of the following primary objectives:

1. To persuade the customer to favor your solution
2. To convey information
3. To clarify your offer and answer questions

All presentations and briefings should be customer focused to address their issues and concerns.

Effective persuasion relies on the following:

1. Reputation and credibility of the speaker
2. Logic of what is said
3. Emotional needs or state of the customer

All three elements are essential.

Some competitive pursuits rely heavily on presentations and videos. It is critical to know and understand the solicitation type early in the pursuit.

PRESENTATIONS TO CUSTOMERS

1 Maintain consistency throughout the pursuit.

2 Keep a balance between content development and delivery.

3 Identify the next achievable sales objective or milestone.

4 Analyze your audience and present logically according to their priorities and needs.

5 Consider the parameters and environment.

6 Include evidence to support your points.

7 Use effective slides and video to support your message.

8 Deliver with confidence.

9 Establish the ground rules, then follow them.

1   MAINTAIN CONSISTENCY THROUGHOUT THE PURSUIT.

Complex pursuits involve multiple bidders and presentations. Unexplained changes in your message cause confusion, doubt, and objections.

See CUSTOMER FOCUS, Proposal Guide.

All briefing material and messaging should reflect consistency with your win strategy and value proposition.

By organizing all of your presentations, videos, and documents in the same customer-focused manner, you will save time, be more consistent, and be more successful in achieving your objectives.

2   KEEP A BALANCE BETWEEN CONTENT DEVELOPMENT AND DELIVERY.

When you plan a presentation or briefing to a customer, spend adequate time developing your content and practicing your delivery.

Presentations are developed using graphics, color, lists, fonts, white space, and style for emphasis.

When organizing your presentation, follow the simple pattern shown below:

* Tell them what you are going to tell them.
* Tell them.
* Tell them what you told them.

Presenters rely on gestures, voice dynamics, eye contact, posture, movement, and facial expressions. These nonverbal messages can either reinforce or contradict the verbal message.

When verbal and nonverbal messages conflict during the delivery of the message, the listener tends to trust the nonverbal elements to determine the meaning.

3   IDENTIFY THE NEXT ACHIEVABLE SALES OBJECTIVE OR MILESTONE.

When preparing your presentation or briefing, begin by answering two questions:

1. What is your objective?
2. What would you like the customer to agree to do next?

The answer to the first is usually broad: to persuade the customer to buy your idea, product, or service, or to validate your offer.

The answer to the second is far more focused: to agree to change a specification, for example, or to commit to attend a product demonstration.

Open your presentation by stating your objective:

Today I will demonstrate how outsourcing network support can save $240,000 annually and free your managers to focus on Global's core activities.

Then, clearly state your desired next step resulting from the briefing. Be sure the customer knows what you expect as a next step in the decision-making process.

©Shipley Associates

4   ANALYZE YOUR AUDIENCE AND PRESENT LOGICALLY ACCORDING TO THEIR PRIORITIES AND NEEDS.

To present effectively, you must understand your customer's priorities and needs. When presenting, state your understanding of their needs and ask for confirmation.

In your (bid, phone request, initial meeting) you asked us to address the following issues:

> *(List the issues.)*

Have we gotten them correct? If so, with your agreement, we will address each one in order.

If you are too early in the pursuit to have a basis to state their issues, then either ask them or cite your understanding and the basis for your understanding.

We agreed to meet today to discuss how we might help you establish bottling facilities in South America. Our experience with other organizations developing manufacturing facilities in South America suggests that most are concerned about the following issues:

> *(List the issues.)*

How would your concerns be similar or different?

Organize your message in order of importance to the customer, unless directed otherwise by the customer. Presentations can be logically organized by order of importance, time, cause and effect, or spatially.

Using the executive summary as the basis for customer presentations is an effective approach to maintain a consistent sales message, save time, and be customer focused.

Figure 1 shows how a presentation can align with an executive summary. Note two differences:

1. Presentations require more emphatic summaries and transitions among main points.

See EXECUTIVE SUMMARY *and* ORGANIZATION, Proposal Guide.

2. Graphics will have to be adjusted for the medium.

Alignment between your written proposal and the briefing is key.

ALIGNING YOUR PRESENTATION AND EXECUTIVE SUMMARIES

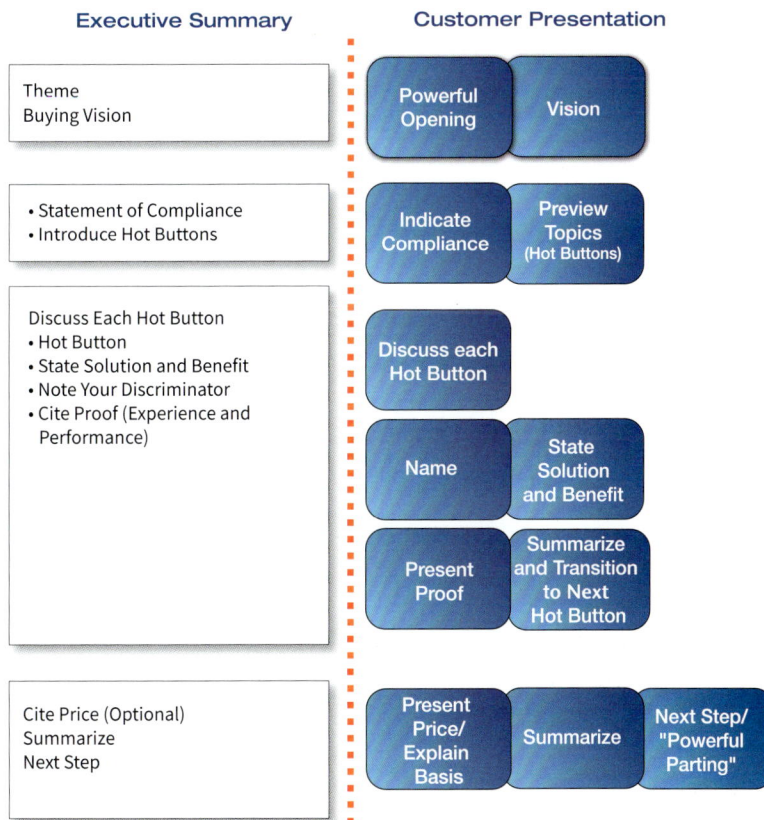

Figure 1. Use the Same Organization for Your Customer Presentation and Executive Summary. *If you organize your customer presentations as shown, you will save time preparing the executive summary and maintain a consistent message. If your executive summary is prepared first, simply add slides as needed, following sound slide preparation guidelines.*

5   CONSIDER THE PARAMETERS AND ENVIRONMENT.

When planning your presentation or briefing, consider the location, time allocation, number of attendees, technology, and other factors.

The location and room type will determine the amount of space for the presentation and type of visuals you can use.

The time allocation will affect the depth of content and amount of detail you can provide. It is a good idea to clarify time allocation for each topic with the customer in advance.

The number of attendees will affect the delivery medium selected and the design of your graphics. Virtual attendees must be considered as well.

Technology and technology testing are key aspects of presentation preparation. Be as familiar as possible with the overall presentation environment.

6   INCLUDE EVIDENCE TO SUPPORT YOUR POINTS.

Emphasize visual evidence rather than textual evidence, if possible.

Develop adequate support for each main point. Remember evidence of support is not necessarily proof in a scientific sense. Support includes definitions, evaluation criteria, explanations, experience, proof of performance, and testimonials.

Definitions establish a common basis of understanding, and evaluation criteria establish a basis for judgment or comparison.

Explanations are nearly always necessary, but match them to the expertise of the attendees.

Video is a common method for providing evidence and support during briefings.

Experience is the proof that your organization has done this before or has completed similar tasks. When experience is not identical, relate parallel experience from similar subtasks.

Proof of performance is about results. When you completed the task, what was the benefit to the customer or impact on the customer's process? Be clear when presenting proof examples to your customer.

Testimonials or references offer independent proof that the experience and performance cited are real. Testimonials carry emotionally persuasive impact in addition to the facts.

7   USE EFFECTIVE SLIDES AND VIDEO TO SUPPORT YOUR MESSAGE.

Effective slides and video should highlight key messages, not display every point. Think of slides as billboards, not text ads. Videos should be professional and compelling.

Slides or videos should support your message rather than become the message. Presenters have problems when their slides or videos serve too many additional purposes:

- Cue or prompt the speaker
- Support participants' note taking
- Review key points for audience members' subsequent use or study
- Substitute for written papers, guides, or case studies

Keep the following in mind when designing presentation graphics and video:

1. Keep text simple on slides and video segments:
   - Keep slides to one thought, concept, or idea.
   - Use a sentence headline that states your key point on all but title slides. Left justify headline text.
   - Limit lists to two-to-four items and six words per line.
   - Minimize bulleted lists because they do not show the links between items.
   - Replace bulleted lists with graphical support for the key point stated in the title.

©Shipley Associates

– Use one or two fonts or typefaces (at the most).

– Highlight with bold, italics, or color. Highlight key numbers. Avoid underlined text.

2. Keep the graphics uncluttered:

– Use images, graphics, or visual arrangements of text. Connect arrangements of text with lines or arrows.

– Show only key numbers when the actual number is important.

– Show only trend lines when the trend is your key point.

3. For slides, guide eyes to the main point:

– Use larger type.

– Use an arrow.

– Use animation or a video clip.

– Leave white space between visual elements, rather than white space for borders. When projected, white space on the border is less noticeable.

– Use animation and builds with dense slides.

4. Organize clearly:

– Use an image on each title slide that orients the audience to your key message, objective, or subject.

– Follow title slides with an introductory or mapping slide that previews direction.

– End with a concluding slide that restates your initial assertion. Incorporate your opening image and summary support image on this concluding slide.

5. Follow these additional suggestions:

– Use a landscape style permitting larger print and longer, easier-to-read phrases.

– Use 28 point or larger type for titles and 18-24 point for body text, depending upon room size.

– Keep the grammatical structure of bullet points parallel, making content easier to understand and present.

– Proof carefully; do not rely exclusively on spell checking software.

– Use numbers in display lists when you may want to refer to a few specific items.

– Use phrases, not sentences.

See COLOR *and* GRAPHICS, Proposal Guide.

Choose colors and templates carefully. Consider your corporate image, the audience, and your objective. Some audiences comment on the background or motion while missing the presenter's point.

Many decorative images in standard presentation templates actually detract from your message and reduce audience recall. Reverse print on dark backgrounds must be either larger or bolder.

8   DELIVER WITH CONFIDENCE.

Confident delivery demands rehearsal. Rehearsals enable you to test six critical aspects of your presentation:

- **Timing**—Does it match the customers' expectations?

- **Intonation and Emphasis**—Do you hit each point correctly?

- **Technology**—Can you use all hardware, software, lights, and screens? Do the visuals project correctly and clearly for all viewers? Are video links functional?

- **Confidence**—Have you rehearsed to enable you to focus on your customers and to adjust to their reactions?

- **Audience Reaction**—Does the test group get your message? Are you customer focused?

- **Questions and Answers**—Are questions allowed during or after your presentation? Do you want to encourage questions? How will questions affect timing? In team presentations, who will respond? How do you plan to respond?

Practice answering questions.

Black the screen when presenting key points that are not supported by a slide. Focus the audience on the presenter, not the screen.

9   ESTABLISH THE GROUND RULES, THEN FOLLOW THEM.

Follow customers' ground rules or establish them collaboratively. Collaboration promotes acceptance.

In less formal situations, frequently check the customer's understanding and acceptance. Participation keeps the customer's attention.

Presentation experts differ on how and when to allow questions. No single approach is best in all situations. One approach is to ask the audience to hold questions for the end. With this approach, nervous presenters can stay on topic and on schedule. However, interactivity is lost, and the presentation can end dully when questions abruptly cease.

Another approach is to encourage questions during the presentation to involve customers, gauge reaction, and tailor content. With this approach, presenters must be skilled enough to stay on topic and on schedule. Allow interruptions if you have adequate presentation skills.

For virtual presentations, establish protocols for muting, commenting, and asking questions. Be sure everyone's audio and screen sharing is working. Rehearsing virtual presentations is critical due to the variations in platforms and technologies.

Retain enough time with either approach to summarize and close with power and enthusiasm. End on a high note.

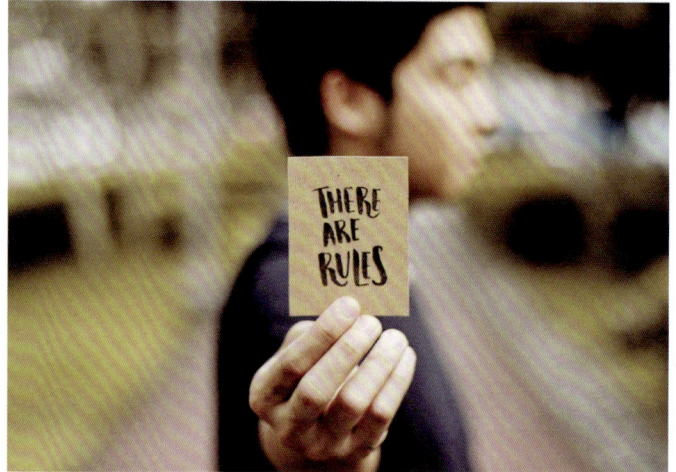

PRICING TO WIN

Pricing to win is a process for achieving the price to win by developing an offer that is competitive within the customer's value system. Essential process inputs include acquisition requirements, the customer's budget, competitors' likely bids, realistic costs to deliver the offered solution, and alternative solutions.

Understanding pricing to win requires common definitions and perspectives on evolving trends in business development best practice. First, key definitions:

- **Price** is the amount of money expected, required, or given in payment for the solution.

- **Cost** is the cost to the seller to supply the solution. If the seller makes a profit, then the price exceeds the cost.

- **Price to compete** is your interim estimate of the customer's perception of a competitive range before final requirements are known. Use it to guide initial solution design.

- **Price to win** is the combination of price and capability yielding a probability of win that meets the seller's strategic objectives based on the requirements and evaluation process. Hence, price to win is not just a number. Rather it is a number linked to a set of capabilities that generate specific measurable benefits to the buyer.

- **Pricing to win** is the process for achieving or arriving at the price to win and is the focus of this topic section.

In markets involving complex sales, business development practices tend to evolve in this order:

- Professional sales techniques are implemented, first tactical, then strategic.

- Professional proposal planning and management processes are implemented.

- Formal capture planning and management processes are implemented.

- A formal pricing-to-win process is implemented.

Visionary managers initiate each wave. When competitors reduce the sector leader's competitive advantage by emulating the leader's processes, the leader initiates the next wave of improvements.

"The same general conditions that facilitate a company's ability to use other business development best practices contribute to that company's ability to build and sustain pricing to win and competitive assessment best practices."

Final Report: Benchmark Study on Implementing PTW/ CA Capability in a Company, Business Development Institute International, 31 March 2011.

PRICING TO WIN

1 Integrate pricing to win as a fundamental aspect of your business development lifecycle.

2 Recognize basic customer buying types to anticipate their buying behaviors.

3 Determine the customer's addressable budget.

4 Consider the customer's expected price.

5 Estimate and refine the price to compete based upon competitors' bids and actual award prices on prior similar contracts.

6 Estimate and refine a price to win using an opportunity-based, bottom-up approach.

7 Compare likely bids and solutions using the winning price window (WPW).

8 Develop a strategy to achieve the price to win.

9 Incorporate customer evaluation processes into your pricing strategy.

10 Recognize the impacts of game changers, including political, economic, social, technological, legal, and environmental (PESTLE) factors or events.

11 Refine your solution based on changes in the competitive landscape.

12 Refine your strategies based on changes in your solution or competitive landscape.

13 Re-assess your pricing strategies post-award and update your pricing-to-win database.

From an academic perspective, pricing to win is a subset of strategic pricing, an active academic research topic in economics, purchasing, industrial marketing, and business development. Academic research focuses on the importance of internal and external pricing factors when pursuing transfer, cost-plus, parity, second market, complementary product, or low-cost pricing strategies. Internal factors relate to the selling organization. External factors relate to competitors, customers, and customers' buying environments (as in regulated markets).

Academic, B2B, and government sector pricing-to-win language differs. Academics largely focus on consumer and mass markets, which are easier to analyze and model. Organizations pursuing major, one-off government and B2B contracts, the focus of this topic section, use government-focused terms because the leading pricing-to-win practitioners are in the government-focused sector. Non-profits might have different definitions of profit, fee, price, cost, and cost-sharing, but the fundamentals apply.

Leading business development professionals view pricing to win as a strategic capability and competition-sensitive advantage. The most capable organizations have pricing-to-win departments, employ full-time practitioners, and often contract with independent consultants to cross-check their internal analyses.

Some organizations rely entirely on consultants, valuing their independent perspective and part-time cost. However, many others continue to rely on capture managers, account managers, program managers, cost volume managers, and their senior management team to arrive at an acceptable price to win on an ad hoc basis grounded in their experience.

Capture Guide pricing-to-win guidelines are applicable to a single major opportunity or groups of similar opportunities. Placed in context:

- Strategic competitor analysis focuses broadly on the capabilities, capacities, personalities, and market penetration strategies of your competitors.

- Tactical competitive analysis focuses on the same items in the context of a single opportunity.

- Pricing to win focuses on the trade-offs between the customer's requirements, budget, and values; your objectives, capabilities, solution, and costs; and competitors' likely objectives, capabilities, solution, costs, and strategies.

1 INTEGRATE PRICING TO WIN AS A FUNDAMENTAL ASPECT OF YOUR BUSINESS DEVELOPMENT LIFECYCLE.

Few sellers quote a price without considering whether it is a potentially winning price. So pricing to win is an old concept under a new label, often executed in an ad hoc fashion based upon the seller's personal experience. Sellers' internal processes, techniques, and roles blur as managers attempt to distinguish pricing from costing, identify internal and external factors, separate facts from opinion, reduce bias, and assign roles. Similarly, independent pricing-to-win consultants use different terms and processes, tout different data sources as discriminators, and bring different experience with customers, markets, technologies, and competitive environments.

Embrace common processes and definitions as your first pricing-to-win integration step. Figure 1 depicts the Shipley Business Development Lifecycle by phase at the top, aligned with a table listing relevant pricing-to-win activities by phase and concluding decision gate. The activities listed in column two are notional, repeated, and adapted to each opportunity.

See DECISION GATE REVIEWS; *and the entire* Business Development Lifecycle Guide.

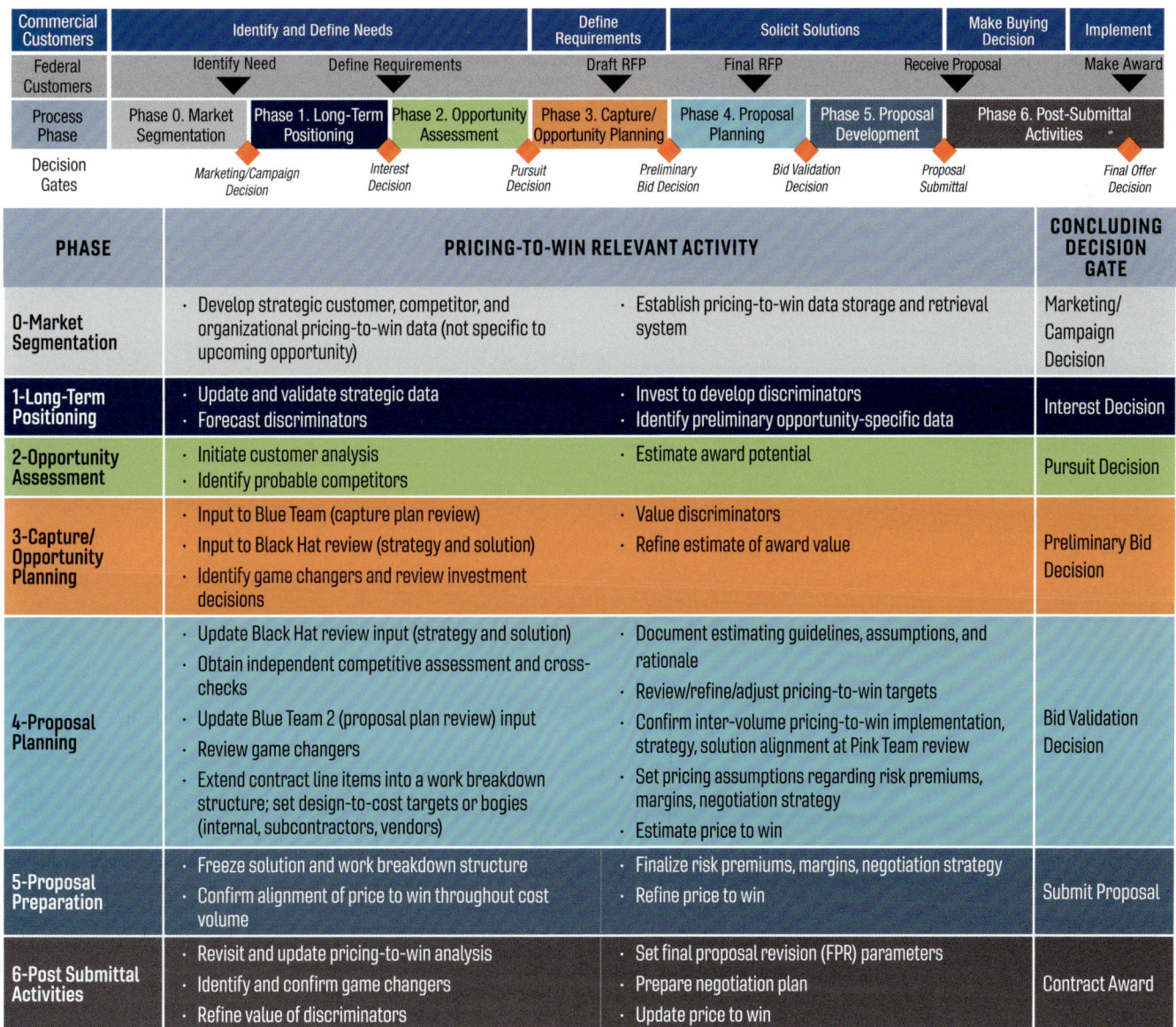

PHASE	PRICING-TO-WIN RELEVANT ACTIVITY		CONCLUDING DECISION GATE
0-Market Segmentation	· Develop strategic customer, competitor, and organizational pricing-to-win data (not specific to upcoming opportunity)	· Establish pricing-to-win data storage and retrieval system	Marketing/ Campaign Decision
1-Long-Term Positioning	· Update and validate strategic data · Forecast discriminators	· Invest to develop discriminators · Identify preliminary opportunity-specific data	Interest Decision
2-Opportunity Assessment	· Initiate customer analysis · Identify probable competitors	· Estimate award potential	Pursuit Decision
3-Capture/ Opportunity Planning	· Input to Blue Team (capture plan review) · Input to Black Hat review (strategy and solution) · Identify game changers and review investment decisions	· Value discriminators · Refine estimate of award value	Preliminary Bid Decision
4-Proposal Planning	· Update Black Hat review input (strategy and solution) · Obtain independent competitive assessment and cross-checks · Update Blue Team 2 (proposal plan review) input · Review game changers · Extend contract line items into a work breakdown structure; set design-to-cost targets or bogies (internal, subcontractors, vendors)	· Document estimating guidelines, assumptions, and rationale · Review/refine/adjust pricing-to-win targets · Confirm inter-volume pricing-to-win implementation, strategy, solution alignment at Pink Team review · Set pricing assumptions regarding risk premiums, margins, negotiation strategy · Estimate price to win	Bid Validation Decision
5-Proposal Preparation	· Freeze solution and work breakdown structure · Confirm alignment of price to win throughout cost volume	· Finalize risk premiums, margins, negotiation strategy · Refine price to win	Submit Proposal
6-Post Submittal Activities	· Revisit and update pricing-to-win analysis · Identify and confirm game changers · Refine value of discriminators	· Set final proposal revision (FPR) parameters · Prepare negotiation plan · Update price to win	Contract Award

Figure 1. Integrate Pricing-to-Win Activities with Your Business Development Lifecycle. *Every phase of the business development lifecycle includes activities related to pricing to win. These activities are interdependent with solution development and refinement and capture strategy.*

2 RECOGNIZE BASIC CUSTOMER BUYING TYPES TO ANTICIPATE THEIR BUYING BEHAVIORS.

See VALUE PROPOSITIONS.

Understanding customers' buying types helps you zero in on a winning price. Consider three types of customers:

- **Budget-limited customers** cannot afford the capability they want but will spend all their available budget and usually be disappointed.
- **Capability-satisfied customers** buy only what they need at the lowest available price.
- **Best-value customers** trade price against capability. Educated ones understand the trade-offs between value and price. Naïve ones mistakenly believe they can purchase the desired capability at an unrealistically low price.

Under U.S. federal procurement regulations, best value has specific legal meanings in addition to the larger context of trading price against capability. Two types of best value selection processes can be used: trade-off and lowest price technically acceptable. Trade-offs allow

Recognize customer buying types as a simplification applicable to most markets. Often buying decisions are made by committees comprised of individuals with different issues and concepts of value.

higher prices or lower technical capabilities to be selected when an offer is judged to yield the best overall value. Extra capability can be rewarded. Conversely, the lowest price technically acceptable process mandates selection of the lowest-priced offer among those that are at least minimally compliant. In that case, no value is assigned to additional capability.

By understanding the type of customer you are dealing with, you can better identify and position your price to win. Keep in mind that price to win is a combination of price and capability.

If the customer perceives equal capabilities, a rational customer will select the solution with the lowest price. Hence, differentiate your offer if you want the customer to pay more for your superior solution. How much more you can charge depends upon the customer's perception of your added value and whether they have sufficient budget.

Given sufficiently long lead times, you might be able to persuade and help the budget–limited customer to obtain a larger budget; convince the capability-satisfied customer that either some portion of a competitor's extra capability is unnecessary or some aspect of your solution is essential, or conversely that they need more capability (adds value); or educate the naïve best-value customer. If not, then align your solution with the customer type or no-bid. Ignoring this reality might be the single greatest reason bidders lose.

3 DETERMINE THE CUSTOMER'S ADDRESSABLE BUDGET.

Customers typically don't spend all available funding on external purchases of goods or services. They reserve some portion to cover expenses associated with the purchase, and the remainder is the amount likely to be available for a purchase, referred to as the addressable budget.

Determine how much of the customer's budget is addressable by identifying patterns from prior budgets. Customers typically deduct or reserve a portion of the budget for these types of items:

- Project management costs
- Risk reserves to cover potential cost increases, errors or omissions in the specifications, or changes in quantities
- Scope creep

- Agency or departmental overheads (sometimes required to support other programs)
- Fees for ancillary services, such as information technology, communications, engineering or technical support, quality assurance, test support, etc.
- Travel and temporary duty surcharges
- Buying agency or purchasing department surcharges

Determining the customer's budget and funding profile might be as easy as asking. As a rule, the earlier in the buying process, the less fixed the customer's budget. Bid requests might state the budget, especially on task orders.

Glean budget information from websites, public statements, and news releases. Determine if overall budgets have increased or decreased over prior years and whether this trend might affect this purchase. For example, one company bidding on a state services job resisted adapting its solution despite the governor's public announcement that all department budgets would be cut by 20 percent. Needless to say, it did not win.

Figure 2 is a relatively simple illustration of how the addressable budget might be estimated based on historic reserves and deductions. The percentages shown should not be extrapolated to other programs.

	BUDGET (MILLIONS)	PERCENT
Budget line-item	$250	100
Less:		
Project management overhead	$17.5	7
Risk reserve	$7.5	3
Contracting/purchase expenses	$7.5	3
Agency reserve	$7.5	3
Addressable budget	$210	84

Figure 2. Determining Maximum Addressable Budget. *Given the history that 16 percent of the budget has been reserved as shown and $250 million budgeted, the maximum addressable budget is $210 million.*

As the opportunity matures, repeatedly analyze the customer's addressable budget in greater detail. Refine your budget analysis by considering these questions:

- What is likely to happen with overall funding? What is the year-to-year trend? How might this trend affect this purchase?

- What is the typical hold-back percentage? Is the amount a percentage of the total contract, a percentage of named components, a fixed charge per item, or a combination with a maximum charge?

- What is the price breakdown by probable or actual contract item?

- Will they seek or insert cost or revenue-sharing, bonding, seller financing, or mandatory set-aside requirements?

- Are small, minority, or disadvantaged business terms included?

- Will they make or consider multiple awards, dividing the available funds? If so, what are the probable maximum and minimum awards? Will the awards be for similar amounts or allocated according to past performance, capability, or price?

- What is the funding profile: timing, type, and source? When will funds be authorized and then available, and does the authority to spend end or extend into subsequent budget cycles?

In general, confident, experienced buyers are more comfortable disclosing and discussing their addressable budget. Less confident and experienced buyers might resist, believing buyers will automatically propose at the maximum. If so, emphasize your need to develop a realistic solution that they can afford.

- Do funding provisions restrict what can be purchased? For example, capital funds often cannot be used for operating and support costs.

- Does the source of funds, whether budgeted, borrowed, or generated by fees, restrict the use, amount, or predictability?

- Does the customer management team have incentives that influence the funding profile? For example, some outsourcing expenses are intentionally back-loaded to show greater savings in the initial years, either to improve management bonuses or in anticipation of improved out-year revenues.

- What is the contract type, and what are the associated allowable margins or reserves?

- What historical "cost adjustments" has this customer made when evaluating your proposals and competitors' proposals? Consider risk adjustments implied by past performance and those associated with the proposed technical and management solution.

- Is there an ante, a requirement for an item, service, or capability that will not be paid to be developed as part of the contract? An ante might comprise research and development funds, pre-engineering, testing, bonding, warranty, or transition and start-up expenses. While some government purchasing regulations limit such requirements, they are often encountered in commercial practice and may be found in a modified sense with government customers. *See COSTING*

- What are the logistics and support implications? Often 60 percent of procurement funds are reserved for operations, spares, field support, depot support, operational integration, information technology, upgrades, and technology refreshes.

4   CONSIDER THE CUSTOMER'S EXPECTED PRICE.

Individual, business, and government buyers all have price expectations. Individuals might research typical prices, business buyers prepare expenditure requests, and government organizations typically follow regulated, defined processes.

U.S. Government regulations often require the buying organization to prepare should-cost analyses, independent cost estimates (ICE), or independent government estimates (IGE) before issuing bid requests. B2B organizations typically require an expenditure request that includes a detailed business case, schedule, project description, and cost plan for purchasing approval, even when funds are budgeted.

Customers employ multiple methods when preparing should-cost estimates:

- Comparing the total cost to the total cost of other, similar purchases
- Using detailed parametric or bottom-up estimating models
- Hiring a consultant to develop a should-cost estimate
- Relying on competitors' estimates or white papers
- Extracting an estimate from public sources
- Issuing a Request For Information (RFI)

The more complex the sale, the more likely customers will have prepared some type of cost estimate. Ask customers to share their estimates and/or estimating methods with you.

5   ESTIMATE AND REFINE THE PRICE TO COMPETE BASED UPON COMPETITORS' BIDS AND ACTUAL AWARD PRICES ON PRIOR SIMILAR CONTRACTS.

This is a top-down approach based on both prior customer awards and competitors' bids relative to those awards. In general, this approach resembles a prospective buyer or seller in a consumer market who attempts to determine the market price of an item or service.

Early in the sales cycle, estimate and cross-check your estimate of the price to compete. Begin with the customer's should-cost analysis, if available. Examine customer buying trends, seeking evidence of how those expectations might evolve. Even during preliminary discussions, focus on solutions near the price to compete.

As the pursuit continues, repeatedly refine your price-to-compete estimate to establish a leading position with the customer. Consider previous contracts awarded to likely competitors compared to addressable budgets for those procurements. The awarded prices on those contracts are good preliminary indicators of where competitors positioned their offers relative to customer budgets. Use your findings to estimate where competitors might position their offers on the current procurement. While the most relevant contracts are those issued by the same customer, similar contracts awarded by other customers offer good insight.

Arrive at a price to compete after comparing your estimates from various sources. Develop your solution with that price to compete in mind.

No single method works consistently. Adapt your approach to exploit the best available data. Figure 3 illustrates a purchasing pattern based upon prior awards. Estimate the price to compete based on similar customer and competitor buying history.

	CONTRACT	WINNER	BUDGET	AWARD	YEAR	PORTION AVAILABLE
Purchase History	Alpha	Global	10	8	20X2	0.80
	Beta	AeroMax	20	16.4	20X3	0.82
	Delta	Beacon	5	3.8	20X4	0.76
	Gamma	Global	12	10	20X5	0.83
Next Purchase	Omega		16	13.1-13.4	20X6	0.82-0.84 (?)

Figure 3. **Estimating the Price to Compete Based on Award History.** *Given historic data on the Alpha, Beta, Delta, and Gamma contracts, two patterns seem evident: 1) The percentage of addressable budget seems to be increasing slightly over time, and 2) Smaller purchases appear to require a larger percentage reserve, assuming common items are being purchased. Therefore, the anticipated Omega contract was estimated at 0.82 to 0.84, implying a price to compete of 13.1 to 13.4. Most analysts would target towards the lower end, at about 13.*

©Shipley Associates

6 ESTIMATE A PRICE TO WIN USING AN OPPORTUNITY-BASED, BOTTOM-UP APPROACH.

Focus on your primary competitors. If you are competing in a crowded market, focus on types of competitors. Rely on your tactical competitive analysis to outline competitors' likely solutions, and then estimate how they will price each solution.

While the following steps appear relatively direct, pricing-to-win analysts find the process challenging, iterative, time-consuming, and frustratingly subjective. Analysts on complex systems bids report spending months developing and refining their analyses.

At a high level, estimate an opportunity-based, bottom-up price to win using the following process:

- Develop a Work Breakdown Structure (WBS) for each competitor or type of competitor. To reduce the bias of the immediate architects of your probable system, enlist the assistance of uninvolved designers of similar systems who are familiar with competitors' system design and delivery approaches.

- Price competitors' systems using a bottom-up approach. Price WBS components based on their prior bids. Adjust prices to correct for changes in rates, methods, technology, sources, and other relevant factors.

- Sum WBS element prices, and then adjust the total using competitive intelligence regarding competitors' immediate business pressures and objectives. Consider current or anticipated backlogs, margin or profit expectations, strategic direction, and prior tactical responses to competitive pressures. Consider their relationship with the customer, incumbent or non-incumbent status, and even the personalities of key members of their management team. How committed are they to winning this bid?

- Consider the strengths and weaknesses of competitors' solutions. How might they respond by adapting their solutions and pricing? How might the customer value these changes?

- Assess your relative position by preparing a summary matrix depicting competitors' solutions and your solution.

- Select a price to win—a combination of price and capabilities—that provides your desired win probability. You might select a lower price at higher capability than you expect competitors to offer. But, business considerations might also drive you toward other postures. For example, you might deliberately offer a higher price with greater profit margin, depending on the customer's recognition of greater value in your solution, rather than blindly bidding the lowest possible price. Base your price to win on your understanding of how the customer will evaluate offers and select the winner.

- Retain your assumptions and analysis for subsequent iterations as you obtain new and improved intelligence.

Determining competitors' probable solutions, strategies, and pricing is often assigned in part or entirely to a Black Hat review team, depending upon the capability of the team and maturity of the organization's pricing-to-win process.

Organizations with mature pricing-to-win capabilities will often independently analyze competitors' solutions and prices, providing input to the Black Hat review team. If so, the Black Hat review team cross-checks this input and focuses on probable capture strategies and gaming aspects. If pricing-to-win input is lacking or immature, the Black Hat review team attempts to fill the gap, but they often lack the time to develop new data or confirm explicit and implicit assumptions.

Cross-check estimates from as many sources as possible. Compare the top-down results described in Guideline 5 with the bottom-up results described in Guideline 6. Employ different analysts, sources of data, analytical methods, and parameters. Verify the currency, accuracy, and assumptions implicit in analysts' data.

See COLOR TEAM REVIEWS.

7   COMPARE LIKELY BIDS AND SOLUTIONS USING THE WINNING PRICE WINDOW (WPW).

The WPW in figure 4 depicts the customer's view of their options plotted in two dimensions, price and capability. The WPW is a conceptual tool, intended to help you assess alternatives and arrive at a price to win.

The boundaries are defined as follows:

- Maximum budget is the maximum amount the customer has budgeted.
- Addressable budget is the amount the customer has available for a purchase after deducting expenses associated with the purchase.

- Minimum credible budget is the amount below which the customer doubts the credibility of obtaining an acceptable solution.
- Minimum acceptable capability is the minimum capability acceptable to this customer.
- Maximum justifiable capability is the maximum capability that this customer can justify. While more capability might be possible and available, this customer does not perceive a practical use; it would be considered gold plating.

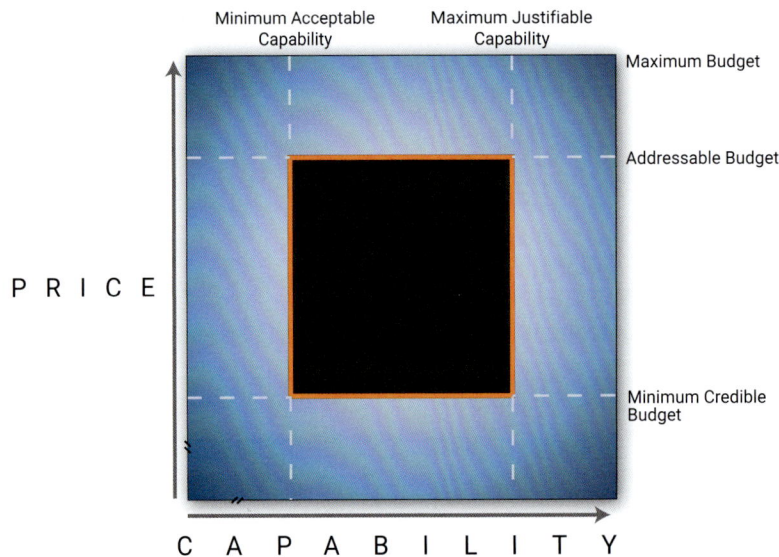

Figure 4. Winning Price Window. *Use the WPW to compare and contrast competitors' probable positions relative to yours. The absence of a scale reflects the relative nature of your assessment. For example, is your price higher or lower than competitors, and is it within the customer's budget parameters? Do not expect quantitative precision.*

Over time, the WPW becomes smaller, as shown in figure 5, as the customer better understands organizational needs, potential solutions, and relative values. Your pricing-to-win process objective is to iteratively and more accurately define the boundaries of the WPW, and then to favorably position your price to win versus competitors.

©Shipley Associates

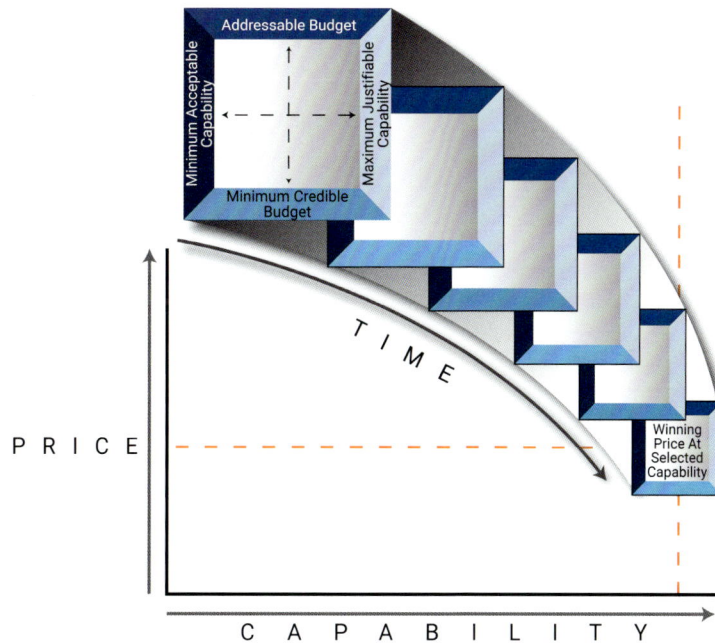

Figure 5. Narrowing the Winning Price Window. *The WPW contains the winning price. Conceptually, these price-capability boundaries narrow as the customer better understands organizational needs and the values offered by potential solutions. Your theoretical but rarely achieved goal is to identify the actual award price prior to submitting a bid.*

8   DEVELOP A STRATEGY TO ACHIEVE THE PRICE TO WIN.

Your price to win is a combination of your solution and price. Improve your position by analyzing the relative costs and benefits of existing and potential features of your solution. Add features that offer the greatest added value at minimum relative cost. Eliminate expensive features that offer relatively minimal benefit.

For many organizations, developing a strategy to achieve the price to win marks the transition between the work of pricing-to-win analysts and the capture team that develops, prices, and refines the solution and then works collaboratively with the customer, trying to influence the customer to prefer that solution. To minimize bias, many pricing-to-win analysts resist working on the solution, as they often must reassess the refined solution. Accurately assessing a solution that you helped develop is difficult.

Ask your capture team to refine the solution, considering the following alternatives:

- Lower costs by teaming and adjusting work shares.
- Absorb development costs, adjust assumptions regarding risk, payback period, cost of capital, and development of prototypes or development models.

- Supplement design costs using internal or external research and development funds.
- Establish new cost centers (to reduce the cost of corporate overhead allocations).
- Modify assumptions about the placement of proposed personnel within pay grades (e. g., at the 25% vs. 50% or 75% levels).
- Adjust the span of control to reduce management positions.
- Change managers to task leads so that they are presumed to contribute to productive work, not just manage.
- Adopt processes/tools that enhance productivity.
- Rework task estimates based upon requirements rather than historic costs (modify implicit assumptions).
- Develop creative warranty approaches.
- Adjust margin.
- Increase capability by adding valued features/discriminators.
- Decrease capability within the WPW.

Developing and implementing a strategy to achieve the price to win are primary capture team responsibilities.

- Decrease capability below the minimum limit by persuading the customer to alter their perception of needs and values.
- Raise customer capability expectations by helping justify higher capabilities not available from competitors (creating discriminators).

- Maximize profit while still offering a lower price to win than competitors.
- Consider noncompliant solutions or offers.

9 INCORPORATE CUSTOMER EVALUATION PROCESSES INTO YOUR PRICING STRATEGY.

Extending the principle that the only relevant view is what the customer believes, the customer's method of valuing solutions is the only relevant approach.

Note: Examples in this section were developed to emphasize the importance of the customer's pricing evaluation process and not to suggest deceptive pricing tactics. However, ignoring the customer's price evaluation model is naïve.

Customers' evaluation processes can dramatically affect the relative competitiveness of your solution. Customers with a rigidly defined and disciplined evaluation process, most common in government markets, seek to equalize evaluations to minimize bias, whether real or perceived. As a result, the evaluation is often based on the prior contract rather than the probable need.

For example, a telecommunication services contract might specify a technology and quantity that was typical but will become obsolete. Suppose the past contract included a line item for 1,000 pagers. The contract price was $100 per month, for an extended line item annual cost of $1.2 million. Realizing few people continue to carry pagers, Bidder A assumes only 5 pagers will be ordered under the new contract, so the contract prices pagers at $5 per month, even though their internal cost will be $90 per month. The evaluated price, $5 each x

1,000 pagers x 12 months would be $60,000, a $1.14 million annual savings over the existing contract. But if the estimated quantity is correct, the cost to supply the pagers will be $90 each x 5 pagers x 12 months, or $5,400. Bidder A might then enrich the overall profit margin by quoting a higher margin on a different line item evaluated at lower-than-anticipated purchase quantities.

A similar tactic is applicable to labor categories and rates or tasks and prices that the customer will weigh heavily during evaluation but seldom purchase. Many indefinite delivery indefinite quantity (IDIQ) contracts are evaluated assuming a type and quantity of services, but the actual purchases will be under subsequent, individual task orders. Savvy bidders might attractively price their offering under the expected formula, knowing from historical information that the customer will purchase a different labor mix.

Within an individual task, a bidder might propose a working task leader rather than a task manager, knowing that the customer assumes that managers only manage, while a task leader performs productive work. Even if the rates for the task lead and task manager are identical, the evaluation process might presume more direct labor hours are required when a task manager is proposed.

©Shipley Associates

10 RECOGNIZE THE IMPACTS OF GAME CHANGERS, INCLUDING POLITICAL, ECONOMIC, SOCIAL, TECHNOLOGICAL, LEGAL, AND ENVIRONMENTAL (PESTLE) FACTORS OR EVENTS.

A game changer is information that invalidates your implicit pricing-to-win assumptions. Confirm the existence of game changers by reviewing prior major losses, especially surprise losses. Did the award go to a little known or unidentified competitor, for an unexpectedly low price, or to a new or unknown technology? Were the contract terms, timing of key events, or involvement of unknown personnel a surprise? If so, you encountered game changers.

Game changers might originate from the customer, competitors, your organization, or external situational factors. Note that similar game changers affect both competitors and your organization. Figure 6 lists common game changers by origin.

Some external situational game changers involve trends, such as global warming or the growing scarcity of specific resources. At what point do trends become relevant and significant?

Other game changers are sudden and more difficult to forecast, such as war, earthquakes, tsunamis, or industrial accidents. While you might not be able to predict certain events, you might opt to propose contract terms and conditions to reduce your risk.

Add game changers to the contingency portion of your capture plan, and then repeatedly review and update them.

COMMON GAME CHANGERS		
CUSTOMER	*COMPETITORS AND YOUR ORGANIZATION*	*PESTLE (POLITICAL, ECONOMIC, SOCIAL, TECHNOLOGICAL, LEGAL, AND ENVIRONMENTAL)*
• Budget change (size, funding category, timing) • Schedule change • Key personnel change • Revised priorities, objectives, or direction • New requirements • Gain or loss of strategic importance	• Merger, acquisition, divestiture • Loss/change of key personnel • Major cost or schedule overruns on other contracts • Teaming shift • Financial pressures from markets, management, or creditors • Changes in strategic objectives, processes, or organization • Recent losses or wins, related or not	• Changes in government, elected, or regulatory officials; war or conflict • Changes in financial markets, cost and availability of resources • Shift in social conventions or mores • Shift in the capability, availability, or cost of new technologies • Changes in laws, regulations, or the interpretation of regulations • Changes in the environment (incremental climate change, industrial accident, abrupt climate event)

Figure 6. Potential Game Changers. *Game changers invalidate your pricing-to-win assumptions. Identify reasons customers, competitors, and your organization might not act as anticipated. Determine if and how significant trends will affect this procurement. For example, will a growing emphasis on "green" initiatives really affect this customer's evaluation?*

11   REFINE YOUR SOLUTION BASED ON CHANGES IN THE COMPETITIVE LANDSCAPE.

A continuing business development challenge is minimizing bias in pricing-to-win activities while implementing the result in capture planning activities.

Attaining a price to win is iterative. Repeat the tactical activities listed under Guideline 8 when changes in competitive intelligence dictate. Given new information, changes in assumptions, or identification of game changers, repeatedly refine your solution.

Arguably, refining your solution is a capture team activity rather than a pricing-to-win activity. Base solution refinements on the customer's perceptions rather than your own views of what you know to be correct.

If dealing with a budget-limited customer, ask:

- Have we identified and removed non-essential features that add cost but might appear to offer minimal commensurate value?
- Can we identify elements that could be made optional if the customer needs to further reduce acquisition cost?
- Can we restructure the offering to better meet the funding profile?

If dealing with a capability-satisfied customer, ask:

- Have we met the customer's minimum capability expectations?
- Have we included capabilities that could be eliminated to lower our price and yet remain competitive?

- Can we add or substitute features offering greater capability and value than our competitors?
- Can we convince the customer to raise expectations, making it harder for competitors to meet requirements?
- Have we reviewed competitors' likely offerings to identify new or overlooked approaches that we could incorporate into our solution at lower cost?

If dealing with an educated best value customer, ask:

- Have we maximized and prioritized the value-cost trade-offs for major solution features?
- What changes maximize value at the minimum cost?
- Have we confirmed and reinforced the customer's understanding of best value?

If dealing with a naïve best value customer, ask:

- Have we attempted to educate our naïve customer?
- Do we have sufficient access, time, and resources to educate them?
- While we might disagree with their assessment, can we modify our proposed solution at acceptable risk? If not, should we no-bid?

12   REFINE YOUR STRATEGIES BASED ON CHANGES IN YOUR SOLUTION OR COMPETITIVE LANDSCAPE.

Assuming that you have refined your solution per Guideline 11, focus on influencing the customer to prefer your solution. You must convince the customer that your refinements add value, offer improved capabilities, prices, or both.

Update your Integrated Solution Worksheet, shown in figure 7, part of the capture plan template. If sufficiently early in the process, use it to collaborate with the customer, identifying and confirming the underlying issues and requirements. If the requirements are defined, use it to help refine the underlying issues, your solution, competitors' potential solutions, discriminators, gaps, strategies, and tactics.

Concentrate on the final two columns. Assign responsibility for each action item to a single person whether they complete the action or direct the completion. Simply changing your solution without explaining how your changes benefit the customer is off-putting to the customer and often worsens your position.

The only aspect of capture strategy that improves your position with the customer is the tactical implementation. Internally focused aspects might be satisfying, but they do not improve your position.

ShipleyAssociates®	Integrated Solution Worksheet							
Item No.	Customer Issues	Customer Requirements	Available Solution	Gap	Competitor Solution	Discriminators	Strategy	Action Required
1	System must be available.	8 hr. response time.	2 hr. response time	1 hr	3 hr. response time	Faster response but more expensive?	Emphasize no additional cost with cellular.	Show current response time. Show photo-service with cell phone.

Figure 7. Update Integrated Solution Worksheet. *Assuming this was completed in your capture plan, update it row by row. Focus primarily on the last two columns: Strategy and Action Required. Add columns or link each row to a specific implementation action plan. When time and resources are limited, prioritize and focus on key actions.*

13 RE-ASSESS YOUR PRICING STRATEGIES POST-AWARD AND UPDATE YOUR PRICING-TO-WIN DATABASE.

After proposal submittal, re-evaluate your position with the customer. While the order will vary depending upon the customer and procurement, anticipate taking the following types of post-submittal actions:

- Respond to customer requests for clarifications, seek feedback, and anticipate revised requirements.
- Support past performance investigations visits by senior members of the buying team.
- Prepare for structured presentations and interchanges.
- Prepare and submit requested proposal revisions.
- Prepare a formal negotiation plan.
- Negotiate a final contract.

After proposal submittal, repeat your pricing-to-win process in a focused, abbreviated form:

- Revisit your competitive position and price to win in the WPW. Concentrate on the short list of remaining competitors.
- Reassess the positive and negative value gaps of your discriminators. Validate your quantitative value assessments.
- Read between the lines of customer statements. Are they subtly suggesting a preference or giving you hints about what may be necessary to close the deal?
- Have you detected any game changers on the part of the customer or competitors?
- Revisit your solution. Consider potential revisions within procurement parameters.

- Re-price revisions. Cross-check pricing assumptions.
- Update your strategy in writing. Then specify your tactics for each anticipated event.
- Prepare to concisely and clearly link, explain, and justify changes in your solution and pricing.

See VALUE PROPOSITIONS; POST-SUBMITTAL ACTIVITIES, Business Development Lifecycle Guide.

When invited to negotiate a contract, prepare a negotiation plan. In some business negotiations, the negotiator loses sight of the goal, pushes too far, and loses the opportunity to achieve the initial goal. Successful negotiations are 80 percent preparation and 20 percent execution.

Identify your interests and those of your customer. Develop clear criteria to evaluate and measure options. Successful negotiators establish a zone of potential agreement, setting high and low outcome objectives. Consider the following facets:

- Quantify the value of the potential deal to you and the customer.
- Secure the support of your management and teammates on the parameters of an acceptable deal.
- Determine your bargaining range: opening position, target, and minimum acceptable.
- Estimate the customer's range: opening position, target, and maximum acceptable.
- Determine your leverage, a function of the quantified value of your discriminators. Base concessions on quantitative value assessments.

- Develop a preferred negotiation agenda, listing issues in decreasing order of importance, that you and possibly your customer will want to discuss. Propose and justify your agenda, but prepare to adapt to the customer's agenda.

- Identify potential ethical issues and how you might resolve them.

- Prepare for extended negotiations. Avoid making concessions due to time pressures by anticipating and minimizing the impacts to your team.

- Structure your negotiating team with clearly defined roles, much like an oral presentation or proposal.

- Take careful notes, clarify questions before answering, debrief immediately after every session, and then prepare for the next session.

- Win or lose, document lessons learned and other findings in your competitive intelligence database. Begin preparing for your next opportunity, whether with this customer or other customers, this competitor or other competitors.

SALES COMMUNICATION

Sales communications include any document sent to a customer that is designed to advance a potential sale. Effective written communications are customer focused, clear, concise, and well organized.

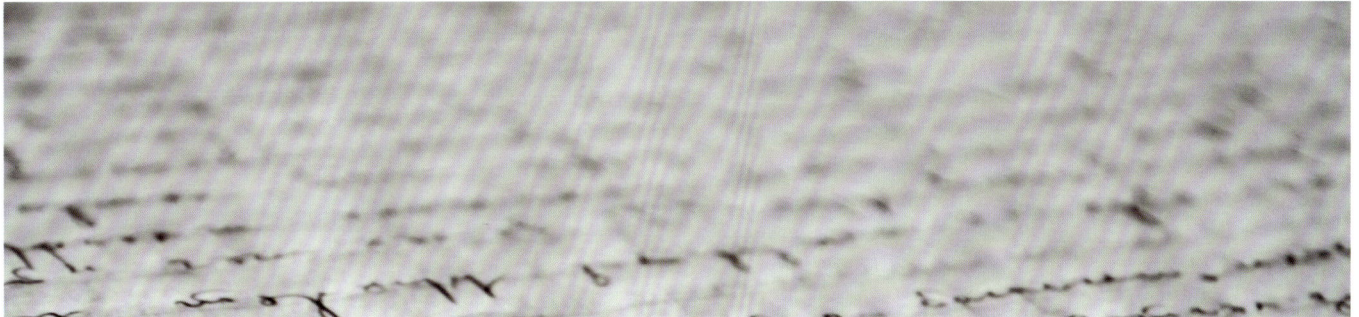

The purpose of each sales communication is to advance the sale to the next achievable objective, clearly supported by the benefits to the customer. Writers must be able to answer three questions:

1. What is my purpose in drafting this communication?
2. What do I want the reader to do next?
3. What do I want the reader to know?

When sales communications fail, the writer often failed to answer the previous three questions. Clear and correct writing is an effective way to help customers understand you and accept your ideas. Poor writing causes confusion, potential distrust, and possible rejection of your ideas.

Written communication includes letters, emails, texts, and other forms of communication. Never minimize the importance of your message based upon the mode of communication.

The process described for strategizing, organizing, drafting, and revising effective sales letters is similar to the approach recommended to prepare executive summaries and letter proposals. Both are specialized forms of sales letters.

Many types of written communications occur during a typical sales cycle. Note how the objective of each changes as the sale advances.

See CUSTOMER FOCUS, ORGANIZATION, EXECUTIVE SUMMARY, *and* LETTER PROPOSALS, Proposal Guide.

See SAMPLE TEMPLATE 5.

The most effective capture managers are sales professionals, like it or not. Hence, capture managers write, review, and approve sales communications to their customers.

SALES COMMUNICATION

1 Follow the disciplined POWeR™ writing process to quickly and consistently write effective sales communications.

2 Use the Strategy Template to strategize your sales communications.

3 Follow the Four-Box organizational structure.

4 Draft quickly and uncritically, following your Four-Box Template.

5 Revise to add value, clarity, and brevity to your message.

1   FOLLOW THE DISCIPLINED POWER™ WRITING PROCESS TO QUICKLY AND CONSISTENTLY WRITE EFFECTIVE SALES COMMUNICATIONS.

The best sales professionals plan to advance the sale with every client contact, including their communication. Sometimes writing a message is easy; everything flows. Other times, writers struggle and dislike the result. Resorting to tailoring previous messages is often expedient but ineffective because no two customers have identical needs.

The only way to quickly and consistently prepare effective sales communications is to follow a disciplined process, one that you understand and have practiced. Following a consistent process helps you focus on your key messages within a consistent framework.

Consistently write effective sales communications by following this five-step POWeR™ writing process:

P lanning

O rganizing

W riting

e xamining

R evising

The acronym POWeR has four uppercase letters and a lower case e. The uppercase letters represent stages or steps that the writer controls. The lowercase e represents the examining stage where other people are asked to suggest improvements before the message is revised.

Follow these steps when you prepare any kind of sales message. Substeps in each phase are summarized in figure 1.

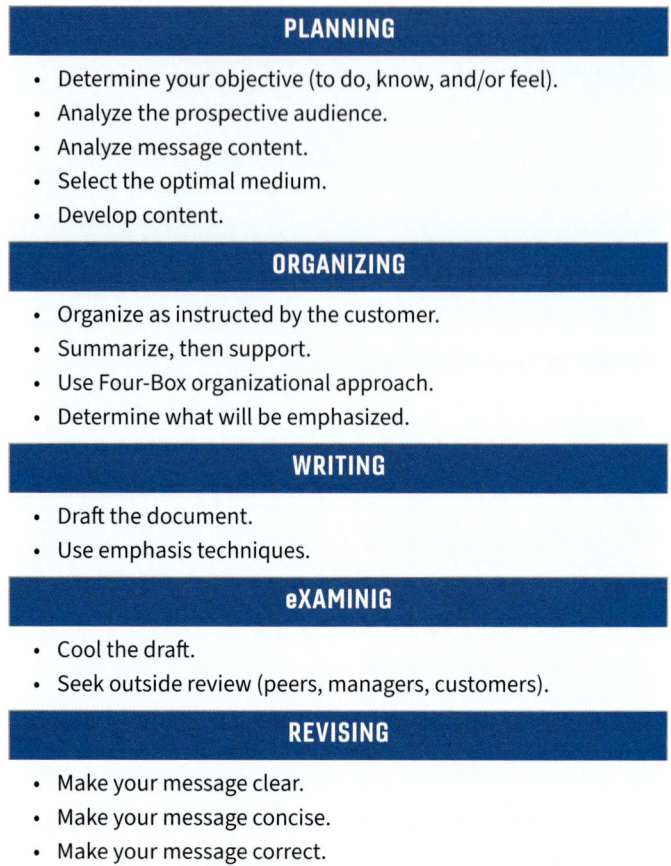

PLANNING
- Determine your objective (to do, know, and/or feel).
- Analyze the prospective audience.
- Analyze message content.
- Select the optimal medium.
- Develop content.

ORGANIZING
- Organize as instructed by the customer.
- Summarize, then support.
- Use Four-Box organizational approach.
- Determine what will be emphasized.

WRITING
- Draft the document.
- Use emphasis techniques.

eXAMINIG
- Cool the draft.
- Seek outside review (peers, managers, customers).

REVISING
- Make your message clear.
- Make your message concise.
- Make your message correct.

Figure 1. Improve Communication Effectiveness and Efficiency by Using the POWeR™ Writing Process. *This five-step process is the most effective and efficient way to develop written and oral messages. This approach is implicit within the business development processes and tools discussed in this* Capture Guide.

2   USE THE STRATEGY TEMPLATE TO STRATEGIZE YOUR SALES COMMUNICATIONS.

Prepare your communication strategy by completing the Strategy Template shown in figure 2. Use the Strategy Template every time until you are thoroughly comfortable with this process.

Many sales documents fail because they are vague and unclear, accurately reflecting the fuzzy thinking and minimal planning of the author. Ask three questions to test the strategy of any sales document:

- What was the writer's purpose?
- What does the writer want the reader to agree to do next?
- What does the writer want the reader to know?

The first question is broad. The second is focused. The third provides context. The purpose of most sales documents is to obtain action or to inform. Action is required to advance the sale, which is the preferred purpose. To inform is a relatively weak purpose.

An effective sales message motivates the customer to the desired action because of the persuasive information in the document.

What does the customer need to know that would persuade the customer to take that action? A customer-focused strategy is based on the assumption that people act in their own best interest. If you are looking for a win-win situation, then your customer's objectives and your objectives must align.

Sales documents in complex sales often have multiple readers, including the decision maker and others who influence the decision maker. List the various customers or readers, then list their issues. Whenever possible, develop issues collaboratively with customers.

The Strategy Template is most useful when developing a new document. Experienced and skilled writers can skip this template under two conditions:

- *You are revising an existing document.*
- *You are confident your strategy is correct.*

As your skills improve, go directly to the Four-Box Template found in Guideline 3.

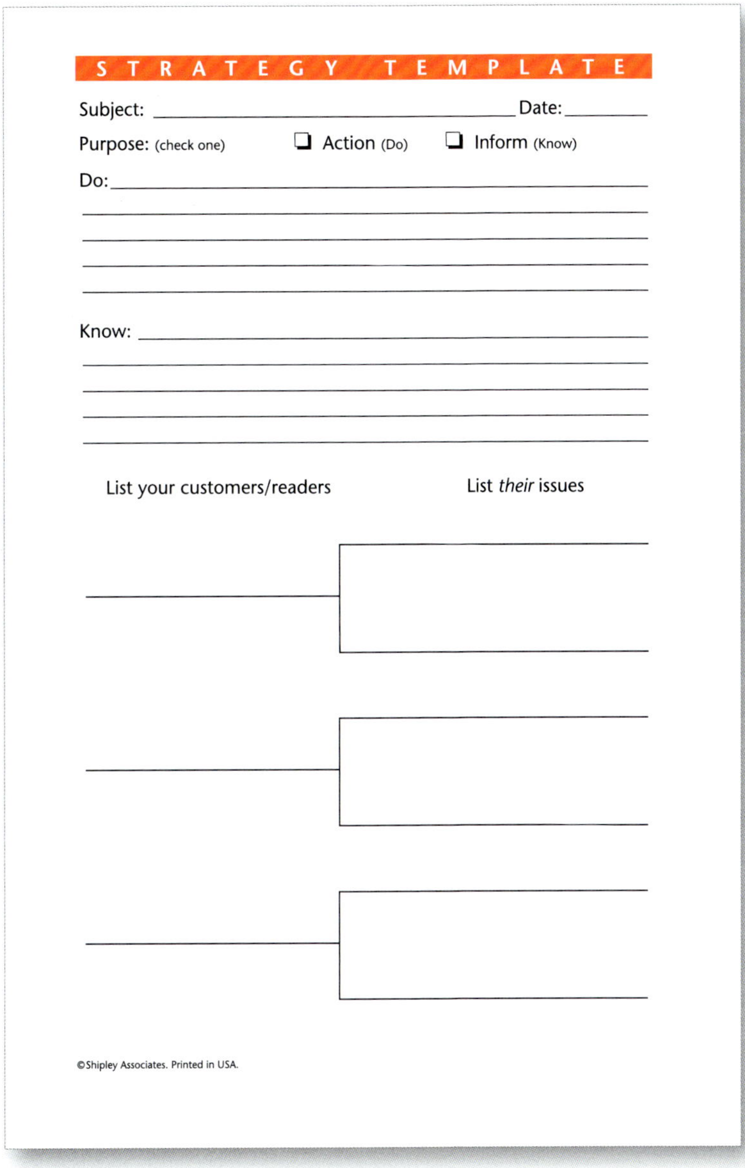
STRATEGY TEMPLATE

Subject: ____________________ Date: ________

Purpose: (check one) ❏ Action (Do) ❏ Inform (Know)

Do: ____________________

Know: ____________________

List your customers/readers

List *their* issues

©Shipley Associates. Printed in USA.

Figure 2. Use the Strategy Template to Develop Your Message. *Using the Strategy Template will help you develop a more persuasive strategy. Avoid two errors: (1) Dismissing the Strategy Template as too obvious, and (2) Filling it with empty jargon.*

3 FOLLOW THE FOUR-BOX ORGANIZATIONAL STRUCTURE.

Use the Four-Box Template shown in figure 3 to present your message in a customer-focused, persuasive style. Use the annotations in the margin and within the template as a guide. Your ideas will evolve as you move from the Strategy Template to the Four-Box Template. Expect imperfection.

Draft an informative subject line or heading. Summarize your most significant Do/Know statements. Try to include benefits and features. Make it as short as you can while still being fully informative.

Begin with a signal word to immediately announce the action desired and to signal the content to the reader. Typical signal words vary with your purpose:

ACTION PURPOSE

DO:

- Proposal
- Recommendation
- Request
- Invitation

See CHOOSING CORRECT WORDS, CUSTOMER FOCUS, *and* LISTS, Proposal Guide.

INFORMATION PURPOSE

KNOW:

- Agenda
- Notice
- Announcement
- Response

GOOD EXAMPLE:

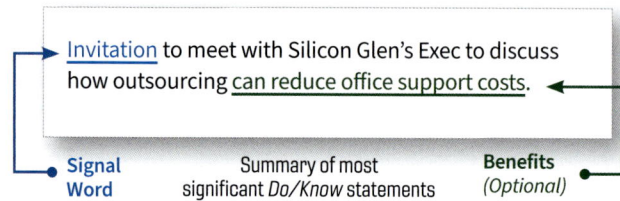

Invitation to meet with Silicon Glen's Exec to discuss how outsourcing can reduce office support costs.

Signal Word — Summary of most significant *Do/Know* statements — **Benefits** *(Optional)*

©Shipley Associates

FOUR-BOX TEMPLATE

Box 1: Summary
Signal your purpose in a clear heading.
Include a theme statement linking the most important benefit to features of your proposal.
Summarize the essence of your message. State what you want the reader to do, know, or feel.

Clear Heading
Theme Statement
Summary

Box 2: Introduction
Preview organization of the document. Organize around the points most likely to influence the reader.
Subordinate topics in a proposal should be customer hot buttons or major issues.
If possible, link to a customer source.

Introduction

Subordinate Topics
Subordinate Topic 1
Subordinate Topic 2
Subordinate Topic 3
Subordinate Topic 4
Subordinate Topic 5
Subordinate Topic 6

Box 3: Body
Maintain the same organizational scheme introduced in Box 2.
Provide convincing details for the reader, including benefits, discriminators, the solution, proof points, and previous experience. Consider visuals to help convey your message.
Eliminate extraneous details that are interesting to you but do not support your purpose.

Topic 1:
Topic 2:
Topic 3:
Topic 4:
Topic 5:
Topic 6:

Box 4: Review
End by clearly stating the next realistically achievable step. Summarize why the customer should select you.
Emphasize important benefits.
If there is no desired next step, or space is very limited, consider skipping Box 4.

Copyright 2017 Shipley Associates   1

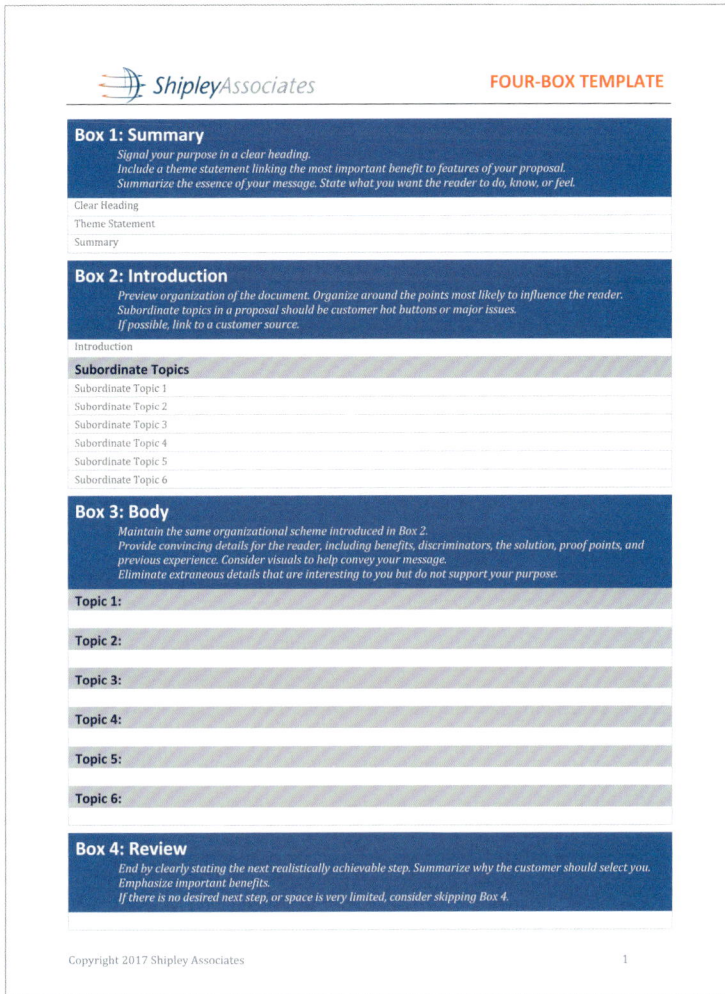

In Box 1, use setups if needed to connect to a previous event. Most readers are initially trying to place your sales document in context. Keep your setups short. Often a short phrase will suffice:

Good examples

As you requested in our January 15 meeting, . . .

In our September 15 phone conversation, you said coping with rapid change and reducing cost were driving your fiscal year planning by . . .

Then summarize the customer's overall need in a customer-focused manner. Customer ownership of the need must be explicit.

In Box 2, establish the customer's issues, tying them to the overall need and making ownership explicit. For emphasis, introduce issues in a display list. List them as the customer did or in decreasing order of importance to the customer.

In Box 3, link all of your solution information to one of the customer's issues. If you cannot forge the link, your information is irrelevant. Eliminate irrelevant or extraneous information. Address each client issue in the order introduced in Box 2.

In Box 4, restate your main ideas, linking the benefits to the customer. Indicate the action required, and directly state the next step. Be proactive. Avoid ending with stale jargon or cliches.

Figure 3. The Four-Box Template. *Use this template to convert your strategy from the Strategy Template into a customer-focused, clearly organized, and persuasive sales document. Follow the suggestions in the template. Use this template to organize every sales letter.*

4   DRAFT QUICKLY AND UNCRITICALLY, FOLLOWING YOUR FOUR-BOX TEMPLATE.

Most sales professionals find that after completing the Strategy Template and Four-Box Template, their documents almost write themselves.

Draft quickly, expecting imperfection. Writing is creative; revising is critical. If you try to do both at the same time, you will do neither well, and the process will take much longer.

Frequently refer to the Strategy Template and Four-Box Template to stay focused.

5   REVISE TO ADD VALUE, CLARITY, AND BREVITY TO YOUR MESSAGE.

Revise the sales document in three stages to save time. Fix the major items before the minor items. View revision as an opportunity to improve your sales letter. This is a realistic goal if you have followed the first three steps. If not, you often feel the urge to start over.

Follow the three-step revision process outlined in figure 4.

Few of us can see our own mistakes. Always ask someone else to review your documents.

The Peer Review Template, shown in figure 5, is a tool designed to help peers and managers constructively review sales communications.

FIRST STAGE: BE CLEAR

Subject Line

- Begin with a signal word.
- State what the reader should do or know.
- Include benefit (optional).

Objective

- State up front.
- Be specific and clear.
- Include setups.
- Use if necessary.
- Keep short.

Customer Focus

- Name customer before yourself.
- State benefits before features.
- Make hot button ownership explicit.
- Tie hot buttons to your solution.

Content and Organization

- Summarize then preview your content.
- Organize around customer's hot buttons.

Key Information Highlighted

- Use informative headings and subheadings.
- Use lists.
- Use white space for emphasis.
- Use **boldface**, *italics*, CAPITALS, or color.
- Use clear graphics with action captions.

SECOND STAGE: BE CONCISE

Paragraphs

- Use six lines maximum.
- Use one major idea per paragraph.

Sentences (15-20 word maximum)

- Use active voice—Who does what?
- Use strong verbs.
- Cut false subjects—it, there.

Words

- Cut gobbledygook.
- Cut wordy phrases.
- Solve word problems.

THIRD STAGE: BE CORRECT

Proofread Thoroughly

- Check grammar, punctuation, spelling, word choice, and number usage.

Know Where to Find the Rules

- Consult industry-appropriate style guide.
- Consult a current dictionary.
- Consult specialized references.

Figure 4. Revise in Three Stages. *In the first stage, address content. Make sure you present the right message about the customer's issues and offer real value. In the second stage, make your message as concise as possible. In the third stage, correct spelling, punctuation, and grammar. Careless errors suggest potential poor quality elsewhere.*

P E E R   R E V I E W   T E M P L A T E

What was the writer's purpose?

What did the writer want the reader to agree to do/know next?

Would the requested action be the next realistically achievable step most likely to advance this sale?   ❏ Yes   ❏ No

If not, what do you recommend?

List the customer's/reader's hot buttons:

-
-
-
-

©Shipley Associates. Printed in USA.

Figure 5. Peer Review Template. *Managers and peers can improve their coaching of writers by: (1) Comparing the results of the Peer Review Template with the information found in the Strategy Template and the Four-Box Template and (2) Evaluating sales documents using only the Peer Review Template. If this template is difficult to complete, the document is unlikely to be successful.*

©Shipley Associates

SCHEDULE AND ACTION PLAN DEVELOPMENT

Schedule and action plan development are essential to visualize, implement, and monitor progress of the capture plan. Unscheduled tasks are rarely completed.

Common scheduling and action plan principles apply to capture plans. Preparing a realistic schedule requires a clear understanding of each task, the situation, capability of assigned talent, and adequate support resources. Just developing the schedule clarifies your understanding of the task.

Adapt the complexity of the capture schedule to the market sector, value, and importance of the opportunity to your organization, time frame, and available resources. For example, a geographically distant and unfamiliar customer will require more time, expense, and visits to position than a proximate, prior customer.

Scheduling capture efforts is more difficult than scheduling proposals. Capture activities might be limited by customer procurement requirements and shifting end points. In addition, the earlier you discover the opportunity, the less you and your customer are likely to know about the procurement schedule.

Customers often modify critical procurement milestones, meaning you cannot reliably schedule capture activities. You will not know when customer-centric capture activities must end.

See BID DECISIONS *and* PROCESS, Proposal Guide.

Apply a disciplined yet adaptive approach to scheduling capture and action plan activities. Your challenge is to complete positioning.

Guided by your action plan, act and react as your knowledge of the customer, opportunity, competition, and potential solution evolves. Managing a capture schedule or action plan will never be precise.

Figure 1 summarizes some of the similarities and differences between capture and proposal schedules.

DIFFERENCES	
CAPTURE SCHEDULES	**PROPOSAL SCHEDULES**
Longer and more variable time span from the pursuit decision through program initiation	Shorter and less variable time span from the bid decision to proposal submittal and lessons-learned documentation
Based on milestones, gate reviews, and customer activities	Driven by proposal due date(s)
Uncertain dates driven by customer decisions and competitors' tactics	Dates driven primarily by customer deliverable dates and internal resources and minimally by competitors' tactics
Built after pursuit decision and extended through program initiation	Build backwards from proposal due date
Permitted customer-facing activities might be limited after bid request is issued	Customer deliverable due dates do not limit internally focused proposal preparation tasks
SIMILARITIES	
Requires a single manager to lead the effort and manage the schedule	
Requires established budget to support approved tasks	
Assigns a single person the responsibility to complete each task, with start and end dates	
Arranged to minimize sequential tasks, and maximize parallel tasks	
Requires senior leadership buy-in and participation in gate reviews	

Figure 1. Differences and Similarities of Capture and Proposal Scheduling. *The timing and focus of the schedules differ, but many scheduling guidelines are common.*

SCHEDULE AND ACTION PLAN DEVELOPMENT

1 Create, align, and adapt the capture schedule to the customer's actions, your organization's business development framework, the resources available, and the selling environment.

2 Create an action plan to schedule and monitor capture activities.

3 Minimize sequential tasks; maximize parallel tasks.

4 Delegate intelligently.

5 Assign a person to each task with start and end dates.

6 Use gate reviews to complete action.

7 Over-Communicate.

©Shipley Associates

1   CREATE, ALIGN, AND ADAPT THE CAPTURE SCHEDULE TO THE CUSTOMER'S ACTIONS, YOUR ORGANIZATION'S BUSINESS DEVELOPMENT FRAMEWORK, THE RESOURCES AVAILABLE, AND THE SELLING ENVIRONMENT.

Consider three questions:

> 1. What phase-critical and time-sensitive activities must be completed immediately before circumstances change?
>
> 2. What key activities must be completed to meet your management's expectations?
>
> 3. What items must be presented at the next gate review?

Consider the following phase-critical and time-sensitive activities:

- Access to the customer might be restricted after solicitation documents are released. If so, gathering intelligence early is vital to making an informed pursuit decision, developing your capture strategy, and positioning your solution as the preferred solution. Schedule customer intelligence gathering and solution positioning activity as early as possible, and continue until restricted.

- If your strategy requires teaming, you must identify the optimal partner and negotiate a teaming agreement before they team with a competitor. Schedule teaming discussions promptly after completing your competitive analysis and capture strategy.

- If your solution requires key personnel, identify and reserve or recruit them before they are committed to other activities, programs, or competitors.

- If new technology is required, use lead time to develop and verify that technology before promising it to the customer. Ideally, persuade the customer to specify your technology in the bid request.

- If past performance requirements will be critical, identify appropriate experience and performance examples within your organization or via teaming partners. Ideally, preview this experience and performance with the customer, scheduling site visits or interviews, if possible.

With the next gate reviews identified, focus on scheduling the key activities required to prepare the mandatory inputs and meet management's expectations.

Once time-sensitive activities are identified, consider typical, key capture planning actions. Refer to figure 2 for general capture steps:

See DECISION GATE REVIEWS.

See SAMPLE TEMPLATE 4.

- Manage the capture process
- Build relationships
- Gather and analyze data
- Develop and implement strategy
- Engage proposal support

Add, delete, or compress depending upon the time and resources available, customer's buying schedule, and selling environment. While key activities vary and dates might shift, include every gate and color team review on your capture planning schedule.

	KEY ACTIVITY	ACTIVITY LEADER	START DATE	DUE DATE	COMMENTS
MANAGE THE CAPTURE PROCESS	**Develop capture plan** ❑ Populate, validate, and update capture plan ❑ Hold review sessions to ensure team is moving forward				
	Determine key management actions ❑ Provide oversight for opportunity, key relationships, intelligence, strategy, and actions ❑ Establish capture/bid & proposal budget ❑ Transition from capture to proposal planning				
BUILD RELATIONSHIPS	**Form and train capture team** ❑ Select capture manager ❑ Initiate a capture team (SMEs) ❑ Define specific roles and responsibilities ❑ Train capture team ❑ Hold kickoff meeting to initiate capture activities				
	Expand customer relationships ❑ Identify customer, program, and procurement organizations ❑ Define customer buying cycle ❑ Create a customer contact plan ❑ Collaborate on value propositions				
GATHER AND ANALYZE DATA	**Perform program/opportunity assessment** ❑ Gather relevant opportunity/program data ❑ Analyze, validate, and update data ❑ Determine gaps and update findings as opportunity evolves				
	Perform customer assessment ❑ Gain clear understanding of customer requirements ❑ Identify/validate customer issues, wants, needs, and hot buttons ❑ Determine Source Selection Authority and key decision makers				
	Perform competitor assessment ❑ Determine key competitors ❑ Validate data from multiple sources ❑ Populate Bidder Comparison Chart ❑ Assess strengths and weaknesses from Bidder Comparison Chart ❑ Determine critical gaps and discriminators				
	Perform self (organization)-assessment ❑ Assess strengths and weaknesses from Bidder Comparison Chart ❑ Determine critical gaps and discriminators ❑ Create strategy statements to highlight key messages				

Continued • • • • • • • ➤

©Shipley Associates

	KEY ACTIVITY	ACTIVITY LEADER	START DATE	DUE DATE	COMMENTS
DEVELOP AND IMPLEMENT STRATEGY	**Determine Price-to-Win (PTW) strategy** ❏ Gain understanding of customer budget and pricing history ❏ Learn what competitors are charging for similar work ❏ Create a should-cost analysis from customer perspective ❏ Align PTW strategy with customer, competitor, and should-cost findings				
	Develop win strategy ❏ Lay out key actions needed to win				
	Initiate teaming strategy ❏ Determine customer subcontracting requirements ❏ Build teaming strategy to complement your capabilities ❏ Initiate teaming discussions ❏ Formalize through executed teaming agreements				
	Develop high-level proposal solutions ❏ Lay out key points and issues for technical, management, past performance, and cost/price proposal volumes ❏ Document high-level solution on an Integrated Solution Worksheet				
	Initiate Black Hat activities and review ❏ Determine most threatening competitors ❏ Create capture strategies through the eyes of competition ❏ Incorporate key findings into capture plan				
	Determine program execution strategy ❏ Plan ahead to determine key actions necessary to begin work on Day One of contract award				
	Turn strategies into action plans ❏ Populate action plans with key strategies ❏ Manage specific tasks within each action plan				
ENGAGE PROPOSAL SUPPORT	**Identify proposal team** ❏ Select proposal manager ❏ Determine resource needs ❏ Integrate with capture team				
	Develop proposal management plan ❏ Transfer key capture data to proposal management plan ❏ Develop storyboards				
	Hold proposal strategy session ❏ Determine which actions may evolve into proposal messages ❏ Review strengths, weaknesses, discriminators, features, and benefits ❏ Turn strategy statements into win theme statements				
	Develop draft executive summary ❏ Populate executive summary with important key messages to drive proposal messages ❏ Share draft executive summary with proposal team				
	Collect high-level proposal collateral ❏ Gather potential documentation (i.e., past performance, resumes) ❏ Validate appropriateness of data for proposal use ❏ Manage data collection				

Figure 2. Planning Potential Capture Activities. *Determine which activities are needed for each capture opportunity. Eliminate, condense, or expand as appropriate. Align these actions with gate review deliverables, then assign the activity leader, start date, and due date.*

See SAMPLE TEMPLATES 1–2.

Capture plans evolve over time. While the contents of a capture plan might look daunting, build and refine the content as you progress. Add increasing levels of detail over time and keep the data current with frequent updates.

Typically, you will identify key activities, add them to your schedule, but then lack sufficient resources to complete some activities. One option is to simply delete the activity and hope for the best, using the available resources as efficiently as possible. Alternatively, schedule the activity, but leave the task unassigned to highlight the lack of resources to management.

See DECISION GATE REVIEWS.

Adapt your capture schedule to the selling environment. While much of this discussion has focused on sales cycles measured in months, a sales cycle measured in days requires a highly compressed and streamlined process.

For example, if you will be responding to 5-day task order requests, your capture activity will focus on collaboratively developing task requirements with the customer or, at minimum, be the first to discover that a task order request will be issued.

Gate reviews will be short and few, but you should still address the key activities identified in this guideline.

2   CREATE AN ACTION PLAN TO SCHEDULE AND MONITOR CAPTURE ACTIVITIES.

Simple timeline charts are adequate for smaller capture plans.

Because capture managers seldom manage direct reports, adapt your scheduling approach to your organization. If you use a common calendaring tool, enter events in your calendar and invite assignees to accept the event. Use online calendars to coordinate your capture schedule.

One of the best ways to keep capture tasks on schedule is to publish the schedule prominently and review it regularly. When assignees see their names on a late or incomplete task, it often prompts them to complete their tasks.

3   MINIMIZE SEQUENTIAL TASKS; MAXIMIZE PARALLEL TASKS.

Clear task descriptions, quality standards, and start-and-end dates empower contributors to work in parallel with minimum conflict. If you hear contributors say they are waiting on someone else to finish his or her task before they start, you have sequential tasks and might be in trouble.

Capture managers frequently handle unnecessary sales tasks. It is important to mention, however, that the capture manager role should take precedence over personal direct-sales tasks.

4 DELEGATE INTELLIGENTLY.

Assign tasks to people with the expertise, time, willingness, and managerial support to complete the task. While the expertise and time suggestions are obvious, some individuals just refuse to accept capture tasks. For example, some people say: "I'm not in sales. I don't do that." Alternatively, identifying a supportive but less knowledgeable person might be a better choice.

Perhaps the greatest management challenge is identifying whether the manager of the person assigned to a task is fabricating support. Capture tasks compete with previously scheduled tasks, which are often linked to revenue. Rather than refuse support, these managers set priorities for their direct reports, perhaps stating: "Support the capture plan, but first complete your assigned, billable work."

Efficient organizations support capture activities at all levels. If that is not the ethic in your organization, seek support from your senior management sponsor, present a persuasive justification to the manager of the person assigned to the task, or reassign it.

Simply eliminating the task from your schedule because you lack the resource sets a dangerous precedent. Consider leaving the task open and discussing it at the next gate review. If you lack critical information, why are you sure that you will win?

5 ASSIGN A PERSON TO EACH TASK WITH START AND END DATES.

People are rarely assigned full-time to a capture effort, including the capture manager. Establish realistic hours, schedule the task and subtasks, manage completion, and return them to their other responsibilities.

Assign one person primary responsibility, even if multiple people contribute. In some cases, that person might not be the primary content expert or the person with the largest role, just the person who will make sure the task is completed.

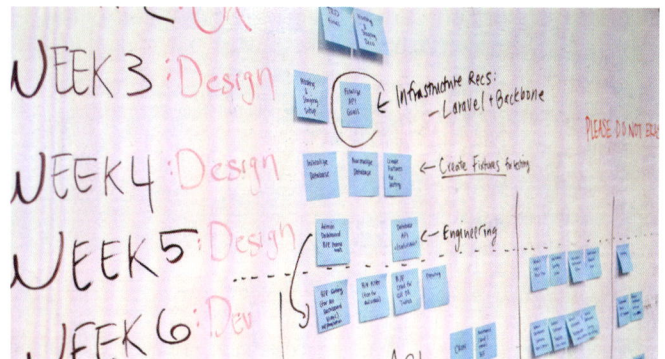

6   USE GATE REVIEWS TO COMPLETE ACTION.

An incomplete capture plan and its qualitative general statements are early warning signs of no-bid decisions.

See SAMPLE TEMPLATE 8.

Make gate review guidelines comprehensive and constructive.

The comprehensiveness of a review increases as the capture progresses. Because early reviews are shorter, develop summary charts that highlight exceptions. Consider a graphic that rates tasks by risk for executives to easily evaluate.

Be constructive by praising the task owners and their managers for the green tasks. Be prepared to offer constructive options for the red and yellow tasks. The gate review might be your only opportunity to secure senior management support.

7   OVER-COMMUNICATE.

When managing tasks assigned to indirect reports, maintain visibility and urgency through regular, repeated communication. Balance the medium, frequency, urgency, and tone.

Be considerate, as frequent messages or intrusive, inconvenient mediums irritate team members. Some of the most irritating time wasters are unnecessary late-night or weekend calls; over-addressing, hitting reply all, and blind copying on emails; and overly large, frequent, and long teleconferences.

Figure 3 summarizes the merits of increasingly varied team communication and schedule management options.

COMMUNICATION AND SCHEDULE MANAGEMENT OPTIONS	MERITS
TEXT MESSAGE	Immediate, creates a sense of urgency, but reserve for relatively simple, informational messages. As texting increases, the messages are more easily forgotten.
EMAIL	Works for everyone, but messages are often obscured by extensive email traffic. Email does leave a trail, which improves accountability. Create a group list for standard messages. Limit the address list for other messages to individuals who need to take or approve the requested action. Make sure that messages to newly added people are not automatically diverted to their *junk* folder. Avoid *reply all* when the message could be more appropriately handled by replying only to the sender.
PHONE CALL	Immediate, but leaves no trail. People forget details; written follow-up is often constructive.
CONFERENCE CALL	Set and communicate the agenda. Schedule when you can maximize participation. Set and observe time limits. Adapt the medium, from small-group, web-video to large-group teleconferences. New, low-cost, flexible options are introduced frequently. If not handled professionally, accountability can be a problem. (*See* VIRTUAL TEAM MANAGEMENT, **Proposal Guide**)
LIVE MEETING	As the most expensive option, reserve meetings for the most important, sensitive, or confidential events. Given a limited capture budget, reduce the cost of live meetings by scheduling meetings concurrently with other events, locating a low-cost venue, or use an alternate medium.
INSTANT MESSAGING	Immediate, usually includes a pop-up notification on the user's phone or computer. Best suited for shorter messages.

Figure 3. **Capture Team Communication and Schedule Management Options.** *Select a communication medium appropriate to the importance and urgency of your message and to individuals who must be involved.*

©Shipley Associates

SOLUTION DEVELOPMENT

Solution development involves the design and development of consistent technical and management approaches, coordinating relevant past performance, and a winning price window. Approaches to solution development vary greatly based on the industry and markets in which you compete.

A capture manager is often involved in helping gather information for the solution that will most likely meet the customer's needs, motivators, and requirements. Collaborating early with the solution team is vital to sharing insight gained during the sales/capture activities and interactions with the customer.

Your team's solution development can be broken into five key topics to plan for during pursuit efforts:

- **Technical**—How you will solve the key technical requirements (stated and derived)
- **Management**—How you will manage the customer's program to a successful conclusion

- **Past Performance**—Relevant past performance examples that align with your offer and solution
- **Price**—Determining a pricing strategy and pricing window that puts your offer in the competitive range for evaluation.
- **Risk**—Identify major technical and programmatic risks and show how you define and identify, manage, monitor, control, and retire risk to the program.

SOLUTION DEVELOPMENT

1 Understand best practices for solution development.

2 Collaborate with the customer on a notional solution.

3 Consider the technical solution.

4 Determine the likely management solution.

5 Map out relevant past performance.

6 Determine a winning price within the competitive range.

1   UNDERSTAND BEST PRACTICES FOR SOLUTION DEVELOPMENT.

Collaborate with the customer to develop a solution that addresses the customer's issues and hot buttons and fits within the winning price. Start early. Do not push a predetermined offering on an unwilling buyer. Lead the customer toward a mutually satisfactory approach differentiated from competitors, as shown in figure 1.

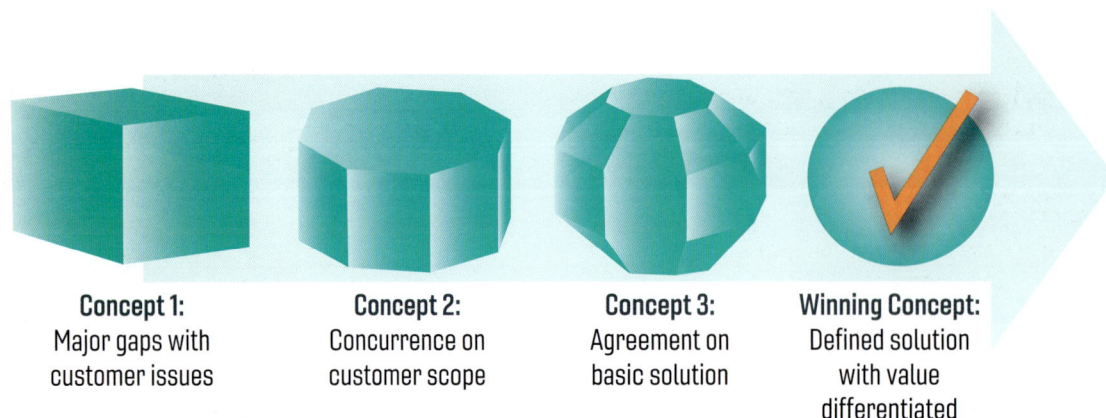

Concept 1: Major gaps with customer issues

Concept 2: Concurrence on customer scope

Concept 3: Agreement on basic solution

Winning Concept: Defined solution with value differentiated

Figure 1. Progression of Customer-Focused Solution Development. *With the benefit of lead time, you can progress with the customer from a crude structure that perhaps leaves gaps around some customer issues, through a concurrence on general scope, to an agreed basic solution.*

Follow these suggestions as you develop a customer-focused solution:

- Make sure the solution is explicitly linked to customer requirements and issues—customer focus is key!
- Integrate the solution development efforts with other capture activities.
- Set a "solution freeze date" and stick to it.
- Use tracking tools to monitor progress of solution development throughout the business capture cycle.

As you transition the opportunity to the proposal team, prepare to present the solution at the proposal kickoff meeting.

Coordinating with the proposal team means that when the customer gets your final proposal, the solution seems familiar. The customer will already understand any difficult technical concepts and the value trade-offs.

2   COLLABORATE WITH THE CUSTOMER ON A NOTIONAL SOLUTION.

Early in the capture process, the customer may not yet be aware of some important issues. You should help the customer understand them, especially when they impart a favorable position to your prospective solution. Shaping your customer's understanding of issues is one of the most productive things you can do. Make the customer a better-educated buyer so your eventual proposal can be understood for its true merits. If possible, encourage the customer to develop requirements that actually favor a solution you can provide.

Determine which of the following categories are most important to the customer early in the pursuit process. Then, shape your solution to solve the most important customer issues:

- **Needs:** user requirements, operational necessities, mission fulfillment

- **Wants:** "nice to haves," future growth, redundancy, agency prestige

- **Program requirements:** key design specifications, maintenance, data and documentation, delivery rate, critical path

- **Cost concerns:** total cost, budget profile

- **Hidden agendas:** internal politics, outside pressure, supplier continuity, incumbent replacement

- **Risks:** cost overruns, schedule slippage, technical failure, quality

You should constantly strive to isolate the customer's major issues. These can be anything the customer worries about, anything that keeps management awake at night. What are the customer's goals, and what issues affect those goals?

One of the main goals of the capture manager, especially early in an opportunity's lifecycle, must be to identify, describe, and confirm the customer's hot buttons. Figure 2 explains factors of a hot button.

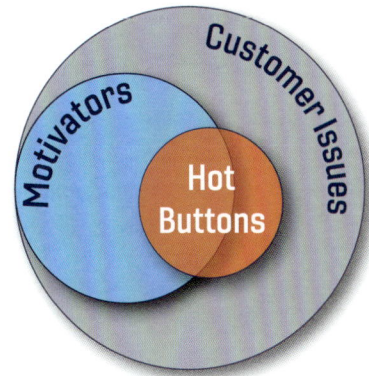

Figure 2. Issues, Motivators, and Hot Buttons. *Issues can be anything the customer worries about. Motivators are the main objectives the customer wants to achieve with the acquisition. Hot buttons are the most important factors that will swing the source selection decision to one offeror or another.*

Understanding these issues helps shape a solution that will meet customer's needs and expectations.

3   CONSIDER THE TECHNICAL SOLUTION.

Establish your solution development team as early as possible. Determine who the key stakeholders and technical experts are and clarify roles and responsibilities.

The technical solution details how you will accomplish the technical work to achieve the customer's mission, performance, and problem-solving objectives.

The solution must link mission and requirements to the customer's issues that resulted in the procurement in the first place. It must link issues with answers, answers with improvements, and improvements with risks and mitigations.

The technical solution must convey a story about how our approach delivers career-building success to the customer while solving a complex web of technology, process, program, and engineering problems that result in an elegant solution that delivers.

Consider starting with the *end of the story*: What results do you want your technical solution to provide for the customer?

4   DETERMINE THE LIKELY MANAGEMENT SOLUTION.

The same principles used to develop the technical aspects of your solution will apply to the management solution. Service contracts are often inextricably linked, so it may be best to develop them simultaneously. Figure 3 shows an integrated approach to developing a sound management solution.

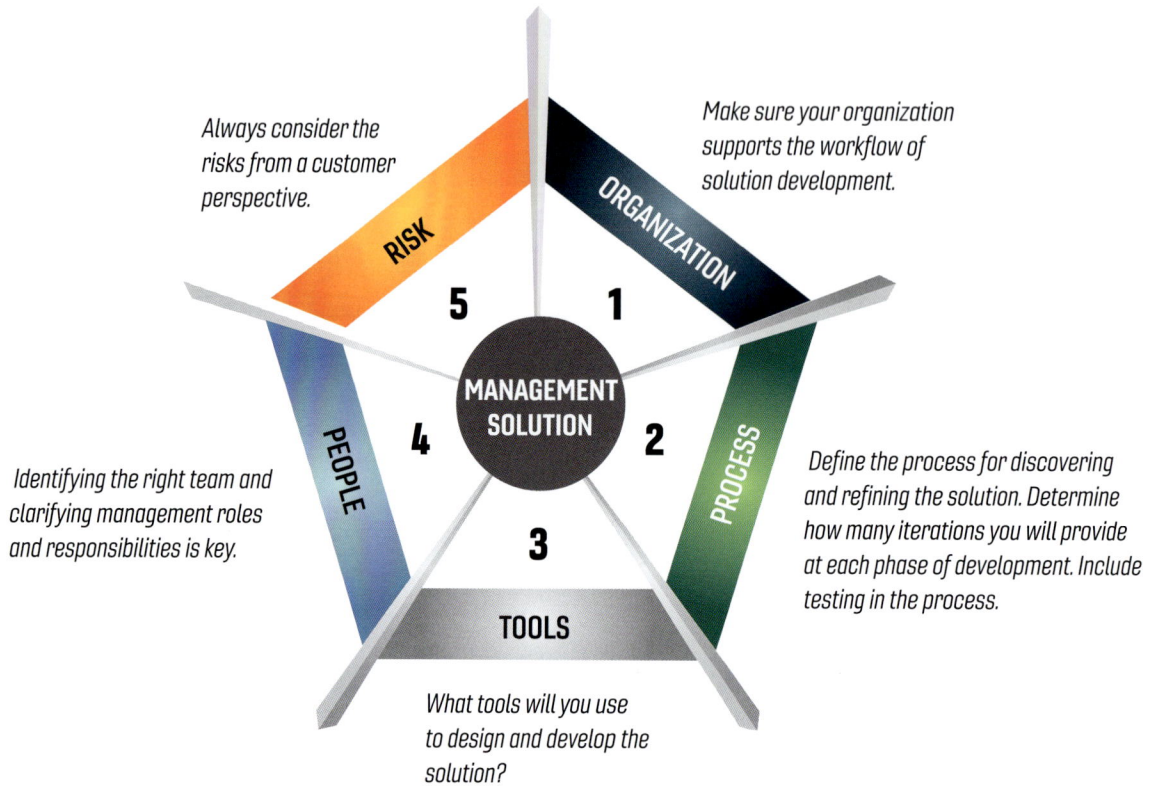

Always consider the risks from a customer perspective.

Make sure your organization supports the workflow of solution development.

RISK

ORGANIZATION

5   **1**

MANAGEMENT SOLUTION

PEOPLE

4

2

PROCESS

3

TOOLS

Identifying the right team and clarifying management roles and responsibilities is key.

Define the process for discovering and refining the solution. Determine how many iterations you will provide at each phase of development. Include testing in the process.

What tools will you use to design and develop the solution?

Figure 3. An Integrated Management Solution Development Approach. *This approach addresses the people, process, tools, organization, and risk elements for developing a management solution.*

You should have an integrated view of how to run a successful program that encompasses all critical aspects from the customer's perspective into a singular management environment that produces technical, quality, schedule, cost, risk, and mission success.

The depiction may be more complex but approximates a layered method demonstrating how all management parts work together. Under positive direction of the program manager, you can achieve the desired results of the mission or mission support.

5 MAP OUT RELEVANT PAST PERFORMANCE.

Relevant experience is the same or similar work your company has done; past performance indicates how well you did that work.

To be relevant, the example does not need to be for the identical product or service. The example should only cover something similar enough to provide reasonable indicators of expected performance capability and risk.

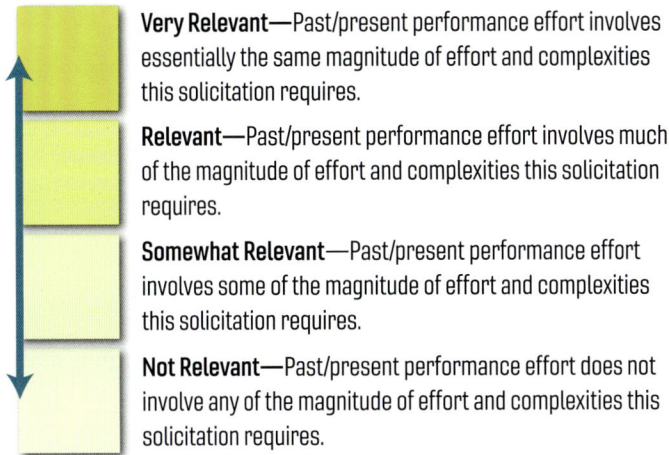

Very Relevant—Past/present performance effort involves essentially the same magnitude of effort and complexities this solicitation requires.

Relevant—Past/present performance effort involves much of the magnitude of effort and complexities this solicitation requires.

Somewhat Relevant—Past/present performance effort involves some of the magnitude of effort and complexities this solicitation requires.

Not Relevant—Past/present performance effort does not involve any of the magnitude of effort and complexities this solicitation requires.

Some organizations choose not to bid on an opportunity if they do not have relevant past performance.

Specific, minimum past performance evaluation factors include the following:

- **Quality of service.** How well did a contractor perform previously contracted work, as reported by the customer?

- **Cost controls.** How well did the contractor adhere to the contracted price? Even on fixed price contracts, where the government is insulated from price risk, government buyers are painfully aware that the quality of the goods or service can fall if the contractor gets into financial trouble.

- **Timeliness.** Projects are jeopardized when contractors deliver late. On cost-reimbursable contracts, costs go up.

- **Business relationships.** Customers desire a contractor who is easy to work with, responsive to changes in needs, and won't abuse the change order process. Good business relationships indicate that a contractor fully appreciates the nature of the work, has the skills and resources to complete it, and holds the customer's interests in high regard.

You can leverage corrected past performance deficiencies as strong management skills. Include information on how you've learned from the problem, instituted corrective or preventive procedures, and won't make the same mistake again:

- Verify past performance deficiencies have been corrected
- State the actions taken to correct problem

Past performance is a key aspect of solution development and should be started early in the capture process.

6   DETERMINE A WINNING PRICE WITHIN THE COMPETITIVE RANGE.

As a capture manager, you must help determine a price that will put your company within the competitive range.

The customer doesn't want to buy less than is needed, but also won't buy more than can be foreseen or justified to be useful. Likewise, there are both upper and lower limits on budgets that influence prices customers are willing to pay. The minimum credible budget depends on:

- Customers history buying similar products or services in the past
- Should-cost analyses
- Market surveys
- Other bids received

In other words, a prudent and educated buyer knows you get what you pay for and sets price expectations accordingly.

See PRICING TO WIN.

As capture manager, be part of the process for narrowing the price window during capture activities.

SUPPORTING THE PROPOSAL

Supporting the proposal while continuing your capture activities is essential to ensuring capture and proposal strategies are aligned and implemented in the proposal.

Ideally, you can sometimes win an award without submitting a competitive proposal. The reality is that few customers are permitted to award a contract—or want to award a contract—without soliciting competitive bids, even when they have a preferred vendor. Government regulations or corporate purchasing guidelines often require competitive proposals, usually from three or more bidders.

Capture activity continues in parallel with proposal planning, preparation, and review. Customers might limit contact with bidders, but the rules vary by country, market, purchasing environment, customer, and opportunity.

Capture management and proposal management require different skills, and few individuals have both skill sets. Most capture and sales professionals welcome professional proposal support. Capture managers and proposal managers can most effectively engage proposal support by following the guidelines in this section.

Keep the responsibilities and goals of the core capture team in mind:

- Capture/opportunity manager: Owns the opportunity and the customer—the goal is to win.
- Proposal manager: Owns the proposal—the goal is a quality, winning proposal.
- Program manager: Owns the solution—the goal is a profitable, deliverable solution.

Each of the guidelines comprises activities that engage some aspect of proposal support, whether managed or completed by the capture manager or the proposal manager.

SUPPORTING THE PROPOSAL

1 Seek proposal manager input when preparing the detailed proposal budget.

2 Extend the capture strategy into the proposal strategy.

3 Integrate the extended capture team in key pre-proposal activities.

4 Draft the executive summary.

5 Influence the selection of the best core proposal team members.

6 Support the proposal kickoff meeting.

7 Define and manage customer contacts.

8 Participate in but do not facilitate color team reviews.

9 Help analyze the final bid request and lead the Bid Validation Decision gate review.

10 Lead, guide, or contribute to post-bid submittal interactions with the customer.

 ©Shipley Associates

1 SEEK PROPOSAL MANAGER INPUT WHEN PREPARING THE DETAILED PROPOSAL BUDGET.

The first task of a capture manager is to prepare the capture plan. A key element is to estimate and secure a budget for proposal support activities. Seek input from proposal support to estimate the cost to prepare the proposal. Proposal professionals are the only people likely to have relevant cost metrics. When proposal managers prepare the budgets, they are more committed to completing proposals within those budgets.

Two primary proposal preparation cost elements are the cost to design the solution and the cost to prepare the documents.

The cost to design the solution depends on whether the solution is new, a variant of a prior design, or essentially the same as a prior design.

The cost to prepare the proposal documents is directly related to the page count. The value of the contract is relevant but often less important; $500 million contracts have been awarded based on 35-page proposals.

Formally solicited and evaluated proposals are often more costly to prepare because everything must be written for the proposal. More generic bid requests tend to contain more boilerplate or general requirements. Consequently, boilerplate response materials are more easily adapted, which reduces the per-page proposal preparation cost.

When asking a proposal manager to estimate proposal preparation cost, anticipate the following questions:

See PRODUCTION, Proposal Guide.

- How many volumes and copies of each volume, and what is the page count/limit by volume?
- How similar is the solicitation to prior solicitations from this customer?
- Is your probable solution defined?
- How similar is the solution to prior solutions?
- How long is the preparation period?
- What and how many color team reviews are planned?
- Do you anticipate draft and final solicitations? Extensions?
- Do you anticipate orals or a finals briefing after submittal?
- Is a demonstration required?
- What additional plans are required before, with, or after the proposal is due?
- Are cost and pricing data and estimating rationale required as part of the cost volume?
- What access and availability can we count on from content experts?
- Have you identified and can you supply relevant experience and past performance data?
- Will travel be necessary?

Estimating proposal preparation cost is as much art as science, and the science is based upon realistic scoping and reliable metrics.

2 EXTEND THE CAPTURE STRATEGY INTO THE PROPOSAL STRATEGY.

See COLOR TEAM REVIEWS and WIN STRATEGY DEVELOPMENT.

Capture strategy is your plan to win a specific, definable opportunity. Strategy statements include strategic and tactical aspects. The strategic aspects define your position, and the tactical aspects define the actions that you will take to implement that strategy. Your capture strategy should have been reviewed as part of the Blue Team review.

Extending your capture strategy into the proposal strategy might be the single most important interaction that a capture manager has with the proposal manager. Align capture and proposal messages.

Extending capture strategy into proposal strategy is not as simple as transferring capture strategy statements from the capture plan to the proposal management plan. The strategy or positioning portion is the same, but the tactical implementation changes. The following brief example is extended in "Win Strategy Development," Guideline 8.

Capture strategy example:

What: (position).

We will emphasize our ability to complete the design-build of a distribution center on time.

By: (action).

Taking the customer on a plant tour of the XYZ distribution center in Orlando, FL.

Proposal strategy example:

What: (position).

We will emphasize our ability to complete the design-build of a distribution center on time.

By: (action).

Including in our proposal photos of the XYZ distribution center in Orlando, FL.

Consider scheduling a second Blue Team review to improve the quality of your proposal strategy.

If so, the focus shifts:

Blue review 1   *Focuses on capture strategy.*

Blue review 2   *Focuses on proposal strategy.*

If you have a second Blue Team review, consider errors of omission and alignment as well as the correctness, comprehensiveness, and specificity of strategy statements.

Preparing strategy statements gives the proposal team context they need to prepare a compelling proposal.

©Shipley Associates

3 INTEGRATE THE EXTENDED CAPTURE TEAM IN KEY PRE-PROPOSAL ACTIVITIES.

Integrate proposal support, program management, engineering, and key teaming partners in proposal planning, solution development, work share, Work Breakdown Structure (WBS) development, and price-to-win (PTW) activities.

Your primary focus as the capture manager is to win the contract. While proposal support, program management, engineering, and key teaming partners also want to win, they report to other managers with potentially conflicting objectives.

Successful teams are based upon trust, so successful team leaders focus on building and maintaining trust among team members.

Improve your capture success by integrating and aligning the activities of your extended capture team members. Review and clarify the roles, focus, relationships, responsibilities, and authorities of team members. If not, two outcomes are likely, both risky:

- The quality of the solution and proposal suffers.
- Technical and programmatic risk increases.

Team members make different assumptions, both explicit and implicit, which significantly impact cost and risk. Vaguely defined and poorly understood solutions and approaches will be described vaguely in the proposal, decreasing the persuasiveness and win probability.

The proposal manager is responsible for preparing a compliant, responsive proposal that appears to be the product of an integrated team. Help the proposal manager define contributors' roles and gain the support of contributors' managers. The capture manager usually has greater influence than the proposal manager, so back your proposal manager.

See PROPOSAL MANAGEMENT PLAN, Proposal Guide.

Just as project managers prepare project plans, proposal managers prepare Proposal Management Plans (PMPs). Multiple elements of the PMP can be extracted, adapted, and aligned from the capture plan, as shown in figure 1.

Collaborate with the proposal manager on capture and proposal plan updates and encourage adapted reuse. Figure 2 lists PMP contents and potential material sources.

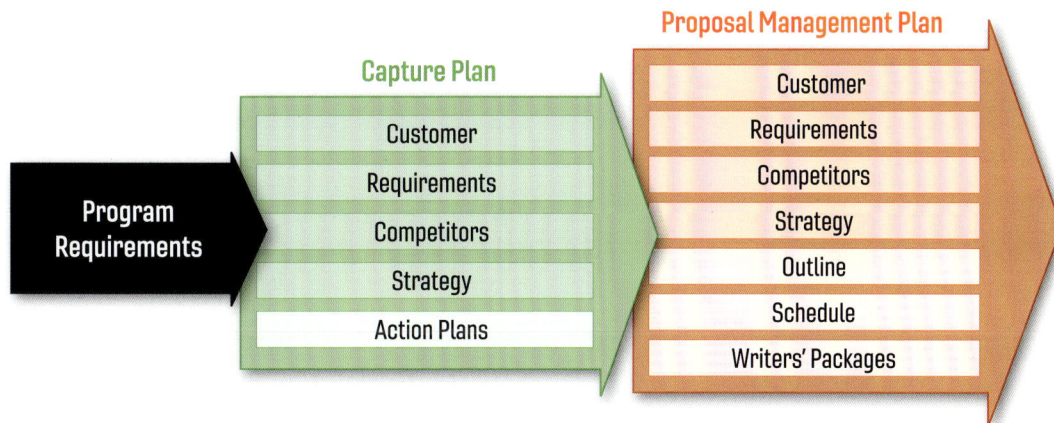

Figure 1. Capture Plan Transition. *For large proposals, or when there are many teaming partners, the proposal manager may decide to collect essential planning documents under a single file. In such cases, much of the background information from the capture plan can be reused. The proposal manager adds proposal-specific information such as the outline, schedule, and individual writer's instruction packages.*

Sample Proposal Management Plan (PMP) Content

1.0	*Proposal Project Summary*	*Appendix 1: Proposal Development Schedule*
2.0	*Customer Profile*	*Appendix 2: Proposal Outline, Cross Reference of RFP Require-ments, and Writing Assignments*
3.0	*Competitive Analysis*	
4.0	*Proposal Strategies and Themes*	*Attachment 1. Writers' Information*
5.0	*Staffing, Roles, and Responsibilities*	*Attachment 2. Preliminary Executive Summary*
6.0	*Proposal Operations*	

Figure 2. Proposal Management Plan Content. *Help the proposal team by providing as much capture information to them as possible.*

4   DRAFT THE EXECUTIVE SUMMARY.

The executive summary should be the first item written for a proposal and the last item revised.

Develop the draft executive summary over time, adding and correcting the content as your understanding of the customer, customer requirements, bid request, competitors, your strategy, and your solution evolve.

See EXECUTIVE SUMMARY, Proposal Guide.

The capture manager is often the primary owner of the executive summary but seldom the only writer. The capture manager should prepare the initial draft and present it at the Preliminary Bid Decision gate review and the proposal kickoff meeting. Include, at minimum, these items:

- Customer's buying vision
- Hot button issues (citing sources or owners)
- High-level solution requirements
- Primary proposal theme(s)

Distribute your draft executive summary at the proposal kickoff meeting.

Schedule the Preliminary Bid Decision gate review only if you can present an executive summary draft containing this information.

Avoid these common executive summary mistakes:

- Preparing the first draft by adapting an executive summary from a prior submittal. These drafts are never quite right, they are seldom sufficiently customer focused, and you will resist making subsequent changes.
- Preparing the executive summary last, just prior to the Red Team review. You lose the opportunity to guide proposal contributors and vet the executive summary with your management and potentially the customer.

See PRESENTATIONS TO CUSTOMERS on how to align the executive summary and a customer presentation.

A quality executive summary draft offers proof that you understand the customer and have a credible capture strategy.

Ask the Blue Team and others to critique the draft executive summary in its current form. Realizing the importance, many capture managers prepare the first draft of the executive summary. Others delegate first draft writing to the proposal manager, especially if they have strong writing skills and have written executive summaries. Either way, the capture manager retains primary responsibility and ownership.

Use executive summary drafts to brief internal management, obtain buy-in, and refine your proposal strategy. Senior managers will review a draft executive summary when they would not bother to review a capture plan.

Use the executive summary to brief your extended capture team, including the proposal team, program management, engineering, and key teaming partners and their management.

Distribute and review the draft executive summary at the proposal kickoff meeting. When proposal developers understand your primary messages, they can align their drafts. Equally important, having and sharing a draft executive summary at proposal kickoff convinces contributors that they will be competently managed and their contributions will lead to a win.

Preview executive summary information and drafts with trusted coaches in the customer's organization or former customer employees if legal, permitted, or practical. Alternatively, screen key points in customer presentations.

Drafting a customer-focused, concise, comprehensive, and persuasive executive summary is difficult. For guidance, refer to the Executive Summary topic section, attend training, and request independent reviews from customers and outside consultants. Often senior managers are too invested to

constructively critique executive summaries produced within their own organization.

5   INFLUENCE THE SELECTION OF THE BEST CORE PROPOSAL TEAM MEMBERS.

Help identify and secure the best talent for key proposal roles. Your goal should be:

- Make the right people available; don't try to make the available people right.

The right people are invariably overbooked and assigned to ongoing tasks. Capture managers often prefer to avoid getting too deeply involved in proposal preparation. While you might be confident that the customer prefers your solution and organization, they are usually bound by what is in your proposal.

Discuss the selection of these key proposal team members with your proposal manager:

Technical volume leader: Select a technical manager in the program area who is technically knowledgeable and can locate expertise on technical sub-areas. Ideally, volume leaders can communicate vertically and laterally, are respected by management and peers, and can resolve technical issues on multiple levels. The ideal technical volume lead can draft technical sections if needed, but most importantly, can coach technical contributors.

Management volume leader: The ideal management volume lead is the person who will manage the program. If the designated program manager is not the management volume lead, ask the assigned person to write as if he or she will be the program manager. Focus on key individuals' responsibilities, authorities, specific work processes, and working relationship with the contracting organization. The management volume lead typically must prepare or manage the preparation of a series of plans: quality assurance, configuration management, risks assessment, transition, subcontracting, and small and minority business.

Cost volume leader: Select a person with solid costing experience who can construct a compliant, traceable, clearly organized document that convinces the customer that your costs are reasonable and realistic. Ask the cost volume lead to collaborate with the program manager and key teaming partners to define work shares, the WBS, the Contractor Statement of Work (CSOW), cost assumptions, and estimating guidelines. The cost volume lead should assist the price-to-win specialist and collaborate with fellow volume leads to ensure the solution they cost and price is identical to the solution proposed in other volumes.

Lead proposal writers: Support the proposal manager's efforts to obtain lead writers who have been successful on major proposals. Ideally, lead writers do not have to be trained, closely supervised, coddled, or micro-managed. Ask lead writers to mentor less experienced writers. If the only writers available are inexperienced, secure funding to train the writing team. Just-in-time, opportunity-specific training typically saves far more writing time than the time required for the training. Even when writers are experienced, make sure the proposal manager schedules brief, focused training sessions to review writing standards and reinforce best practices.

6   SUPPORT THE PROPOSAL KICKOFF MEETING.

While the proposal manager usually plans and conducts proposal kickoff meetings, the capture manager briefs the proposal team on the customer, opportunity, and competition. Proposal contributors commit their best efforts when they believe this particular management team is prepared and committed to win.

Overview the capture strategy, including actions planned, actions completed, customer feedback, teaming partners, potential subcontractors and vendors, and probable competitors. Stress the alignment between capture and proposal strategy, and endorse the proposal strategy, which will be briefed by the proposal manager.

Whether alone or in concert with the program manager, the capture manager reviews teaming considerations, qualifications, and teaming partners' roles and introduces key participants from the teaming partners.

Include teaming partners in the proposal kickoff. If confidentiality or disclosure considerations prevent including teaming partners, note why teaming partners are absent, and conduct a separate kickoff with teaming partners. Include key proposal personnel in the teaming partner kickoff, whether in person or virtual.

7   DEFINE AND MANAGE CUSTOMER CONTACTS.

As the team interfaces with the customer, the capture manager should define, schedule, and manage customer contacts, including bidders' conferences, site visits, and questions regarding solicitation documents.

Note: Capable proposal managers often handle questions about the bid request and post-submittal clarifications. As capture manager, delegate these activities if you are confident they will be handled competently.

Every contact should be managed so that the outcome advances rather than impedes the sale.

Early capture activities are easier to manage because the capture manager often plans, attends, facilitates, or arranges these activities. However, bidder conferences and site visits introduce new individuals who might know relatively little about the customer and the opportunity. The usual meeting guidelines apply:

- Name the event leader.
- Plan the event.
- Define each participant's role.

Establish common expectations, objectives, and ground rules with your team prior to the event and with the customer prior to or at the event.

- Prepare and rehearse, if appropriate.
- Follow the facilitator's lead during the event.
- Conclude events by reviewing and confirming next steps.
- Debrief the team immediately after the event, summarize results, inform others as needed, and assign follow-up actions.

Every proposal team will have questions about requirements, conflicts, and omissions in solicitation documents. While the proposal manager, legal, or contracts representative might collect, review, and refine these questions, the capture manager should be aware of each question and strategize with the proposal team regarding if, how, and who will pose questions. Apply the same approach to additional customer questions.

©Shipley Associates

8   PARTICIPATE IN BUT DO NOT FACILITATE COLOR TEAM REVIEWS.

The capture manager participates in color team reviews but is usually too involved in the effort to impartially facilitate color team reviews. Identify an experienced and respected facilitator from inside or outside the organization.

Typical capture manager contributions include the following tasks:

- Brief reviewers on key aspects of the opportunity.
- Remain available to respond to reviewer questions during the review.
- Attend the review debrief, asking clarification questions that help you define constructive follow-up actions.
- Thank reviewers for their contributions.

See COLOR TEAM REVIEWS.

9   HELP ANALYZE THE FINAL BID REQUEST AND LEAD THE BID VALIDATION DECISION GATE REVIEW.

When bid requests change, the capture manager is best positioned to interpret the customer's motivations, issues, and justification for the change. Wise capture managers understand and address the underlying issue. Naïve capture managers simply accept the change.

As part of the core capture team, review the final bid request and identify show stoppers or contingencies. Were any of these contingencies pre-identified in your capture plan? Is the opportunity still congruent with your organization's strategic direction and objectives? If not, revisit your bid decision. Walking away from a bid this late is difficult but better than winning a contract that you cannot afford to complete.

Do other bid request changes affect your strategy, solution, or pricing approach? If so, discuss and define adjustments, request acceptance at the Bid Validation Decision review, and implement adjustments post review.

10   LEAD, GUIDE, OR CONTRIBUTE TO POST-BID SUBMITTAL INTERACTIONS WITH THE CUSTOMER.

The capture manager's post-submittal role varies greatly by organization. Some organizations reassign the capture manager after proposal submittal, delegating the follow-up questions, clarifications, and final bid price to the program manager and proposal manager. Others shift the lead to the program manager, but retain the capture manager to facilitate short list or orals presentations.

If the capture manager will have the primary ongoing relationship with the customer, keep them involved. In the Business to Business (B2B) sector, this might be the account manager. If the program manager will have the ongoing relationship, shift the capture manager to another pursuit.

The capture manager's charge is to win the contract, and you have not won until you sign the contract. In most instances, the capture manager supports but does not lead the following post-submittal activities:

- Questions and clarifications follow most proposal submittals and are typically coordinated by the proposal manager. Regard questions as a positive event; customers usually ask questions because you remain in contention. Strategize each answer and respond with the same discipline and courtesy as in the proposal.
- Site visits are an opportunity to impress members of the customer's evaluation team. While the proposal or program manager might plan these visits, the capture manager should usually facilitate site visits. Site visits are positive signs that you remain in contention.
- Contract negotiations are often led by the seller's contract specialists, supported by the program manager. As

capture manager, brief the lead negotiator regarding key customer participants and customer hot button issues.

- Proposal debriefs are usually requested, scheduled, and facilitated by the capture manager or proposal manager. Request a debrief, win or lose, and keep it constructive. Assign a note-taker. The capture manager should focus on listening, recognizing non-verbal signals, and asking constructive follow-up questions. Leave proposal document questions to the proposal manager, if he or she attends the debrief.

- Protests are best handled by contracts or legal representatives. Capture managers expecting to pursue additional opportunities with the same customer need to create some distance to maintain a positive or at least neutral relationship with the customer.

- Program start-up is often seen by customers as the official handover from the capture manager to the program manager. Introduce or re-introduce key program management personnel, clarify their roles, and reinforce their qualifications. As the long-time face of your organization with the customer, explicitly state your role, if any, in this program and future programs.

If your organization reassigns the capture manager after proposal submittal, then the program manager is already the primary customer contact. Ideally, the program manager has been active in the capture process and is well known by the customer. If not, the capture manager should introduce the program manager before moving to a new assignment.

A capture manager might maintain an ongoing role when pursuing one of the following types of opportunities:

- Task orders under a master ordering contract
- Change orders on a major contract
- Added tasks when supporting a prime contractor

Depending upon the market and selling environment, the capture manager might be identical to an account manager with an ongoing oversight role for all contracted services with the same customer. Alternatively, the program manager on a major program assumes a capture role regarding change proposals and added tasks.

©Shipley Associates

TEAMING

Teaming is a strategy where two or more organizations agree to jointly pursue an opportunity to improve their chances of winning. In a broad sense, teaming can range from informal prime-subcontractor relationships to the creation of a new joint-venture organization.

Capture and opportunity leaders pursue teaming arrangements from different perspectives. The most common reason to team is if the resulting competitive advantage justifies the additional management burden and potential loss of work share.

Organizations pursue teaming arrangements for a number of other reasons:

- Eliminate a competitor.
- Lock up a subcontractor.
- Obtain access to a particular market or customer.
- Meet customer work share requirements.

- Attempt to win more favorable terms from a partner.
- Obtain information about a competitor through the teaming partner.
- Share the financial risk and development cost.
- Obtain access to new processes, methods, facilities, or business confidential information.

Some teaming arrangements are made to qualify for specific types of procurements.

TEAMING

1 Make teaming decisions early in the capture process.

2 Develop selection criteria and carefully analyze potential teaming combinations.

3 Negotiate a common vision as the basis for teaming.

4 Establish a management structure with clear lines of authority.

5 Consult with customers and consider their roles in team formation.

6 Define each teaming partner's work share in advance in a Work Breakdown Structure (WBS).

7 Separate decisions about work share and team management.

8 Address teaming issues, responsibilities, and authorities promptly.

1   MAKE TEAMING DECISIONS EARLY IN THE CAPTURE PROCESS.

The primary reason to make an early teaming decision is the same reason professional sports teams seek the highest possible draft position for new players—you get the best selection. Make early teaming decisions for the following reasons:

- The most advantageous partners are still available.
- The best talent is still available.
- You need a signed agreement to collaborate freely. Teaming discussions take time, involving senior management, attorneys, and formal contracts.
- Funding is easier to obtain early, before funds are committed to other uses.

- Positioning your team with the customer takes acceptance time. The more time you have, the greater the opportunity to influence the customer to accept and prefer your team.
- Teaming partners established early can help you prepare and implement the win strategy.
- Raising difficult issues early during capture allows time for successful resolution or establishing alternate teaming arrangements with other advantageous partners.

Customers gain confidence knowing that teaming arrangements are in place in advance of a solicitation.

2   DEVELOP SELECTION CRITERIA AND CAREFULLY ANALYZE POTENTIAL TEAMING COMBINATIONS.

Develop selection criteria based upon customer requirements and issues, not just counterbalancing strengths and weaknesses of the teaming organizations.

Use a capability matrix showing capability of each teaming partner as it aligns with customer requirements. A matrix will show you strengths and gaps in your combined teaming resources.

For example, a customer would like to fund development of a fuel-efficient vehicle that achieves 200 miles per gallon. Company A is a world leader in diesel and gasoline engine design and manufacture. Company B designs and builds the most efficient electric motors. Company C designs and

builds efficient storage batteries. While the strengths and weaknesses of A, B, and C are complementary, the customer's issue might be how to rapidly and cost effectively integrate all three technologies.

Identify probable selection criteria, including technical, management, past performance, cost, timing, funding, regulatory, social, political, business type, ownership, and legal. Consider hidden or unspoken issues as well as stated requirements. Identify issues that might be driving stated requirements.

3   NEGOTIATE A COMMON VISION AS THE BASIS FOR TEAMING.

In the best teaming relationships, team members share a common vision, strategy, and values. An organization driven to be the low-cost producer is likely to conflict with an organization focused on customer service or technical leadership. An organization with a collaborative management team will conflict with one headed by a CEO with a single-minded approach.

Contrasting visions, approaches, or management values breed conflict, which should prompt you to re-examine the merits of a teaming combination. Team members should recognize the need for each member and respect each member's role and contribution.

Teaming arrangements need to be negotiated, written, and signed as early as possible in the capture phase.

When negotiating a teaming agreement, resolve the prime, subcontractor, and vendor issues, the positional issues, the work share issues, and the intellectual property, cost, and other legal issues. These issues are expanded on in the subsequent guidelines. If left unresolved, these issues can subsequently destroy the team, your ability to form another team, and your credibility with the customer.

Schedule team-building activities promptly after forming your team to improve cooperation and reduce risk. Team building

©Shipley Associates

activities are essential when integrating multi-organizational capture and proposal teams. Cohesive teams built during capture and proposal development reduce your transition risk into program execution.

Team-building activities apply to co-located and virtual teams, and they need not be expensive. Similar principles apply to both types of teams and are not repeated in this topic section.

See VIRTUAL TEAM MANAGEMENT, Proposal Guide.

4   ESTABLISH A MANAGEMENT STRUCTURE WITH CLEAR LINES OF AUTHORITY.

Shared team management does not always work. Some teams rotate management responsibilities on longer-term contracts, but customers are often uncomfortable with potential lapses when management rotates. The best teams see themselves as distinct strategic business units where the primary loyalty of individuals on the team is to the team rather than the parent organization.

Your teaming relationship should be more robust than an arms-length subcontract. Teaming requires greater cooperation and trust than a typical supplier or vendor relationship.

Establish clear lines of authority, especially when individuals from different parent organizations are co-located. Customers want to know the level of authority of each individual to determine who to contact for a quick resolution. Use clear lines of authority to convince the customer that you have well-defined and understood risk mitigation and problem resolution processes in place.

Clear lines of authority apply to any type of teaming arrangement, from joint ventures to Other Transactional Authority (OTA) consortia to project teams within the same organization:

- Insert management organization charts in the proposal.
- Name key managers and key positions, if possible.
- Indicate team members' responsibilities, level of authority by type of decision, preapproved spending limits, and whether they have hiring/firing authority over their own employees and employees of teaming partners.

5   CONSULT WITH CUSTOMERS AND CONSIDER THEIR ROLES IN TEAM FORMATION.

Customers have a stake in teaming combinations, preferred partners, and team contractual arrangements. Review potential teaming combinations and arrangements with the customer, if possible. Whether encouraged by the customer or not, justify why you have teamed, describe the role of each partner, and explain the unique reason that partner was selected. Where appropriate, describe when proposed teaming arrangements have successfully performed on previous efforts with similar customers.

Customers often review your teaming selection criteria as part of their evaluation and source selection process. For example, customers dislike teammates whose primary motivation is to reliably secure a share of the work without competition.

On the other hand, customers like teammates who bring established, collaborative synergies or qualified lower-cost resources to an effort. Customers look favorably on teammates that help them meet one or more socio-economic contracting goals, such as for contracting with small or veteran-owned businesses.

Occasionally, organizations feel compelled to team, either by the customer, their management, or conditions in their market. Forced teaming arrangements increase risk if the partners dislike or prefer to not work together. Consider whether forced teaming is necessary to compete and is worth the increased risk.

6 DEFINE EACH TEAMING PARTNER'S WORK SHARE IN ADVANCE IN A WORK BREAKDOWN STRUCTURE (WBS).

Even at the proposal stage, teams seldom jell until the work share is defined in a written Work Breakdown Structure (WBS). Two things can happen if the work share is not defined; both are risky:

- Tasks are omitted because, "Someone else has those tasks." Omitted tasks are not described or priced, increasing financial and performance risk and decreasing your chances of winning.

- Tasks are included in multiple places, increasing the cost and making you less competitive. Citing different approaches to the same task suggests that you cannot work well as a team.

Appoint a subgroup to develop the WBS, comprising individuals representing every partner. Frequently, work shares must match the funding percentages of the purchasing organizations, specific work locations, and specific subcontractors selected. Typical examples are multinational procurements and export sales that include coproduction or offset requirements.

7 SEPARATE DECISIONS ABOUT WORK SHARE AND TEAM MANAGEMENT.

The organization with the largest work share does not have to be the prime management partner, except when dictated by the customer, such as in government contracts. Where allowed, select the management partner with the best ability to manage the contract or the partner that the customer prefers. Consider the following example:

In this teaming arrangement, Partner A, with 80 percent of the work share, was to be the prime or managing partner to produce training simulators. Partner A was recognized by the customer for excellence in research and development (R&D). They had developed this training simulator, but they had no record of successfully managing a large production contract. Worse yet, Partner A typically delivered R&D contracts late and frequently overran costs.

Partner B, with only 20 percent of the work share, had an excellent record of production contract management experience. Nearly half of the 90-day bid preparation period passed before Partner A would agree to let Partner B become the managing partner.

Note that for some procurements, preferences or requirements for socioeconomic prime contracting or workshare targets may not be known until the final solicitation is issued.

©Shipley Associates

8 ADDRESS TEAMING ISSUES, RESPONSIBILITIES, AND AUTHORITIES PROMPTLY.

Address capture planning; joint customer-facing sales and marketing activities; your proposal preparation process, management approach, and cost allocation; and program or solution development costs. You should also address potential legal concerns, such as allocation of financial risk, intellectual property and licensing, contractual terms and conditions, and legal implications.

Validate your capture strategy with your teaming partners. Assign capture tasks to your partners. Involve them in your positioning and intelligence gathering efforts. Customers doubt repeated claims that you are a team when they only interact with a single organization.

Include teaming partners in key activities:

- Identifying other potential teammates
- Performing competitive assessments
- Facilitating and contributing to capture and proposal review teams
- Making joint presentations to customers
- Validating your capture and proposal strategy
- Identifying relevant past performance examples
- Drafting proposal sections
- Participating in final offer presentations or oral proposal presentations

Capture planning and proposal preparation activities comprise a mini-project that leads to the major project. Both must have clear management structures with clear lines of authority. Seek a common process with common tools, management structure, and approach to covering capture and proposal preparation costs.

Co-locating the proposal or solutioning team is ideal, but often not feasible. Virtual teaming is increasingly required to reduce costs and incorporate input from individuals who are committed to prior tasks or intermittently available.

Few individuals have common visions of what is meant by a virtual team. Managers of virtual teams must deal with four issues, listed in order of importance:

- **Process.** When the process and terms used differ, individuals cannot communicate clearly. Worse, they often do not know it. Teams with a common process and capable proposal manager will prepare a superior proposal in half the time.
- **Culture.** Teams in different time zones create obvious challenges. However, organizational culture variations are often more challenging than national culture variations. Do not underestimate the problems from different organizational cultures and the impact on hardware, software, and process. Individuals who know one platform, one software package, and one process will resist change to the bitter end.
- **Software.** Different operating systems, programs, releases or versions of programs, fonts, print drivers, networks, gateways, and communication protocols usually mean that the teaming partner's input seldom arrives as you thought it would.
- **Hardware.** Contributors often work on different platforms with different capabilities, support needs, and networking characteristics.

Too much of the current focus in virtual teaming is around hardware and software issues. The most difficult and lingering issues involve process and cultural differences.

No organization wants to lose its intellectual property (IP) and establish a competitor. Establish what must be disclosed for efficient contract performance. Licensing under a royalty arrangement is one alternative. Resolve IP issues with your legal team.

While legal arrangements differ in joint-venture, prime-subcontractor, and vendor relationships, most practices in Guideline 8 apply universally.

See VIRTUAL TEAM MANAGEMENT, Proposal Guide.

VALUE PROPOSITIONS

Value propositions establish the value basis for the business relationship. They describe how the seller's solution will improve the customer's business and how that improvement will be measured.

Value propositions are opportunity and customer specific and are developed collaboratively with the customer over the course of the pursuit.

Value propositions go beyond traditional theme statements by incorporating as many of the following elements as possible:

- Quantifies the anticipated business improvement
- Specifies the timing of the benefits
- Specifies the timing of the costs
- States the payback period
- Specifies how the results will be measured and tracked

Because executives, users, and technical buyers have different issues and values, prepare a different value proposition for each type of buyer. For each distinct opportunity, state the total added value of all value propositions in a single summary.

Value propositions are not always presented word-for-word in a proposal or briefing. Rather, the value proposition (offer) is made clear throughout the sales cycle.

VALUE PROPOSITIONS

1 Establish a single sales objective as the first step in developing a value proposition.

2 Apply value propositions as a collaborative selling tool.

3 Use a template to develop value propositions.

4 Develop unique value propositions for each type of buyer.

5 Showcase your value proposition in the executive summary.

6 Address common obstacles to using value propositions.

©Shipley Associates

1 ESTABLISH A SINGLE SALES OBJECTIVE AS THE FIRST STEP IN DEVELOPING A VALUE PROPOSITION.

Shortly after your pursuit decision, draft a brief, precise sales objective that meets the following criteria:

- **Specific**—States what products and services are to be purchased and who will purchase them.

- **Measurable**—Tells how much is to be purchased.

- **Timed**—Cites when the purchase will be made.

- **Result**—States, quantitatively if possible, the result or process change the customer anticipates.

Sample sales objective

Our sales objective is to persuade Global Corporation to outsource information technology (IT) support, currently costing them $2,850,000 annually. Global is seeking an annual cost reduction of 30 percent, commencing May 1, 20XX, and would like the provider to purchase the existing IT assets.

Like most initial sales objectives, not all criteria are met. The purchasing organization is named but not the purchasing individual. Current costs are named, but not the cost of the seller's solution or the cost of the customer's assets. Drafting a sales objective is a good way to determine what additional information you need.

This overall sales objective is the basis for developing a value proposition.

2 APPLY VALUE PROPOSITIONS AS A COLLABORATIVE SELLING TOOL.

One objective of collaborating with the customer to develop a value proposition is to persuade them to award the contract without competitive proposals. The customer must be convinced that the opportunity cost of delaying exceeds the potential savings from competing the contract.

Collaboration between the customer and the seller offers the following potential advantages:

- Both gain a clearer understanding of the customer's objectives and potential benefits.

- Both better understand the actions required of each party, which reduces risk.

- The customer becomes the seller's advocate in the customer's organization.

Value propositions flow directly from the sales objective. The best value propositions are specific. Ideally, authorized representatives of both the customer's and the seller's organizations sign the formal value proposition, and they mutually agree to proceed without competitive proposals.

3 USE A TEMPLATE TO DEVELOP VALUE PROPOSITIONS.

Templates help sellers draft better value propositions in less time. When a template is not used, the result is often vague, qualitative, and hard to measure.

Value propositions should include the following elements:

- Quantified business improvement
- Timing to achieve results
- The solution
- Investment cost
- Payback—financial, efficient, other
- Results measurement and tracking

A template for drafting value propositions is shown in figure 1. Practice developing a baseline value proposition you can tailor with customers on each pursuit.

VALUE PROPOSITION TEMPLATE

> \<Customer Name\> will realize \<quantified business improvement\> by acquiring \<our solution\> for \<total investment cost\>.
>
> Beginning \<implementation date\>, the improvement in \<specific business process or function\> will reach an economic payback in \<timeframe\>.
>
> We have agreed to document the delivered value by \<results measurement and tracking approach\> .

Figure 1. Use a Template to Develop Value Propositions. *The better value propositions are developed with the customer and contain the elements listed. Value propositions sound stronger if the benefits are placed at the beginning.*

4 DEVELOP UNIQUE VALUE PROPOSITIONS FOR EACH TYPE OF BUYER.

Three broad types of buyers are the economic buyer, the users, and the technical buyers.

The **Economic Buyers** give final approval to purchase. They sign the check and retain veto power. Economic buyers tend to be concerned about the trade-off between price and performance. They focus on bottom line impact. While many people may offer input and recommendations, only the economic buyer can give final approval.

While value propositions targeted at individual buyers may overlap, the summary value proposition targeting the economic buyer incorporates all benefits and costs.

The **Users** are the people who judge the potential impact on their job performance. Their personal success is impacted by the sale, so their concerns are often emotional and subjective. Users' issues are reliability, support, ease of operation, maintenance, safety, potential impact on morale, and potential impact on their personal success. Because they use or supervise the use of your product or service, they can undermine a buying decision.

The **Technical Buyers** are gatekeepers. They cannot give final approval, but they can give a final no. Technical buyers often determine the short list. They tend to focus on the features of a product or service against objective specifications established to screen offers.

Technical buyers may not be technical in the scientific sense. Purchasing agents, lawyers, contracts people, and licensing or regulatory authorities are technical buyers. Because technical buyers are primarily focused on how well you meet their screening tests, the better you understand their criteria, the better your chances of getting their recommendations.

Another way to examine buyers is according to their source of power. Power could be economic, control (users), or knowledge (technical). Alternatively, power could be indicated by level of management, such as executive management, middle management, or operations.

Tailor your value proposition(s) to each type of buying influence. The following four value propositions target each type of buyer and are extensions of the earlier example of a single sales objective under Guideline 1:

Value Proposition for the economic buyer

Global Corporation will realize a $3,750,000 reduction in information technology support costs over the next 5 years, commencing May 1, 20XX, by contracting with Computer Heroes, Ltd., at a cost of $2,000,000 per year. Global Corporation will be paid $500,000 for all of Global's IT assets, and Computer Heroes will provide all IT support. Global Corporation will enjoy a 30 percent annual reduction in IT costs, assuming the agreed prices and the same levels of services currently required continue to be required and delivered. All costs will be available to you online and documented in monthly invoices.

Value Proposition for the user

Commencing May 1, 20XX, the department allocations for IT support for the current types and levels of service will be reduced an average of 30 percent. Outdated legacy systems will be transitioned to lower cost, current, commercial off-the-shelf hardware and software. Departmental managers will be free to focus on core management tasks without the distractions of IT issues. All costs will be available and verifiable online and documented in monthly invoices tied to Global work order numbers. With Computer Heroes assuming responsibility for all hardware and software (paying Global $500,000 for the current assets), department managers will no longer have to submit and defend IT capital requests.

Value Proposition for the technical buyer (IT professionals)

Commencing May 1, 20XX, IT professionals will have extensive and varied opportunities for personal growth and advancement within their profession. Computer Heroes will offer positions to all IT employees and will maintain current pay levels for those positions. As an industry leader, all positions will be reviewed and adjusted to industry standards. Opportunities for training and advancement will be offered to all employees on an equal basis through our Intranet website, our employee newsletter, regular all-hands emails, and job site postings.

Value Proposition for the technical buyer (contracts)

Starting May 1, 20XX, all IT support, both employees and assets, will be seamlessly transitioned to Computer Heroes, saving Global Corporation $750,000 per year over current costs. All cost savings will be calculated on the basis of providing identical levels of service and can be verified online by comparing monthly, itemized invoices.

5   SHOWCASE YOUR VALUE PROPOSITION IN THE EXECUTIVE SUMMARY.

If developing value propositions is an integral part of your business development process, weave it into your executive summary.

Begin the executive summary by stating the summary value proposition that targets the economic buyer, the sole person who can sign the check. Follow the summary value proposition with the underlying value propositions. Then present all aspects of your solution against one of the underlying value propositions, substantiating how your approach delivers the value claimed. Conclude by showing how the underlying value propositions add up to the opening summary value proposition.

Use the Four-Box organizational structure discussed in the Executive Summaries section. Integrate your value proposition elements into the theme statement and align value with the hot buttons.

Some aspects of value cannot be quantified. Sometimes, individuals in either customers' or sellers' organizations cannot agree on the quantitative added value. Improving a brand, for example, is difficult to quantify.

See EXECUTIVE SUMMARIES.

Always state the intangible or nonquantified values of your proposed solution. If the quantified added values of competitors' solutions are close to yours, the intangible added values could win the contract. State your quantitative added value before your qualitative added value.

6 ADDRESS COMMON OBSTACLES TO USING VALUE PROPOSITIONS.

Many organizations have difficulty with value propositions. Figure 2 below lists some of the common problems and suggests potential solutions for developing a solid value proposition.

The deep understanding of the customer's business required to develop a value proposition can help discriminate your organization.

Individuals working in regulated markets where contacts between the seller and the customer are limited or prohibited can still benefit from developing value propositions. A quantified value proposition based on reasonable assumptions will be more persuasive than a vague, qualitative claim to offer best value.

REASONS VALUE PROPOSITIONS AVOIDED	POTENTIAL SOLUTIONS
Legal or contracts people refuse to allow any specific statements to limit potential liability.	Carefully state all assumptions and conditions.
Few people understand value propositions as a disciplined concept.	Train all participants in the process.
Short sales cycles limit customer-seller collaboration.	Develop *generic* value propositions that can be tailored.
Excessive targeting of multiple opportunities limits customer-seller collaboration.	Improve Pursuit and Bid/No Bid milestone discipline.
Seller-developed value propositions are summarily rejected by customers.	Find a friendly collaborator, sell on a basis other than *best value,* or no bid.
Customers' distrust of the seller or purchasing restrictions limit or bar collaboration with sellers.	Develop greater trust, or sell on a basis other than *best value*.

Figure 2. Rationale for Establishing a Value Proposition. *Common obstacles to effective use of value propositions can be overcome by applying a more collaborative approach.*

©Shipley Associates

WIN STRATEGY DEVELOPMENT

Win strategy development is an approach for developing an overall plan for winning a competitive bid. Strategy and tactics are often confused. In the purest sense, strategy is your pre-engagement position; tactics are the actions you take to implement your strategy, to convey it persuasively. Both are required to win.

The guidelines for developing a win strategy include preconditioning, targeting, analyzing, and then determining and packaging your solution. A win strategy always takes into consideration your competitive position and requires an understanding of your discriminators.

Organizations that are most effective at winning business have aligned their strategies and processes throughout, including their approach to business development. Their business, market, capture, sales, and proposal strategies and tactics are aligned, coordinated, and consistent.

Misaligned strategies result in inconsistent, confusing, and unclear customer messages. This disconnect prompts customers to doubt your message.

If the following example describes your organization, you can improve your business capture effectiveness:

- Account executives position their solution based on successful previous solutions.

- Individuals write proposals with little direction from capture or sales, using extensive boilerplate due to limited response time and numerous requests to bid.

- When asked to make a final presentation, senior executives deliver standard presentations.

In these examples, messages to the customer are often seller focused. As a result, customers doubt both your understanding of their needs and your commitment to satisfying their needs. You must demonstrate why you are the best solution throughout the capture process.

See SAMPLE TEMPLATE 3.

WIN STRATEGY DEVELOPMENT

1 Clarify strategy at each phase of the business development process.

2 Analyze your current competitive position and discriminators.

3 Define and agree to use common terms and definitions.

4 Define a specific capture objective after your pursuit decision.

5 Identify economic buyers, users, and technical buyers; then list their issues.

6 Rank and combine individual buyers' issues into a set of organizational issues.

7 Use a tool like the Shipley Integrated Solution Worksheet to arrive at a competitive solution that is aligned with the customer's issues and requirements.

8 Prepare a Bidder Comparison Chart (BCC).

9 Draft specific strategy statements that define both what you will do and how you will implement that strategy.

10 Develop a specific value proposition for each opportunity and customer.

11 Create a price-to-win strategy to drive your solution.

12 Use trade-offs to validate your winning approach and ghost the competition.

13 Implement your action plan.

1   CLARIFY STRATEGY AT EACH PHASE OF THE BUSINESS DEVELOPMENT PROCESS.

Strategy might be the most misused word in business. "Strategy" might refer to a position, an action, the entire solution, an aspect of the solution, or a favorite catch phrase or slogan.

To craft and present an aligned message, all members of the selling team must agree to use a common process and common definitions:

BUSINESS STRATEGY
An organization's plan to achieve overall business objectives.

MARKET STRATEGY
An organization's plan to achieve specific market objectives, typically involving multiple sales.

CAPTURE STRATEGY
The plan to win a specific, defined opportunity.

WIN STRATEGY
Perfectly aligned to a capture strategy. It should be opportunity specific and focused on your unique discriminators. It must explain why the customer should choose your solution.

©Shipley Associates

Proposal strategy is a plan to write a persuasive, winning proposal. The proposal strategy is a subset of the capture strategy. The message is the same; only the tactical aspects of implementation differ.

Win strategy is used to describe the over-arching actions required to win an opportunity.

In capture planning, you plan and take actions to convey information that persuades each customer to prefer, or at minimum, favorably regard your organization and solution. You might convey that information in white papers, presentations, meetings, site visits, demonstrations, and media buys or events. In a proposal, you should be conveying identical, aligned information in words, text, and graphics.

2 ANALYZE YOUR CURRENT COMPETITIVE POSITION AND DISCRIMINATORS.

Strategy drives tactics. You always have a position in any sales situation, whether you understand it or not. Developing an effective win strategy requires: (1) Determining your current position, and then (2) Improving it versus competitors' positions.

A discriminator is a feature or benefit that is valued by the customer and unique to you. An effective win strategy always draws attention to discriminators.

Getting an early start developing a strategy saves time and improves the quality of your sales message. When win strategy development is improvised, proposal development is haphazard, uncoordinated, and inconsistent.

Organizations that use a disciplined approach to develop win strategy spend less time clarifying terms and process and have more time to focus on substance and value messages.

3 DEFINE AND AGREE TO USE COMMON TERMS AND DEFINITIONS.

Effective communication requires common terms and definitions. Three of the most universally used and misunderstood terms relating to win strategy are issues, motivators, and hot buttons or hot button issues. The relationship of these three terms is illustrated in figure 1. Issues are customer concerns and worry items that keep them awake at night.

Motivators are the objectives that the customer is trying to achieve:

- Improve profits.
- Increase sales.
- Reduce costs.
- Improve safety.
- Reduce risk.
- Improve quality.

Hot button issues are a consolidated set of issues and motivators, preferably three to five items.

In your communication with the customer, clarify and state hot button issues using the customer's words. Then align your solution or approach to the customer's hot buttons. For example, if a customer is concerned about improving service delivery quality, what aspects of your solution will help them address service delivery quality?

To improve focus, consolidate numerous issues and motivators into three to five hot button issues. Lists of 20 or more items are rapidly forgotten.

All motivators are issues, but not all issues are motivators. For example, training could be an example of a hot button that is an issue but not a motivator. Few customers are motivated to buy because they get to attend training. However, if users were poorly trained on a previous similar purchase, and problems ensued, then training could be a customer's hot button issue.

Customers own issues; sellers own gaps. Concerns that the seller has about a solution or approach are called gaps, the difference between what the customer wants and what the seller can offer.

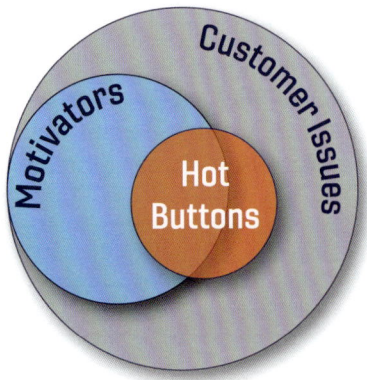

Figure 1. The Relationship Among Issues, Motivators, and Hot Buttons. *Hot buttons are where motivators overlap and become major concerns for the customer.*

Clearly understanding and defining customer hot buttons is critical to the development of a win strategy that can be articulated throughout the sales process, including in the proposal.

4   DEFINE A SPECIFIC CAPTURE OBJECTIVE AFTER YOUR PURSUIT DECISION.

See DECISION GATE REVIEWS.

After you have made a pursuit decision, draft a brief, precise capture objective that meets the following criteria:

- **Specific.** States the products and services that the customer might purchase from your organization, the purchase entity/location, and the person who will make the purchase decision, if known.
- **Measureable.** States the budget and return on investment for the purchase.
- **Timed.** States the timing of the purchase.
- **Result.** States, quantitatively if possible, the benefits and process change the customer anticipates.

Poor Capture Objective

Capture $5 million worth of product and service revenue from Bank-4-U during fiscal year 20XX.

Better Capture Objective

Win a 3-year contract extension to supply and support all copy equipment at Bank-4-U's Reno headquarters. The $3.5 million contract renewal will be awarded on or before June 15, 20XX. Bank-4-U's total cost will remain flat, equaling the current annual cost for identical services.

You often pursue multiple contracts from the same customer. While you might employ common win strategies and tactics, each opportunity is unique and is better addressed individually before you merge tactics. Drawing on your discriminators helps the customer understand the value you bring that is unique to your organization.

5 IDENTIFY ECONOMIC BUYERS, USERS, AND TECHNICAL BUYERS; THEN LIST THEIR ISSUES.

Developing a win strategy requires an understanding of the customer's buying committee. **Economic buyers** are the individuals who give final approval to purchase. They sign the check and retain veto power. Economic buyers tend to be concerned about the trade-off between price and performance. They focus on bottom line impact. While many people may offer input and recommendations, only economic buyers can give final approval.

Users are the people who judge the potential impact on their job performance. Their personal success is impacted by the sale, so their concerns are often emotional and subjective. Users' issues are reliability, support, ease of operation, maintenance, safety, potential impact on morale, and potential impact on their personal success.

Technical buyers are often gatekeepers. They usually cannot give final approval, but they can give a final "No." Technical buyers often determine the short list. They tend to focus on the features of a product or service as measured against objective specifications established to screen offers.

Technical buyers may not be technical in the scientific sense. Purchasing agents, lawyers, contracts people, and licensing or regulatory authorities are technical buyers. Because technical buyers are primarily focused on how well you meet their screening tests, the better you understand their criteria, the better your chances of getting their recommendations.

Another way to examine buyers is according to their source of power. Power could be economic, control (typically users), or technical. Or power could be by level of management, such as executive management, middle management, and operations.

After identifying all the different types of buyers, list the issues of each individual buyer. The most important issues of the entire organization are usually associated with a majority of the buyers. This helps shape the win strategy by placing emphasis on features and benefits that matter most to the customer decision makers.

Customer roles may overlap. For example, the president of a small technical company might be both the economic and technical buyer.

Some sales professionals say that there is only one buyer, the individual empowered to make the final purchase decision. All other types of buyers, such as users or technical buyers, are called influencers.

6 RANK AND COMBINE INDIVIDUAL BUYERS' ISSUES INTO A SET OF ORGANIZATIONAL ISSUES.

One-on-one selling in a business-to-business environment affords the opportunity to address individuals' issues. However, this is not possible when you are preparing a proposal that will be evaluated by multiple buyers, especially in a public sector environment.

Combine individuals' issues into a set of organizational issues that can be addressed in a single proposal or presentation. Rank these issues or hot buttons according to the customer's priorities. This helps shape a win strategy.

Use the rating to determine the relative importance of the group's issues. Take into consideration the individual buyer, the ultimate decision maker and influencers, and the relative importance of that issue to each individual.

See CAPTURE PLANNING, AN OVERVIEW *and* EXECUTIVE SUMMARIES.

7 USE A TOOL LIKE THE SHIPLEY INTEGRATED SOLUTION WORKSHEET TO ARRIVE AT A COMPETITIVE SOLUTION THAT IS ALIGNED WITH THE CUSTOMER'S ISSUES AND REQUIREMENTS.

The Integrated Solution Worksheet (ISW) is a powerful analysis tool used throughout the capture process to develop a win strategy. The ISW is often developed as part of the capture plan. The ISW is shown in figure 2.

Additional uses for the Integrated Solution Worksheet and Bidder Comparison Chart are discussed in CAPTURE PLANNING. AN OVERVIEW; EXECUTIVE SUMMARIES; and TEAMING.

Use the ISW to collaborate with the customer early in the process to define the issues and to ethically help the customer shape and define the requirements.

If the customer already has a solution in mind, the ISW helps define the underlying issues driving the customer's requirements. Analyze your competitive position and discriminators, then work to favorably influence the requirements. Aim to become the customer's preferred provider.

Extend your analysis to outline your solution, identify gaps, outline competitors' likely solutions, and identify discriminators. Then define the strategies and actions required to better position your solution with the customer, as discussed in Guideline 9.

			Integrated Solution Worksheet					
Item No.	Customer Issues	Customer Requirements	Available Solution	Gap	Competitor Solution	Discriminators	Strategy	Action Required
1	System must be available.	8 hr. response time.	2 hr. response time	1 hr.	3 hr. response time	Faster response but more expensive?	Emphasize no additional cost with cellular.	Show current response time. Show photo-service with cell phone.

Figure 2. Integrated Solution Worksheet. *Begin by filling the issues column when you are early in the process. If the customer has identified requirements, fill the requirements column. Then complete each row, linking each item in the row. This process helps identify potential solution gaps and confirms discriminators and strategy.*

8 PREPARE A BIDDER COMPARISON CHART (BCC).

Note: Figures 3 and 4 show alternative approaches to a Bidder Comparison Chart. The figure 3 approach is best suited to smaller, short-response opportunities where the primary focus is on three to five hot button issues. The figure 4 approach is best suited to larger, more complex opportunities where you might identify numerous hot button issues.

A team familiar with the opportunity and likely competitors should meet to analyze hot button issues for each competitor. The BCC is focused on issues, both stated and unstated, and developing strategies and tactics to improve your competitive position.

As a team, use the BCC (or a similar matrix), shown in figure 3, to analyze how the customer's current perception

of your solution and organization compares to your likely competitors' solutions. Use this tool and exercise repeatedly throughout the capture process to measure the effectiveness of your positioning and strengthen your win strategy. Wherever you show a low score, make sure you determine how to mitigate that weakness. Where you show a higher score than competitors, focus on leveraging those strengths.

The BCC results help shape the win strategy and define discriminators.

©Shipley Associates

CUSTOMER ISSUES	WEIGHT	US (SCORE)	COMPANY A	COMPANY B
Specific Experience	30	25	20	15
Low Price	20	5	10	15
Familiarity with Manager Named	20	15	10	10
Ability to Meet Schedule	30	25	21	15
TOTAL SCORE	100	70	61	55

Figure 3. Bidder Comparison Chart. *First list the customer's major issues, then the relative weight of each issue as perceived by the customer. Establish the relative weight of each issue: (1) Use the customer's evaluation criteria, (2) Assign a weight (such as 1-5). Complete each row horizontally, indicating your estimate of the customer's perception of each competitor's ability to satisfy that issue. Compare the products of the weight times the score. The absolute value of the numbers assigned is not important. Only the comparative value matters to help develop a win strategy.*

This approach provides competitive context to your win strategy and position. As shown in figure 4, use data based upon likely customer issues and requirements, relevant strengths and weaknesses of your organization and solution, and relevant strengths and weaknesses of your competitors' solutions and organizations.

The output analysis drives your win strategy, customer messages, and theme statements. A quick checkpoint in win strategy development is to ask the following questions:

- How will we leverage our strengths?
- How will we mitigate our weaknesses?
- How can we exploit our competitors' weaknesses (without naming them)?
- How can we neutralize competitor strengths?

Using a BCC or similar tools helps you establish a strong win strategy.

Information for input and output of a bidder comparison chart

For definitions, discussions, and examples of features, advantages, benefits, discriminators, and theme statements, please go to those sections in the Proposal Guide.

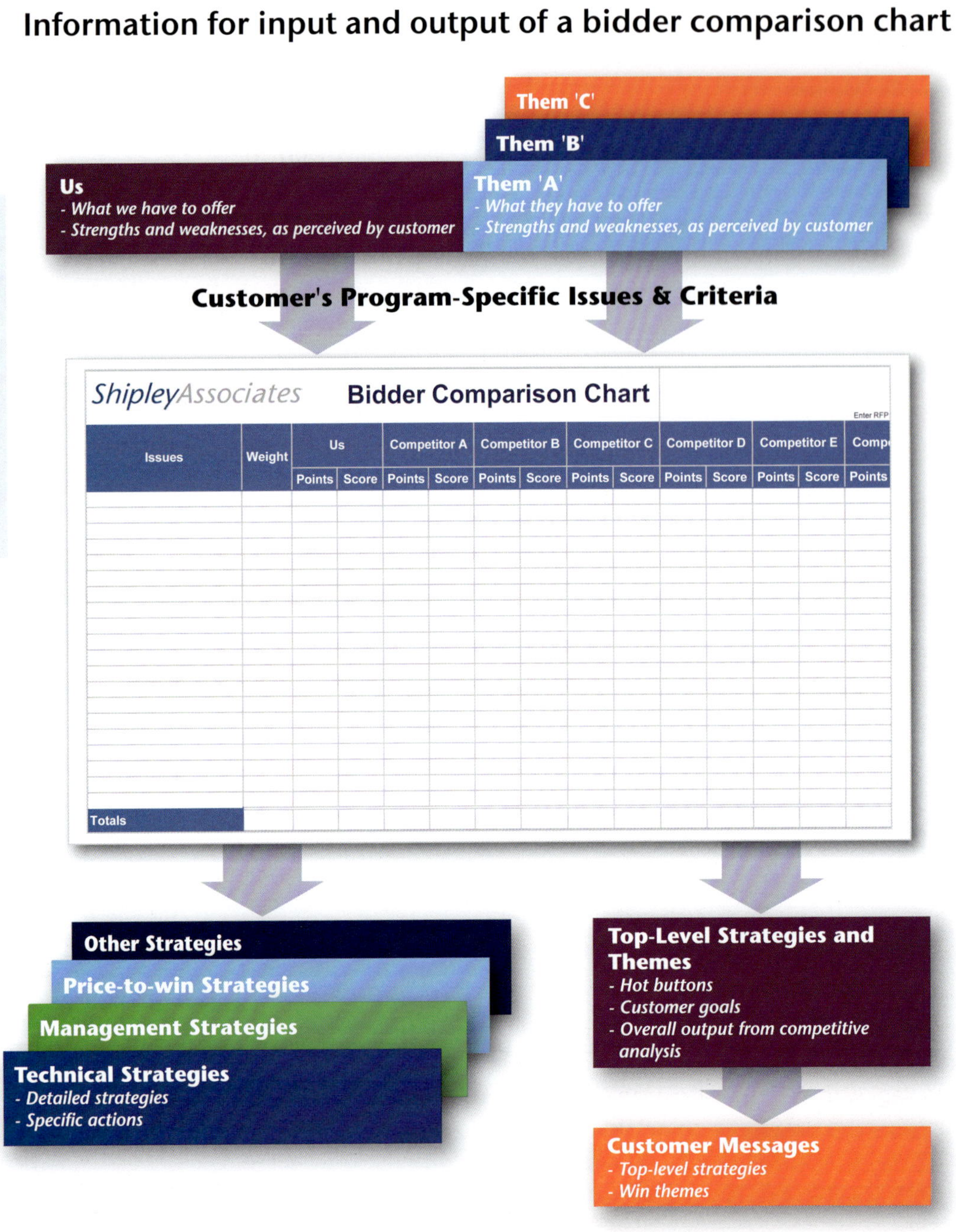

Them 'C'

Them 'B'

Us
- What we have to offer
- Strengths and weaknesses, as perceived by customer

Them 'A'
- What they have to offer
- Strengths and weaknesses, as perceived by customer

Customer's Program-Specific Issues & Criteria

ShipleyAssociates — Bidder Comparison Chart

Enter RFP

Issues	Weight	Us		Competitor A		Competitor B		Competitor C		Competitor D		Competitor E		Comp
		Points	Score	Points	Score	Points	Score	Points	Score	Points	Score	Points	Score	Points
Totals															

Other Strategies

Price-to-win Strategies

Management Strategies

Technical Strategies
- Detailed strategies
- Specific actions

Top-Level Strategies and Themes
- Hot buttons
- Customer goals
- Overall output from competitive analysis

Customer Messages
- Top-level strategies
- Win themes

Figure 4. Customer Issues and Likely Requirements Drive Win Strategy. *Draft at least one strategy statement (per Guideline 9) for every issue listed in the Bidder Comparison Chart. Note that this chart is geared to larger, more complex opportunities.*

©Shipley Associates

9 DRAFT SPECIFIC STRATEGY STATEMENTS THAT DEFINE BOTH WHAT YOU WILL DO AND HOW YOU WILL IMPLEMENT THAT STRATEGY.

Strategy statements are key capture plan elements—they are not "statements" used in a proposal. Collaboratively develop, review, and share win strategy statements across the capture team. Extend each capture strategy statement as you prepare the series of action plans for the capture plan. Note that a single strategy statement might be supported and implemented in multiple action plans.

Win strategy can be influenced in four fundamental ways:

1. Emphasize your strengths.
2. Mitigate your weaknesses.
3. Highlight your competitors' weaknesses.
4. Downplay your competitors' strengths.

Effective strategy statements incorporate both strategic and tactical aspects. The strategic aspect establishes your position. The tactical aspect defines how you will implement the strategy and action steps. Think of the tactical aspect as, "how you will do it."

Strategy statements apply at the capture, proposal, and proposal section levels. Win/capture strategy statements are global and apply to all aspects of the sales cycle.

As the owner of the win strategy, the capture manager or sales executive must ensure that the proposal strategy is aligned with the win strategy. If not, you confuse the customer.

Asking your proposal manager or proposal developers to develop a proposal strategy in the absence of a guiding win strategy is inefficient and reduces your win probability (Pwin). Review your win strategy with the proposal manager, and then ask the proposal manager to draft proposal strategy statements. After reviewing, improving, and approving the set of proposal strategy statements, ask the proposal manager to draft a series of supportive theme statements. A best practice is to develop a theme tree as a series of cascading theme statements that open major proposal sections.

The capture manager or sales executive should prepare a series of win strategy statements similar to the following example, which is an extension of the fourth item in figure 3, the ability to meet schedule.

WIN STRATEGY EXAMPLE	
WHAT:	• We will emphasize our ability to complete the design-build of a distribution center on time.
BY:	• Taking the customer on a plant tour of the XYZ distribution center in Orlando, FL. • Citing three other distribution centers completed on schedule during the past 5 years. • Providing contact names, phone numbers, and quotes verifying our on-time completion of three similar projects.

Given each win strategy statement, the proposal manager then prepares supportive, aligned proposal strategy statements. The capture manager or sales executive should review and approve proposal strategy statements, which are distributed to proposal writers/developers at the proposal kickoff meeting.

See THEME STATEMENTS, Proposal Guide.

ALIGNED PROPOSAL STRATEGY EXAMPLE	
WHAT:	• We will emphasize our ability to complete the design-build of a distribution center on time.
BY:	• Including in our proposal, photos of the XYZ distribution center in Orlando, FL. • Citing three other distribution centers (in a table) in our proposal, all listing the center, place, owner, promised completion date, and actual completion date. • Listing in our proposal, the contact names, phone numbers, and quotes verifying our on-time completion of three similar projects.

Section strategy statements (typically included in proposal storyboards or outlines) are more limited in scope but similar to proposal strategy statements in form, content, and implementation.

Strategy statements and theme statements are often confused. Strategy statements focus on what you plan to do to influence the customer. Strategy statements are internal, never seen by customers. Theme statements are words that you plan to say, orally or in writing, to influence the customer.

Shipley Capture Guide

A well-written proposal strategy statement helps the writer visualize how the strategy will appear on the page. For example, in a solicitation:

- "Describe" or "Discuss" implies text.
- "Show" implies a graphic or proof statement.
- "Include" implies a sketch, drawing, photo, table, flow chart, or graph.
- "Cite" or "Quote" implies evidence of validation.

Often proposal strategy statements and potential theme statements are prepared and distributed to section writers, to guide proposal messaging.

See SAMPLE TEMPLATE 3 for an example of a Strategy Statement Template.

Strategy statements are planning statements. Proposal strategy statements cite what a writer will do when preparing a proposal section. These statements are not actual text or graphics that will appear in the proposal. Customers only see or hear theme statements, one possible result of the strategy statement.

Strengths and weakness of you and competitors are based on customer perceptions, not your perceptions.

Increase theme statement effectiveness in the proposal by taking these actions:

- Assign each theme statement to one or more proposal sections.
- Challenge writers to use the theme statement as drafted or to improve it, usually by making it more specific.
- Confirm that the theme statement was used, improved, or not used because it was not accurate.

10 DEVELOP A SPECIFIC VALUE PROPOSITION FOR EACH OPPORTUNITY AND CUSTOMER.

After targeting and qualifying an opportunity and analyzing your position, freezing your solution is an important milestone. Delaying a solution freeze can result in:

- Members of the selling team presenting generic, vague, and unconvincing solutions to the customer in both presentations and proposals.
- Product and service specialists being compelled to prepare multiple solutions, so the quality of each solution and presentation declines.
- Customers being confused by the options, made uncomfortable with the seller's vacillation, and are generally not persuaded to select your solution.

Value propositions are a disciplined and quantitative way to present your solution and are used by some organizations in B2B selling environments. Sales professionals' presentations and proposals should link solution features to customer benefits. Fundamentally, a value proposition is the summation of the benefits of your solution minus the solution costs:

> Value proposition = Benefits of seller's solution − Cost

Having determined your solution, prepare value propositions for each type of buyer: economic buyer, users, and technical buyers.

Value propositions describe how your solution will improve the customer's business and how the improvement will be measured. Tailor value proposition(s) to each type of buying influence.

Comprehensive value propositions include the following elements and should be considered when developing your win strategy:

- Quantified business improvement
- Timing
- Solution
- Investment Cost
- Payback
- Results measurement and tracking

Develop value propositions collaboratively with the customer. *See* VALUE PROPOSITIONS. Collaboration increases the probability that the customer's organization will accept your quantitative analysis.

This sample value proposition targets the economic buyer:

Global Corporation will realize a $3,500,000 reduction in information technology support costs over the next 5 years, commencing May 1, 20XX, by contracting with Computer Heroes, at a cost of $2,000,000 per year. Global Corporation will be paid $500,000 for all of Global's IT assets, and Computer Heroes will provide all IT support. Global Corporation will enjoy a 30 percent annual reduction in IT costs, assuming the agreed prices and the same services currently required continue to be delivered. All costs will be posted and viewable online and documented in monthly invoices.

The value proposition, or total added value, is the sum of the benefits minus the purchase and implementation cost.

The over-arching value proposition is typically stated in the executive summary as part of the win strategy. If you state a quantified value proposition in the executive summary, consider organizing the executive summary around components of your value proposition. Any quantitative results or claims must be validated with evidence and proof.

Place supporting value propositions targeting the economic buyer, technical buyer, users, and contract managers in the relevant volume summary or major section summary.

11 CREATE A PRICE-TO-WIN STRATEGY TO DRIVE YOUR SOLUTION.

Price and the pricing-to-win approach are essential aspects of win strategy development and capture planning.

Historically, costing and pricing have been approached as separate, confidential, or proprietary issues. Numerous conflicts are implicit:

- Sales and marketing seek the lowest possible price.
- Technical people seek a technically safe price, knowing that technology is uncertain and requirements creep.
- Program managers seek a price that they can deliver, knowing some tasks will be omitted or underscoped.
- Pricers seek a price based on known prior costs.
- Management seeks a strong profit margin, low risk, and low investment.
- Customers seek a low, but realistic, price that is within their budget.

A conceptual view of acceptable price ranges to customers, competitors, and your organization is shown in figure 5 as the acceptable price-to-win window. The winning price is acceptable to the customer, acceptable to your organization, and less or unacceptable to competitors. You arrive at the price-to-win iteratively as you develop increasingly better data about the customer's perceptions, your cost and profit parameters, and the cost and profit parameters of competitors.

Analyze each competitor's acceptable price range by considering their prior pricing strategies. Organizations tend to repeat prior pricing strategies, especially strategies used on winning competitions. A price-to-win analysis without a competitor assessment is incomplete. Pricing to win and competitive assessments go hand in hand.

Figure 5. Conceptual View of Price to Win. *Arriving at the price-to-win window is a process of iteratively reducing the upper and lower limits of what is acceptable to customers, yourself, and competitors. The price to win should be considered when developing a win strategy.*

See PRICING TO WIN.

With various streamlined acquisitions and best-value procurements, customers sometimes vacillate between seeking a collaborative, integrated approach and insisting that bidders keep the technical/management solution entirely separate from the costing and pricing.

Embed cost and price-to-win considerations throughout your business development process, on par with solution development:

- Help the customer triangulate cost/price through should-cost models, cost as an independent variable (CAIV), and grass roots estimating.

- Maintain a consistent approach to costing and pricing across the program, beginning with an integrated set of assumptions to be used as the basis for estimates. Share these assumptions and subsequent changes across your team, including teaming partners when they impact their costs.

Price to win is a strategic management issue, not just a pricing issue. The winning price is not the sum of your estimated costs plus acceptable profit. If your cost plus acceptable profit exceeds your estimated price to win, you need to change your solution or not bid.

©Shipley Associates

12 USE TRADE-OFFS TO VALIDATE YOUR WINNING APPROACH AND GHOST THE COMPETITION.

Trade-offs show you have considered alternatives and selected the best solution for the customer. Instead of simply selecting the first option available or your usual approach, discussing trade-offs demonstrates that you considered the customer's needs, risks, budget, and offered a solution that offers best value at acceptable risk.

You ghost the competition when you raise the specter of competitors' potential weaknesses.

The primary way to downplay competitors' strengths and highlight their weaknesses is through ghosting. Never mention competitors by name. Instead, reject or create doubt about their approaches.

One of the advantages of ghosting is that you do not have to fully justify your position. You only create doubt, as shown in the following example:

We first thought a full design-build approach would be ideal, as it could shorten the time to completion by 3 months. However, with the lack of reliable data on the stability of the soil at the site and the potential for hazardous materials, we have proposed a full site characterization and analysis prior to design. Our conservative approach reduces the risk of construction interruptions and potentially more costly site remediation.

Figure 6 offers some additional ghosting approaches. Use ghosting judiciously. Overuse can annoy the customer.

COMPETITOR'S WEAKNESS	YOU STRESS
Safety problems	Cite your strong safety record. Offer industry averages for comparison.
Labor unrest	Emphasize the importance of a reliable workforce. Note that avoiding the cost of a strike justifies higher hourly wages.
High design cost	Emphasize low overheads and specific industry focus.
Poor reliability	Stress redundant design costs less than lost revenues from poor availability.
Extended downtime	Emphasize your local service center and built-in diagnostics.
Cost overruns	Cite the extra care taken in estimating, material selection, and purchasing.

Figure 6. Use Ghosting to Validate Your Approach and Support Your Win Strategy. *Plan your strategy carefully at the capture and proposal manager levels. Determine what approaches will be introduced for ghosting and where or when they will be raised.*

13 IMPLEMENT YOUR ACTION PLAN.

An effective win strategy always includes an action plan. Like other planning tasks, maintain a balance between strategy development and implementation.

Action planning should hold the capture team members accountable for specific tasks. Assign specific people to tasks with specific due dates. Figure 7 lists some of the reasons strategies are not implemented and suggests improved approaches.

WHY STRATEGIES ARE NOT IMPLEMENTED	IMPROVED APPROACHES
Win strategy actions are not assigned to a single, responsible individual.	Assign one person with resources and completion dates.
No consequence for failure to complete.	Establish regular capture plan (and win strategy) reviews.
Win strategy is regarded as confidential.	Communicate to all team members.
Win strategy is developed late.	Develop and review the win strategy after the pursuit decision. Extend the win strategy to a proposal strategy and distribute at proposal kickoff.
Proposal strategy not evident in drafts.	Use storyboards to flow strategy into sections. Always review drafts with the approved storyboards present.
Writers include unsupported claims.	Insist that all claims must be substantiated.

Figure 7. Improve Win Strategy Implementation. *Follow these recommendations to better implement your win strategy throughout the sales cycle. Balance the time spent planning versus implementing and hold team members accountable for actions and tasks.*

©*Shipley Associates*

SAMPLE TEMPLATES

Sample templates illustrate best practices and alternative approaches to capture planning tools and job aids. The sample templates contain capture planning-related documents in the *Capture Guide* and the *Proposal Guide.* None of the models are intended to be used as is. Use them to improve your understanding of capture planning principles and as a baseline to develop your own documents and tools.

These samples follow the guidelines discussed in this *Capture Guide* and the *Proposal Guide* as closely as possible.

The samples illustrate potential formats and tools used throughout the capture process. Some have been shortened or displayed in a reduced, thumbnail form to make this *Capture Guide* more compact.

The following suggestions will help you use these samples to improve your success when capture planning.

1. Focus on the principles and concepts rather than exact details. Adapt the format, content, and medium to your organization and selling environment.

2. The exact terms and phrases will vary by market and selling environment. Select words that are acceptable and known, and then define terms explicitly for users.

3. Read the notes and adaptation recommendations carefully. Guidelines are not rules, so use sound judgment when tailoring these documents and models.

4. Collect your own models from colleagues, through professional organizations, via industry conferences, and web sources.

5. Refine samples and templates regardless of the source. A best practice is to repeatedly amend and adapt your own documents to make them clearer, easier to use, and more applicable to the immediate opportunity.

SAMPLE TEMPLATES AND CHECKLISTS

1 Sample Capture Plan Template (PowerPoint)

2 Sample Capture Plan Template (Microsoft Word)

3 Win Strategy Statement Template

4 Capture Scheduling Example

5 Sales Letter: Follow-up Communication to Customer

6 Blue Team Review Forms (Strategy Review)

7 Black Hat Review Forms (Competition Review)

Capture plans evolve as new information is gathered and circumstances evolve. Adapt the medium and format, whether text, presentation, collaborative web site, or online database. Suggested modifications to the sample template format shown in this section apply equally to other media.

These sample capture plan templates are consistent with the one used in Shipley's Capture training workshop. The specific elements of these sample templates are starting points to develop a standard plan that meets your organization's needs and typical business opportunities. Augment or delete content for each opportunity. Adapt the style if your management prefers to see evidence of detailed reasoning and analysis.

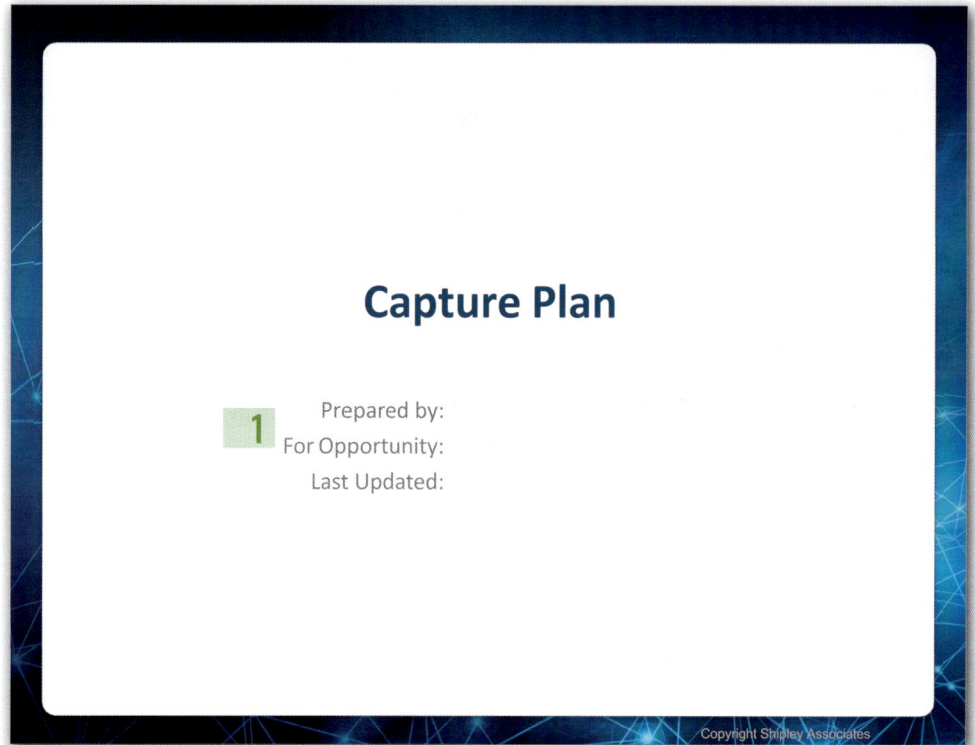

Capture Plan

1 Prepared by:
For Opportunity:
Last Updated:

Copyright Shipley Associates

1 Identify opportunity

- List preparer.
- Update frequently.
- Consider a system that highlights changes for those familiar with prior versions.

Summarize key program elements. Adapt the level of detail to the medium. If presented as a slide, use the Notes feature to add detail for individuals who cannot attend the briefing. Adapt or transfer information from the account plan, if available.

Create the capture plan executive summary after the rest of the plan is as complete as possible. Then update it frequently, at minimum, before each gate and color review. Repeat, support, and expand on executive summary items in the capture plan.

Note: Do not confuse the capture plan executive summary, shown here, with the proposal executive summary.

Executive Summary

Program Overview	
Customer Overview	
Competitive Position Summary	
Summary of Our Solution	
Capture Strategy	
Status	

Copyright Shipley Associates

1 Program Overview
- Summarize the services and products sought. Note the estimated contract value and duration.

2 Customer Overview
- Summarize key customer information.

3 Competitive Position Summary
- List and rank competitors from the customer's perspective.
- List incumbent(s) and teaming combinations, as applicable.
- Link rankings to the Bidder Comparison Chart.

4 Summary of Your Solution
- Outline major solution elements.
- Indicate the potential or actual team, as appropriate.

5 Capture Strategy
- List 3-5 over-arching approaches planned to position your organization and solution as the preferred option.

6 Status
- Summarize current capture efforts.
- Highlight near-term critical tasks, milestones, and required decisions.
- Update frequently.

1-SAMPLE CAPTURE PLAN TEMPLATE (POWERPOINT)

Describe what the customer wants to buy. Consider the Buying Cycle depicted in the top line of figure 2, COLOR TEAM REVIEWS. The customer's concept of the desired solution evolves over the buying cycle. A primary capture goal is to collaboratively shape the solution with the customer. The earlier you start in the buying cycle, the greater your opportunity to influence the preferred solution.

See CUSTOMER INTERFACE.

EXTERNAL ANALYSIS
Opportunity Description

Elements	Description
1 Customer	
2 Program Summary	
3 Key Requirements	
4 Deliverables	
5 Budget and Fiscal-Year Funding Profile	
6 Schedule	
7 Type of Contract	
8 Other: (Specify)	

Copyright Shipley Associates   2

1 Customer

- List the buying organization. Be specific, citing the agency, branch, division, or department. Cite the parent organization, if applicable.

2 Program Summary

- Summarize what is wanted, the customer's envisioned services and/or products.
- Cite the customer's vision and desired outcome: What problem is being solved, pain alleviated, or need satisfied?
- Cite program objectives, if available.

3 Key Requirements

- List requirements by category:
  - Technical
  - Management
  - Key personnel
  - Past performance
  - Cost/price, terms, warranties
  - Security
- Add or delete categories as appropriate.

4 Deliverables

- Services
- Products
- Data

5 Budget and Fiscal Year Funding Profile

- Amount
- Sources (who pays or has the budget)
- Types of funds
- Timing of funding

6 Schedule

- List known buying milestone dates:
  - Industry day
  - Bidders' conference
  - Site visits
  - Draft and final solicitation release
  - Question deadline
  - Proposal submittal
  - Oral presentations
  - Contract award
  - Project initiation
- Highlight near-term dates and update frequently.

7 Type of Contract

- List the type of contract.
- Note if a single or multiple award(s).
- Provide actual or estimated total contract value.

8 Other

- Cite special provisions (data rights ownership, warranties, performance warranties, bonding, insurance).
- Organizational conflict of interest.
- Small, minority, or disadvantaged business requirements.
- Specify contract value by time period.
- Identify length of contract and renewal options.

©Shipley Associates

Extend the customer profile from the account plan, when available. Add detail as you collaborate with the customer, vendors, and anyone who knows or offers information about the customer.

EXTERNAL ANALYSIS

Customer Profile

1 Organization and Key Personnel (stakeholders)	
2 Purchasing or Buying Process	
3 Evaluation Process	
4 Buying History and Trends	

Copyright Shipley Associates   3

1 Organization and Key Personnel

- Describe the organization. Insert or reference organization charts. Good general sources are often available on customers' websites.
- Ask customers to describe their internal structure, especially the immediate buying and user organizations.
- List key personnel.
- Classify personnel as decision makers, influencers, gatekeepers, or potential coaches.

2 Purchasing or Buying Process

- Outline the customer's buying process and how it is managed.
- Note the current position in the buying process.

3 Evaluation Process

- Describe or diagram evaluation steps.
- Link dates to the steps.
- Name and describe probable evaluators.
- List potential evaluation criteria.

4 Buying History and Trends

- List similar purchases made by this organization or individuals who might influence the purchase decision.
- List key parameters of those purchases: program name, location, value, common elements, winners, losing bidders, publicly and privately stated reasons for the selection, and outcomes (performance, schedule, quality, and cost compliance).

1-SAMPLE CAPTURE PLAN TEMPLATE (POWERPOINT)

Hot button issues comprise key customer motivators and concerns or worry items. Record the exact words that you hear repeatedly in conversations or see repeatedly in documents. Substituting terms that you are more comfortable with borders on arrogance or suggests that you are not listening. Guard against citing generally agreed industry lore that is outdated, generic, or not linked to this customer.

EXTERNAL ANALYSIS

Hot Button Issues

1 Hot Button Issues	**2** Background Information / Decision Maker

Copyright Shipley Associates   4

1 Hot Button Issues

- List the most critical issues that will influence the buying decision.

2 Background

- Identify key decision makers.
- Cite the desired future state. Why is this an issue?
- What are the consequences or costs of the current state?

©Shipley Associates

Your competitors' past marketing strategies and approaches are often the best indicators of how they will approach a new opportunity. Predicting what they will do in a particular case is almost impossible unless you have an ongoing and effective competitive intelligence process. Maintain a knowledge base about your competitors' past activities to mine for insights on new capture efforts.

Complete competitor intelligence templates for each competitor. Duplicate capture plan pages if the number of competitors exceeds those in your template.

EXTERNAL ANALYSIS

Competitor Intelligence – Competitor A

Market Approach and Position	
Products and/or Services	
Historical Pricing Patterns	
Business Development	
Customer Relationship	
Relevant Experience	
Past Performance	

Copyright Shipley Associates   5

1 Market Approach and Position

- Indicate focus by job size, customer, and geography.
- Indicate position as leader, follower, new entrant, specialty provider, etc.
- Indicate commitment to the market, importance of this opportunity to future success, and linked or ongoing related work. What is the impact of a loss or no-bid?
- Note how aggressively and flexibly they have pursued similar opportunities.

2 Products and/or Services

- List which services/products are likely to be offered and the source.
- List required adaptations to make them compliant.
- Note if subcontractors or teaming partners are required or probable.

3 Historical Pricing Patterns

- Note if they tend to offer high or low prices.
- Note if they prefer or avoid specific contract vehicles, such as fixed price, cost-plus, performance-based, etc.

4 Business Development

- List typical marketing messages, themes, positioning, and claimed differentiators.
- Note who is involved by name; note the number, type, and experience of management and support staff.
- Note the relative power of management versus individual capture managers or account managers.
- If they contract for site representation, note the role, influence, and effectiveness of this site representative versus direct employees.
- Note if they team and how they integrate teaming partners in selling, strategy development, solution development, and program management. List preferred teaming partners by name or type.

1-SAMPLE CAPTURE PLAN TEMPLATE (POWERPOINT)

5 Customer Relationship

- Does this customer know the organization, division, and management team well? Is it a positive, neutral, or negative perception?

- List personal links or history among individuals in the competitor and customer organization. Have they worked for common organizations or on common projects? Are they linked through professional organizations or common interests?

6 Relevant Experience

- List relevant experience. Relevance might be via common issues, services, people, or products.

7 Past Performance

- Link past performance to prior relevant experience examples, if available. Note how they performed on similar work. Quantitative performance data is difficult to obtain, so cite the source. The most credible performance data to this customer will be about jobs performed for this customer.

- Cite generally accepted industry data for perspective or when actual performance data is not available.

©Shipley Associates

Evaluate each potential competitor based on what the customer is likely to know or believe, not just what you think is true. Customer perceptions are paramount, even when wrong.

Complete competitor intelligence templates for each competitor.

EXTERNAL ANALYSIS

Competitor Intelligence – Competitor A

Customer Perceptions	1 Strengths	2 Weaknesses
	▪ ▪ ▪ ▪ ▪	▪ ▪ ▪ ▪ ▪

3 Customer Issues	4 Available Solution	5 Discriminator	6 Solution Gap

Copyright Shipley Associates   6

1 Strengths
- List known strengths relevant to this opportunity.
- List customer-perceived strengths, even if not real.

2 Weaknesses
- List known weaknesses relevant to this opportunity.
- List customer-perceived weaknesses, even if not real.

3 Customer Issues
- Use the hot button issues listed on the Customer Issues and Hot Buttons page.
- Use the same hot button list for all competitors.

4 Available Solution
- List the probable solution available from this competitor to satisfy each hot button.

5 Discriminator
- List potential discriminator(s). Discriminators are features that: (1) Differ from at least one of the features of competitors' solutions, and (2) Are linked to this customer issue.

6 Solution Gap
- List the difference between the requirement and available solution.
- Gaps can be positive or negative. Note that both positive and negative gaps usually have compensating consequences. For example, a solution that does not meet the capability requirement (negative gap) might cost less (positive gap).

1-SAMPLE CAPTURE PLAN TEMPLATE (POWERPOINT)

Apply the same approach to analyze your position as applied to analyzing your competitors. Guard against bias by seeking input from customer coaches, former employees, industry veterans, and people from your organization.

EXTERNAL ANALYSIS

Our Own Competitive Position

1 Market Approach and Position	
2 Products and/or Services	
3 Historical Pricing Patterns	
4 Business Development	
5 Customer Relationship	
6 Relevant Experience	
7 Past Performance	

Copyright Shipley Associates   11

1 Market Approach and Position

- Indicate your focus by job size, customer, and geography.
- Indicate your position as leader, follower, new entrant, specialty provider, etc.
- Indicate your commitment, importance of this job to your success, and linked or ongoing potential. What is the impact of a loss or no-bid?
- Note how aggressively and flexibly you have pursued similar opportunities.

2 Products and/or Services

- List services, products, and the source that comprise your base offering.
- List adaptations needed to make them compliant.
- Note if subcontractors or teaming partners are required or probable.

3 Historical Pricing Patterns

- Note if your prices are perceived to be high or low. Is that perception accurate?
- Note if you prefer or avoid specific contract vehicles, such as fixed price, cost-plus, performance-based, etc.

4 Business Development

- List your typical marketing messages, themes, positions, and claimed differentiators.
- Note who is involved by name. Note the number, type, and experience of management and support staff.
- Note the relative power of management versus individual capture manager or account managers.
- If you use contract site representatives, note the role and influence of the site representatives versus direct employees.
- If you team, note how you plan to integrate teaming partners in selling, strategy development, solution development, and program management. List preferred teaming partners by name or type.

5 Customer Relationship

- Does this customer know your organization, division, and management team well? Is the perception positive, neutral, or negative?

- List any personal links or history among individuals in your organization and the customer organization. Have these individuals worked for common organizations or on common projects? Are they linked through professional organizations or common interests?

6 Relevant Experience

- List relevant experience. Relevance might be via common issues, services, people, or products.

7 Past Performance

- Link past performance to prior relevant experience examples, if available. Note how you performed on similar work.

1-SAMPLE CAPTURE PLAN TEMPLATE (POWERPOINT)

Base evaluation of your competitive position on customer perceptions rather than internal assumptions or beliefs. When selling, the customer's perceptions are paramount, even if the customer is wrong.

EXTERNAL ANALYSIS

Our Own Competitive Position

Customer Perceptions	**1** Strengths		**2** Weaknesses	
	• • • •		• • • •	
3 Customer Issues	**4** Available Solution	**5** Discriminator	**6** Solution Gap	

Copyright Shipley Associates   12

1 Strengths

- List your real strengths relevant to this opportunity.
- List customer-perceived strengths, even if not real.

2 Weaknesses

- List your known weaknesses relevant to this opportunity.
- List customer-perceived weaknesses, even if not real.

3 Customer Issues

- Use the same list as was used when analyzing competitors.

4 Available Solution

- List your probable solution for each hot button issue.

5 Discriminator

- List potential discriminator(s). Discriminators are features that: (1) Differ from at least one of the competitor's solutions, and (2) Are linked to this customer issue.

6 Solution Gap

- List the difference between the requirement and your available solution.
- Gaps can be positive or negative. Positive and negative gaps usually have compensating consequences.

©Shipley Associates

Complete a Bidder Comparison Chart based on the prior competitive analysis. Complete this comparison for every opportunity, regardless of size.

Collaborate with the capture team to gather unbiased data.

1 **Issues**

- Use the same list of issues from prior competitive analysis.
- Update your analysis regularly.
- List all issues before moving to subsequent columns.

2 **Weight**

- Establish weights based on customer-perceived relative importance.
- Consider the following weighting scheme: 1 = needed; 2 = important; 3 = most important. Other scales are acceptable if you have the knowledge to satisfactorily differentiate importance of issues to the customer.

3 **Points**

- Rank your organization and each competitor on a consistent scale.
- Here is a potential scale to rank your position and competitors' positions:
  - 1–2 = Problem area. Must be improved. Grounds for elimination.
  - 3–4 = Needs improvement. Cause for concern. Negative trend.
  - 5–6 = Average. Adequate. O.K. if customer is seeking marginally compliant solution.
  - 7–8 = Better than average. Strong performance.
  - 9–10 = Substantially exceeds requirements or expectations.

4 **Score**

- Multiply the weight by the points for the issue score.

5 **Totals**

- Total the columns.
- Compare the relative totals. Do they make sense? If not, are you missing an issue? Is the issue weighting too high or too low?
- Avoid changing weights and rankings to get the desired result.
- Review with a knowledgeable, independent authority, if possible.
- Use the Bidder Comparison results to drive win strategy development.

1-SAMPLE CAPTURE PLAN TEMPLATE (POWERPOINT)

This page summarizes your ongoing price-to-win analysis. The overall approach is to bound the winning price into a successively narrower range.

See PRICING TO WIN.

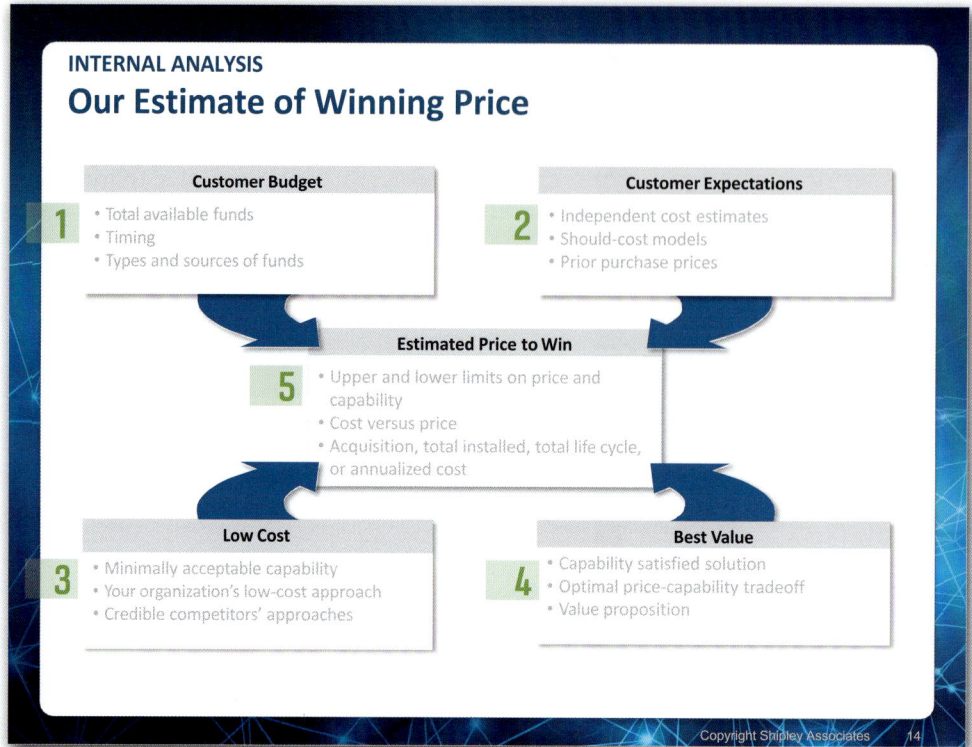

INTERNAL ANALYSIS

Our Estimate of Winning Price

Customer Budget
1
- Total available funds
- Timing
- Types and sources of funds

Customer Expectations
2
- Independent cost estimates
- Should-cost models
- Prior purchase prices

Estimated Price to Win
5
- Upper and lower limits on price and capability
- Cost versus price
- Acquisition, total installed, total life cycle, or annualized cost

Low Cost
3
- Minimally acceptable capability
- Your organization's low-cost approach
- Credible competitors' approaches

Best Value
4
- Capability satisfied solution
- Optimal price-capability tradeoff
- Value proposition

Copyright Shipley Associates   14

---

1 Customer Budget

- Summarize the customer's available budget for the purchase, not total budget for the project. The purchase budget excludes acquisition and internal implementation costs.

- Consider budget timing and cash flow.

- Note the type and source of funds, when relevant (capital investment, operational, budgeted, requested in future budgets).

2 Customer Expectations

- Consider independent cost estimates by the customer or consultants.

- Apply should-cost or parametric pricing models.

- Determine prior purchase prices by this customer for similar products or services.

3 Low Cost

- Identify and price the minimally acceptable capability.

- Determine the lowest cost approach for your organization.

- Consider how competitors could achieve lower prices.

4 Best Value

- Conduct a price-capability trade-off to estimate the customer's willingness to pay more for additional capability. A customer will sometimes pay a margin above a minimum-capability solution's price, but usually no more than 10–15 percent.

- Create a value proposition tailored to the customer's needs. Include a quantified business benefit, timing, and costs of the benefits, a calculated payback period, and methods for measuring results.

5 Estimated Price to Win

- Identify and price the capability-satisfied solution.

- List the customer's probable upper and lower price limits at desired, specified, acceptable, and minimum capability levels. What price is too low to be credible or too high to be affordable?

- Note whether the customer has the flexibility to accept solutions below the specified capability.

- Does the customer care about your perceived margins and underlying cost, or only total price?

- Does the price-to-win need to consider costs/prices in special ways to satisfy the customer, such as total installed, lifecycle, or annualized costs/prices?

©Shipley Associates

1-SAMPLE CAPTURE PLAN TEMPLATE (POWERPOINT)

Extend the Bidder Comparison Chart (BCC) into the Integrated Solution Worksheet (ISW) to outline the parameters of your technical and management solution. Then define the strategy and tactics needed to position your solution as the preferred solution.

The BCC and ISW are the two most important analysis tools in the capture plan.

INTERNAL ANALYSIS
Our Technical/Management Solution

Shipley Associates   Integrated Solution Worksheet

Item No.	Customer Issues	Customer Requirements	Available Solution	Gap	Competitor Solution	Discriminators	Strategy	Action Required
1	2	3	4	5	6	7	8

Copyright Shipley Associates   15

1 Customer Issues
- Transfer the issues listed on the Bidder Comparison Chart.

2 Customer Requirements
- List known or probable requirements linked to customer issues.
- If you see issues without corresponding requirements, consider what might be required.
- If you see requirements without corresponding issues, consider:
  - Have you missed potential issues?
  - Have you erroneously persuaded yourself that something you hope to sell is needed or wanted by this customer? Do you have a solution in search of a customer?

3 Available Solution
- List what you have available now.
- Update as you develop or refine your solution as requirements evolve.

4 Gap
- Note the difference between what is required and your available solution, whether positive or negative. This gap becomes a potential discriminator.

5 Competitor Solution
- List the best competitor's probable solution to each requirement.

6 Discriminators
- List features of your solution that differ from the features of one or more of the competitors' solutions.
- The more important the issue and the greater the difference, the more important the discriminator.

7 Strategy
- List the potential positions that you might take to:
  - Emphasize your strengths.
  - Mitigate your weaknesses.
  - Neutralize competitors' strengths.
  - Highlight competitors' weaknesses.

8 Action Required
- List potential tactical actions that help persuade the customer to accept your strategy or position.
- Because space is limited, expand these actions later when preparing detailed strategy implementation action plans.
- Listing a potential tactic does not commit you to take the action. Implement only those actions that will have the greatest impact within the parameters of your resources, schedule, and the rules of the competition.

1-SAMPLE CAPTURE PLAN TEMPLATE (POWERPOINT)

Specify the composition of your team. Defined broadly, the team might comprise multiple divisions or departments of the same organization, a joint-venture arrangement, or a prime, subcontractors, and various vendors. Some teams include elements of the customer's organization on an ongoing basis or in transition, as in an outsourcing arrangement where the winner takes over an existing function, personnel, and facilities.

Note: Work share negotiations are sensitive, often delayed, and frequently lead to conflicts and pricing errors (both over- and under-pricing). Primes seldom want agreed work shares, while subcontractors seek written contractual commitments.

INTERNAL ANALYSIS

Teaming and Subcontracting

Partner	Role and Work Share	Rationale
1	**2**	**3**

Copyright Shipley Associates   16

1 Partner

- List the organization and points of contact.

2 Role and Work Share

- List their role and agreed work share, if any.
- Document any agreements.
- Include role and workshare for proposal development.

3 Rationale

- Indicate why each teaming partner was selected from the prime's perspective. Possible rationales include:
  - Solicitation requirement
  - Gap in your solution (technical, price, support advantage)
  - Meeting small, minority, or disadvantaged business contracting goals
  - Unique technical or management skills
  - Positive position with the customer
  - Currently on incumbent's team
  - Recommended or requested by the customer
  - Eliminate them from competitors' teams
- Conversely, indicate why the teaming partners either selected or agreed to team with the prime. Use these justifications to position your team as the preferred team.

©Shipley Associates

Strategy statements in a capture plan comprise two elements:

Your desired position: your goal, how you want to be perceived by the customer.

The tactical actions that you will take to improve your position with the customer.

When fully defined in action plans, the tactical actions specify who takes the actions and when they will be taken.

Later, when you begin planning your proposal, you will convert capture strategy statements into proposal strategy statements. The goals will be the same, but the tactical implementation will be about things written or displayed in a verbal presentation; thus, persuading the customer to accept your position.

See WIN STRATEGY DEVELOPMENT.

The first two strategy-development pages are specific to your strengths and weaknesses. The second two reflect competitors' strengths and weaknesses. Often they overlap, as emphasizing your strength often simultaneously high-lights a competitor's weakness.

STRATEGY DEVELOPMENT
Leverage Our Strength

We will leverage our strength in:	By taking these actions:	To achieve:
POSITION	*TACTICS*	*IMPROVED POSITION*

STRATEGY DEVELOPMENT
Mitigate Our Weakness

We will mitigate our weakness in:	By taking these actions:	To achieve:
POSITION	*TACTICS*	*IMPROVED POSITION*

STRATEGY DEVELOPMENT
Exploit Competitor's Weakness

We will exploit our competitor's weakness in:	By taking these actions:	To achieve:
POSITION	*TACTICS*	*IMPROVED POSITION*

STRATEGY DEVELOPMENT
Neutralize Competitor's Strength

We will neutralize our competitor's strength in:	By taking these actions:	To achieve:
POSITION	*TACTICS*	*IMPROVED POSITION*
POSITION	*TACTICS*	*IMPROVED POSITION*
POSITION	*TACTICS*	*IMPROVED POSITION*
POSITION	*TACTICS*	*IMPROVED POSITION*

Copyright Shipley Associates   20

1-SAMPLE CAPTURE PLAN TEMPLATE (POWERPOINT)

The analysis and planning process documented in a capture plan is useless until action is taken. Assigning positioning actions, assessing outcomes, and then adapting subsequent tasks based upon results are the essential role of the capture manager.

One key difference between typical roles of a capture manager and sales professional is that a capture manager coordinates the positioning activities of a large capture team, often including senior management personnel. Most sales professionals focus primarily on individual selling tasks, with less emphasis on managing others to participate in the positioning or selling.

Action plans specify activities to be performed, objectives to be met, assigned personnel, deadlines, locations, costs, and status. Contingencies should be anticipated, and risks must be characterized and mitigated. Adjust the format and content of action plans to circumstances of the opportunity and task management practices of the organization. Use existing scheduling and task management tools to manage capture activities, which are really just important organizational projects.

The sample action plans shown include representative entries. The level of detail shown is usually adequate for management review. Capture team members usually need more detailed information to successfully meet task objectives.

ACTION PLANS
Customer Contact Plan

Contact Objective	Who	When	Where	Cost	Status/ Comments
Initial capability briefing to customer's chief engineer	M. Johnson	April 1, 20XX	DOT Test Laboratory	$1,800 Travel	Delayed till May 15

ACTION PLANS
Intelligence Collection Plan

Intelligence Objective	Who	Need Date	How	Cost	Status/ Comments
Determine funding level for next FY budget	DC Staff	March 15, 20XX	Talk to congr. staff	None (OH)	On track

ACTION PLANS
Our Contingency Plan

Event	Probability	Impact	Response	Status/ Comments
Preferred vendor will not team	Low	Medium	Manufacture parts in-house	Pilot production completed

ACTION PLANS
Solution Development Plan (if required)

Solution Element	Who	Need Date	Cost	Status/ Comments
Demonstrate 1GB/sec autonomous data transfer rate	Dept. H1610	Sept. 15, 20XX	$75K (IR&D)	Auto-synch may delay

Copyright Shipley Associates 24

©Shipley Associates

Include attachments appropriate to your organization. These items might be physically attached or shown as electronic links to a secure website. If you prefer, incorporate them into the body of the capture plan. The list shown in the sample is illustrative but not exhaustive. In general, the largest opportunities will require the most additional information.

EXECUTION AND MONITORING

Capture Plan Attachments

- Capture team organization chart
- Schedule (if needed to augment action plans)
  - Kickoff meeting
  - Management reviews
  - Key milestones from action plans
- Budget (in required corporate format)
- Decision gate review template
- Business and win potential
- Resource plan
- Capture briefing template
- Draft executive summary of proposal

Copyright Shipley Associates   26

2-SAMPLE CAPTURE PLAN TEMPLATE (MICROSOFT WORD)

The same capture plan information shown in presentation form in Sample Template 1 can be maintained using Microsoft Word. The gray text within the document provides instructions on how to use each section.

ShipleyAssociates **Opportunity Planner:** *Information, Analysis, & Strategy*

1.0 CAPTURE/OPPORTUNITY

Opportunity Name	Customer Name	Capture/Opportunity Manager
Enter opportunity name	Enter name of specific buying entity	Enter name of selling entity lead

2.0 OPPORTUNITY DESCRIPTION

Opportunity Summary
Describe what is wanted, the customer's envisioned services and/or products, what problem is being solved or pain alleviated, and objectives if known

Opportunity Value
Enter the estimated total value of the opportunity

Key Requirements
List the requirements by category: technical, management, key personnel, past performance, terms, warranties, security, etc.

Deliverables
List services, products, data, etc.

Opportunity Milestones
Identify start, length of contract, renewal options

Buying Schedule
List known buying milestone dates: industry day, bidders' conference, site visits, draft and final bid request release, Q & A deadline, proposal submittal, oral presentation, contract award

3.0 CUSTOMER OVERVIEW

Organization
Describe the organization

Decision-Makers/Influencers

Name	Role	Hot Buttons/Major Issues
	Classify personnel as decision makers, influencers, gatekeepers, or potential coaches	Track hot buttons, issues, and needs; nuances
(Add rows as needed)		

Evaluation Process
Describe evaluation steps, name and describe probable evaluators, list evaluation criteria

Buying History and Trends
List similar purchases made by this organization or individuals who might influence the purchase decision. List key parameters of those purchases including program name, location, value, common elements, winners, losing bidders, publicly and privately stated reasons for the selection (performance, schedule, quality, cost)

Hot Button/Issue/Evidence/Impact

Hot Button/Issue or Problem	Evidence	Impact
List issue or problem that customer wants to solve	Explain **how the issue or problem shows up**--identify metrics that need to change	Describe, and quantify if possible, the **impact** to the customer
(Add rows as needed)		

*Shipley*Associates — **Opportunity Planner:** *Information, Analysis, & Strategy*

4.0 COMPETITOR ASSESSMENT

[Name of Competitor A]

Summarize their market approach, historical pricing patterns, and estimated price-to-win

Strengths	Weaknesses
List customer-perceived strengths, even if not real	List customer-perceived weaknesses, even if not real

Probable Solution to be Offered	Solution Gaps
List which services/products are likely to be offered and the source, any required adaptations to make them compliant, and any likely subcontracting or teaming	List any potential gaps in the competitor's likely solution

Discriminators
List potential discriminators this competitor may offer. Discriminators are benefits sought by the customer and only available from the competitor.

[Name of Competitor B]

Summarize their market approach, historical pricing patterns, and estimated price-to-win

Strengths	Weaknesses
List customer-perceived strengths, even if not real	List customer-perceived weaknesses, even if not real

Probable Solution to be Offered	Solution Gaps
List which services/products are likely to be offered and the source, any required adaptations to make them compliant, and any likely subcontracting or teaming	List any potential gaps in the competitor's likely solution

Discriminators
List potential discriminators this competitor may offer. Discriminators are benefits sought by the customer and only available from the competitor.

[Name of Competitor C]

Summarize their market approach, historical pricing patterns, and estimated price-to-win

Strengths	Weaknesses
List customer-perceived strengths, even if not real	List customer-perceived weaknesses, even if not real

Probable Solution to be Offered	Solution Gaps
List which services/products are likely to be offered and the source, any required adaptations to make them compliant, and any likely subcontracting or teaming	List any potential gaps in the competitor's likely solution

Discriminators
List potential discriminators this competitor may offer. Discriminators are benefits sought by the customer and only available from the competitor.

Summarize our approach and track record in this market

Strengths	Weaknesses
List customer-perceived strengths, even if not real	List customer-perceived weaknesses, even if not real

Technical/Management Solution	Solution Gaps
List which services/products we are likely to offer and the source, any required adaptations to make them compliant, and any likely subcontracting or teaming	List any potential gaps in our conceptual solution

Discriminators
List potential discriminators our solution provides--discriminators are benefits sought by the customer and only available from us

Experience and Past Performance
List relevant experience and indicate the quality of our past performance

Key Personnel
List key personnel to be proposed on this opportunity

Price To Win

Maximum Budget	Addressable Budget	Minimum Credible Budget	Cost of Minimum Acceptable Capability	Cost of Maximum Justifiable Capability
Maximum amount the customer has budgeted	Amount customer has available after deducting expenses from budget	The amount below which the customer doubts the credibility of obtaining an acceptable solution	Cost of the minimum capability acceptable to the customer	Cost of the maximum capability that the customer can justify

2-SAMPLE CAPTURE PLAN TEMPLATE (MICROSOFT WORD)

ShipleyAssociates   **Opportunity Planner:** *Information, Analysis, & Strategy*

6.0 BIDDER COMPARISON

Issues Add rows as needed	Weight 3 = Most Important	Us 10 = High		Competitor A		Competitor B		Competitor C		Death Star Worst case competitor	
		Points	**Score**	**Points**	**Score**	**Points**	**Score**	**Points**	**Score**	**Points**	**Score**
Issue title	1 - 3	1-10	Wt x Pts								

7.0 WIN STRATEGY

Leverage Our Strength In:	By Taking These Actions:	To Achieve:
Based on bidder comparison, list a position of strength	Name an action we will take—begin with verb	Describe the improved position we will achieve by taking the action
(Add rows as needed)		

Mitigate Our Weakness In:	By Taking These Actions:	To Achieve:
Based on bidder comparison, list a position of weakness	Name an action we will take—begin with verb	Describe the improved position we will achieve by taking the action
(Add rows as needed)		

Neutralize Our Competitors' Strength In:	By Taking These Actions:	To Achieve:
Based on bidder comparison, list a competitor's position of strength	Name an action we will take—begin with verb	Describe the improved position we will achieve by taking the action
(Add rows as needed)		

Exploit Our Competitors' Weakness In:	By Taking These Actions:	To Achieve:
Based on bidder comparison, list a competitor's position of weakness	Name an action we will take—begin with verb	Describe the improved position we will achieve by taking the action
(Add rows as needed)		

8.0 STRATEGIC POSITIONING PLAN

Leveraging Strengths To Improve Our Position

Action	Who	When	Resulting Feature(s)	Associated Benefit(s)	Discriminator
Copy from "By Taking These Actions" column in Section 7.0, *Win Strategy*	Enter name of person assigned	Enter completion date	List new features gained by completing the action	Describe the benefits to the customer provided by the new feature(s)	Are these benefits only available from us? Y/N
[Add rows as needed]					

Mitigating Weaknesses To Improve Our Position

Action	Who	When	Resulting Feature(s)	Associated Benefit(s)	Discriminator
Copy from "By Taking These Actions" column in Section 7.0, *Win Strategy*	Enter name of person assigned	Enter completion date	List new features gained by completing the action	Describe the benefits to the customer provided by the new feature(s)	Are these benefits only available from us? Y/N
[Add rows as needed]					

Neutralizing Competitors' Strengths To Improve Our Position

Action	Who	When	Resulting Feature(s)	Associated Benefit(s)	Discriminator
Copy from "By Taking These Actions" column in Section 7.0, *Win Strategy*	Enter name of person assigned	Enter completion date	List new features gained by completing the action	Describe the benefits to the customer provided by the new feature(s)	Are these benefits only available from us? Y/N
[Add rows as needed]					

Exploiting Competitors' Weakness To Improve Our Position

Action	Who	When	Resulting Feature(s)	Associated Benefit(s)	Discriminator
Copy from "By Taking These Actions" column in Section 7.0, *Win Strategy*	Enter name of person assigned	Enter completion date	List new features gained by completing the action	Describe the benefits to the customer provided by the new feature(s)	Are these benefits only available from us? Y/N
[Add rows as needed]					

©Shipley Associates

*Shipley*Associates

Opportunity Planner: *Information, Analysis, & Strategy*

9.0 INTELLIGENCE COLLECTION PLAN
Maintaining Vigilance on the Opportunity

Intelligence Objective	Source(s)	Who	When	Findings
Describe the intelligence we need to gather or monitor	List possible sources of intelligence	Enter name of person assigned	Enter date the intelligence is needed to be useful	Enter or update the intelligence gained
[Add rows as needed]				

10.0 SOLUTION DEVELOPMENT PLAN
Developing a Validated Customer Solution and a Winning Team

Solution Element	Potential Gap	Action(s) To Close Gap	When	Who
Describe how we will solve the customer's problems and resolve issues	List any weakness or gap in our solution	Enter the actions to take to close the gap and validate the solution with the customer	Enter date the gap must be closed	Enter name of person assigned
[Add rows as needed]				

11.0 CONTINGENCY PLAN
Preparing for Changing Circumstances

Potential Event	Probability	Impact	Contingency Response	Who
Describe an event that could affect our positioning	High/Medium /Low	High/Medium /Low	Describe the action(s) to be taken if the potential event occurs	Enter name of person assigned
[Add rows as needed]				

12.0 CUSTOMER CALL PLAN

Point of Contact, Contact Info	Who	When	Purpose of the Call	
			What is the next decision the customer needs to make?	
			Questions to Ask	**Answers to Your Questions**
	Name of person who will call	Due date	List questions you want to ask the customer	Include answers to your questions asked
			Questions the Customer May Ask You	**Answers to Questions Asked**
			List questions the customer may ask	How will you respond to questions asked?

ShipleyAssociates

STRATEGY STATEMENT TEMPLATE

This template is used to organize and communicate the specific actions that comprise our win strategy. These statements improve the focus of the Capture Team and our reviewers on discriminating our proposal from those of our competitors.

Strategies to Leverage Our Strengths
We will **leverage our strength** in [Specify] by taking the following action(s): [List Specific Action(s)] …to achieve: [list objectives]
We will leverage our strength in [Specify] by taking the following action(s): [List Specific Action(s)] …to achieve: [list objectives]
We will leverage our strength in [Specify] by taking the following action(s): [List Specific Action(s)] …to achieve: [list objectives]
We will leverage our strength in [Specify] by taking the following action(s): [List Specific Action(s)] …to achieve: [list objectives]

See WIN STRATEGY DEVELOPMENT.

ShipleyAssociates

STRATEGY STATEMENT TEMPLATE

We will **mitigate our weakness** in [Specify] by taking the following action(s): [List Specific Action(s)] …to achieve: [list objectives]
We will mitigate our weakness in [Specify] by taking the following action(s): [List Specific Action(s)] …to achieve: [list objectives]
We will mitigate our weakness in [Specify] by taking the following action(s): [List Specific Action(s)] …to achieve: [list objectives]
We will mitigate our weakness in [Specify] by taking the following action(s): [List Specific Action(s)] …to achieve: [list objectives]

©Shipley Associates

ShipleyAssociates

STRATEGY STATEMENT TEMPLATE

Strategies to Take Advantage of Competitor Weaknesses

We will **exploit our competitor's weakness** in [Specify] by taking the following action(s):
[List Specific Action(s)]

...to achieve:
[list objectives]

We will exploit our competitor's weakness in [Specify] by taking the following action(s):
[List Specific Action(s)]

...to achieve:
[list objectives]

We will exploit our competitor's weakness in [Specify] by taking the following action(s):
[List Specific Action(s)]

...to achieve:
[list objectives]

We will exploit our competitor's weakness in [Specify] by taking the following action(s):
[List Specific Action(s)]

...to achieve:
[list objectives]

ShipleyAssociates

STRATEGY STATEMENT TEMPLATE

Strategies to Neutralize Competitor Strengths

We will **neutralize our competitor's strength** in [Specify] by taking the following action(s):
[List Specific Action(s)]

...to achieve:
[list objectives]

We will neutralize our competitor's strength in [Specify] by taking the following action(s):
[List Specific Action(s)]

...to achieve:
[list objectives]

We will neutralize our competitor's strength in [Specify] by taking the following action(s):
[List Specific Action(s)]

...to achieve:
[list objectives]

We will neutralize our competitor's strength in [Specify] by taking the following action(s):
[List Specific Action(s)]

...to achieve:
[list objectives]

1 Title your schedule.

2 List key activities and milestones

3 Map your schedule based on expected RFP date.

4 Show critical milestones such as meetings or deadlines.

5 Show estimated time to complete tasks.

1 Capture Schedule and Milestones

Capture Activity **2**	**3** Apr-20	May-20	Jun-20	Jul-20	Aug-20	Sep-20	Oct-20	Nov-20
OSG & Market Research	■							
Govt Sales Partner Strategy Complete	◆							
CEO / CEO Meeting	◆ **4**							
Research Govt Sales CRM Opportunity	■							
Build Relationship with Client	■■■■■■■■■■■■■							
Proof of Concept / Demo Prep	■							
Demo Presentation		◆						
Proposal Creation - Govt Sales CRM		■						
Govt Sales Prop Submission		◆						
White Paper #1 - CRM Replacement		■ ◆						
Award of Govt Sales CRM				◆				
Draft RFP - CRM Replacement						◆		
Review / Submit Comments on DRFP						■ ◆		
Final RFP - CRM Replacement							◆ **5**	
Proposal Creation - CRM Replacement							■	
Award of OSG CRM Replacement								◆
Project Start								◆

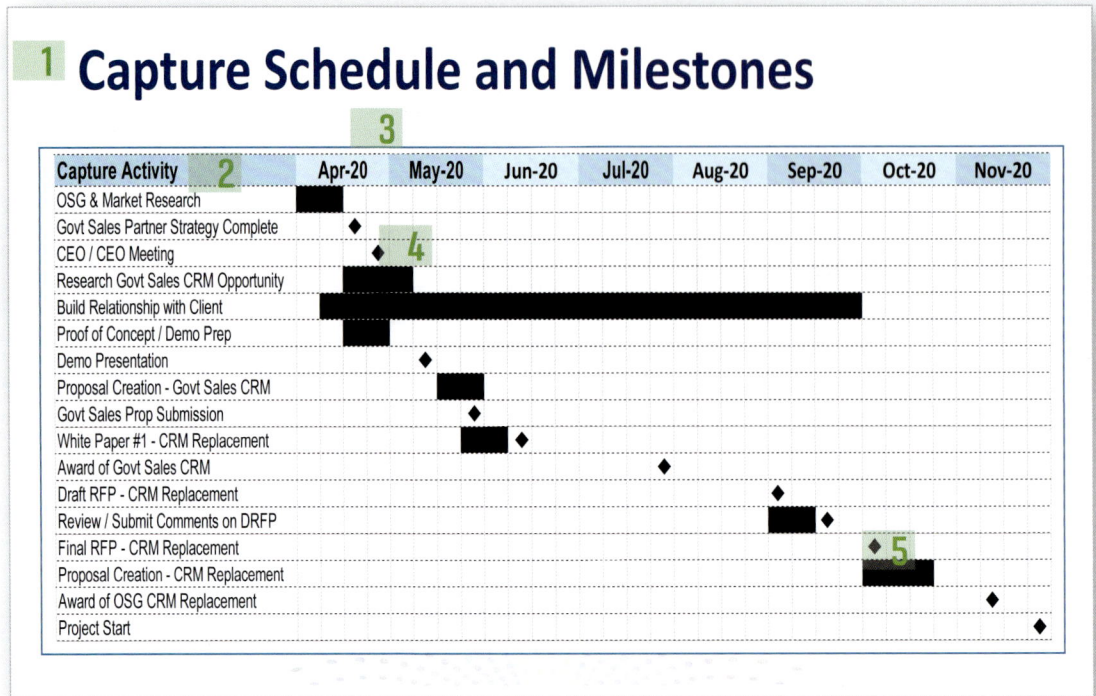

Schedule key capture activities and assign individuals to specific tasks. A schedule helps manage accountability.

©Shipley Associates

1 The informative subject line begins with a signal word, Invitation, that signals the writer's objective, then states what and why. The why is an anticipated benefit to the customer.

2 Capitalizing only the first word in a title is an acceptable and increasingly common practice. Select a style and use it consistently in the same document.

See HEADINGS, Proposal Guide.

3 The short setup refers to and summarizes a previous conversation.

See SALES COMMUNICATION.

4 The customer's issues are stated and ownership is explicit.

See CUSTOMER FOCUS, Proposal Guide.

5 Both subheadings mirror the issues in the introduction.

See SALES LETTERS.

6 Note how most paragraphs begin by referring to the customer, improving the overall customer focus of the letter. Benefits are stated before features.

See CUSTOMER FOCUS *and* FEATURES, ADVANTAGES, AND BENEFITS, Proposal Guide.

7 The seller proactively sets a follow-up time, justifies the timing as being in the best interest of the customer, and restates potential benefits.

February 16, 20XX

Tom Tidy
Vice President, Administration
Silicon Glen Manufacturing
75 Research Park Drive
San Jose, CA 95321

1 **Subject:** **Invitation to meet with Silicon Glen's Executive Committee to discuss how outsourcing can reduce office support costs**

2 Dear Tom:

3 In our February 15 phone conversation, you said coping with rapid change and reducing costs were driving your FY20XX planning and were vital to Silicon Glen's survival. You said that if cost reductions of up to 30 percent were possible, you would set up a meeting with Silicon Glen's Executive Committee.

4 You indicated two issues concerned all Silicon Glen executives:

- Accelerating new product development
- Driving down costs at Silicon Glen

Accelerating new product development

5 Executives are frequently distracted by routine support issues. When the agreed office services are provided by Office Imaging (OI), executives can focus on product development.

Your executives can monitor the status of any support task on-line using our ISO 9000 certified Customer Care® management software. An on-site manager uses the same package to select and manage all outside vendors as required. You can also use the latest, most cost-effective imaging products, a big help to time-constrained managers and designers.

Driving down costs at Silicon Glen

Silicon Glen's office support costs will decline or OI will not offer a contract. We will collaborate with you on a detailed cost analysis with the results committed contractually.

6 Your cost reduction is partially based on OI's greater buying power on equipment and supplies. We further reduce your cost by sharing the site management load with other current contracts in your immediate area.

Shipping costs of your extensive training and support manuals can be cut by 80 percent because we can print and ship locally, including your international locations.

While not yet discussed, most of our new clients are concerned about the future of transferred employees. Actually, OI can offer real advancement opportunities in their career fields that are often not available in highly technical organizations like Silicon Glen.

7 Due to the urgency of your planning cycle, I will call you next Monday to confirm the date and time of our meeting to further discuss how OI can help you accelerate product development while reducing costs. You may call me at 800-555-5555 if I can answer any questions.

Sincerely,

Sarah R Williamson

Office Imaging
1000 Hollister Parkway
San Andreas, CA 94301
415.322.0001
www.officeimaging.com

ShipleyAssociates — BLUE TEAM PLANNER

Opportunity Name	
Capture Manager	
Blue Team Review Lead	
Blue Team Date/Time	Blue Team 1 ☐ Blue Team 2 ☐
Meeting Location	

Blue Team Members		
1.	7.	13.
2.	8.	14.
3.	9.	15.
4.	10.	16.
5.	11.	17.
6.	12.	18.

Capture Manager Lead Checklist	Completed	Not Applicable	Comments/Notes
Capture Budget, Schedule, Organization	☐	☐	
Expanded External/Internal Analysis	☐	☐	
Strategy Statements and Action Plans	☐	☐	
Initial Technical Solution	☐	☐	
Initial Management Solution	☐	☐	
Initial Business Solution (Price To Win)	☐	☐	
Past Performance Baseline	☐	☐	
Blue Team Review Instructions	☐	☐	
Copies of Customer Briefing	☐	☐	
Blue Team Review Assessment Worksheet	☐	☐	
Blue Team Comment Sheets	☐	☐	
	☐	☐	

Proposal Manager Checklist	Completed	Not Applicable	Comments/Notes
Schedule Blue Team Meeting	☐	☐	
Arrange Meeting Room	☐	☐	
Arrange Video Conferencing	☐	☐	
Develop Meeting Agenda	☐	☐	
Develop In Briefing	☐	☐	
Conduct White Team Debriefing	☐	☐	
Review/Revise Blue Team Instructions	☐	☐	
Conduct Out Briefing	☐	☐	
	☐	☐	

©Shipley Associates

ShipleyAssociates

BLUE TEAM REVIEW FORM

Capture / Proposal Plan	
Capture Manager	
Proposal Manager	
Date of Review	

Summary – Strengths

1.
2.
3.

Summary – Weaknesses

1.
2.
3.

Summary – Major Recommendations

1.
2.
3.

Blue Team Reviewer		**Phone Number**	
		Email Address	
Blue Team Lead		**Phone Number**	
		Email Address	

Name of Capture / Proposal Team Member(s) Addressing Issue	Date	Resolved	Not Applicable	Resolution Comments/Notes
		☐	☐	
		☐	☐	

Additional Comments:

ShipleyAssociates

BLACK HAT PLANNER

Opportunity Name	
Capture Manager	
Black Hat Leader	
Review Date	
Review Time	
Location	

Black Hat Members and Competitor Team Assignments

1.		7.	
2.		8.	
3.		9.	
4.		10.	
5.		11.	
6.		12.	

Capture Manager Checklist	Completed	Not Applicable	Comments/Notes
Capture Plan	☐	☐	
Competitive Assessment	☐	☐	
Price-to-Win	☐	☐	
	☐	☐	

Black Hat Leader Checklist	Completed	Not Applicable	Comments/Notes
Schedule Black Hat Meeting	☐	☐	
Enlist Black Hat Reviewers	☐	☐	
Develop Agenda	☐	☐	
Schedule Space/Conferencing Facilities	☐	☐	
Bidder Comparison Chart	☐	☐	
Notes on Competitive Intelligence	☐	☐	
Black Hat Instructions	☐	☐	
Black Hat Assignments	☐	☐	
Black Hat In Briefing	☐	☐	
	☐	☐	

©Shipley Associates

ShipleyAssociates

BLACK HAT REVIEW FORM

Overview

The Black Hat team will work through strategies, solutions, and intelligence gaps throughout this review. The Black Hat leader will document those findings as you develop them. However, since you know the competitor you are simulating better than the rest of the group, we ask that you document significant changes to our solutions and/or strategies you believe we must make to improve our positioning. Please also identify any intelligence gaps regarding that competitor.

This information may overlap, underlap or supplement the group's documentation, but will add to the clarity and completeness of the Black Hat deliverables.

Capture Plan/Opportunity Name	
Reviewer	
Date	
Competitor Simulated	

Our Solution Changes Driven by Black Hat Findings – Technical, Management, Small Business, etc.

1.
2.
3.
4.

Our Strategy Changes Driven by Black Hat Findings – Capture Actions, Ghosting, etc.

5.
6.
7.
8.
9.
10.
11.
12.

Competitive Intelligence Gaps Identified by Black Hat Findings

13.
14.
15.
16.

©Shipley Associates

Index

©Shipley Associates

©Shipley Associates